MW00353370

The Accidental Plague Diaries

THE

ACCIDENTAL PLAGUE

DIARIES

A COVID-19 PANDEMIC EXPERIENCE

ANDREW DUXBURY MD

The Accidental Plague Diaries: A COVID-19 Pandemic Experience

Development Editing by Steve Peha
Layout and Design by Steve Peha
Cover Illustration by Jeannie Duxbury

Printed in the United States of America.

Published by:

Singular Books
An Imprint of Platform Publishing
543 NE 84th St.
Seattle, WA 98115

www.platform-publishing.com

ISBN: 978-0-9972831-4-3

For Alyn and Alison,
who always knew I had a book in me.

ACKNOWLEDGMENTS

NO BOOK EMERGES LIKE ATHENA from the author's mind full and complete. It takes the proverbial village to nurture it and allow it to reach maturity.

I owe a debt of gratitude first and foremost to Steve Peha, my editor and publisher, who first saw the possibilities in my late night musings and was able to help me shape them into a coherent whole.

Additional debts are owed to my sister, Jeannie Rae, for her art work, Harper Wood, for proofing an unwieldy manuscript, Maree Jones for getting the word out, and R. Daniel Walker for making me look half way presentable in my photograph.

I also give thanks to my friends who volunteered to beta read the manuscript and told me that it was worth pressing on, and to the hundreds and hundreds of readers of my original essays who commented, responded, messaged, engaged, and otherwise let me know that maybe I was on to something.

Lastly, a special shout-out to Stephen Sondheim for having provided the soundtrack to my adult life and teaching me the lesson that the perfect word is always out there if you can just find it.

TABLE OF CONTENTS

And now was acknowledged the presence of the Red Death. He had come like a thief in the night. And one by one dropped the revellers in the blood-bedewed halls of their revel, and died each in the despairing posture of his fall. And the life of the ebony clock went out with that of the last of the gay. And the flames of the tripods expired. And Darkness and Decay and the Red Death held illimitable dominion over all.—Edgar Allan Poe, *The Masque of the Red Death*

PROLOGUE

Like It Was

TUESDAY | DECEMBER 31, 2019

NEW YEAR'S EVE ISN'T AN EASY TIME FOR ME. It hearkens back to a clash between youthful reverie and adult reality.

When I was a child in the 1960s and 70s, I realized that I would be alive not just for the turn of a century, but for the turn of a millennium. I would be 36 years old on New Year's Eve 1999, an ancient age to childhood me and, as I slipped into young adulthood, I started to speculate about where life might take me and where I would spend that fateful night.

I completed college at Stanford University, medical school at the University of Washington, and residency/fellowship in geriatric medicine at the University of California, Davis. That took me up to 1993.

Along the way, I came out as a gay man, forged a long-term relationship with my husband Steve (marriage wasn't legal yet for same sex couples, but we considered ourselves married), and was hired by UC Davis as a faculty member in their Section of Geriatrics. Steve and I had a happy life in our Arts and Crafts bungalow in midtown Sacramento, settling into a life of work, civic engagement, and taking advantage of all the things the greater San Francisco Bay area had to offer.

It all came crashing down in 1998 when an internal struggle at UC Davis between the School of Medicine and the Health System led to the sudden defunding of the Section of Geriatrics (including my salary) and I was told I would need to seek employment elsewhere. Generally, in academia, you are given a year to job search and find a good fit. I was given two months.

The sudden collapse of the program rendered those of us associated with it toxic and unable to find jobs in West Coast academic health systems. So Steve and I, spurred on by the need for a quick transition and a continuing paycheck, ended up in the Deep South where I found a job with the University of Alabama at Birmingham, whipping their ambulatory geriatric clinical programs into shape. We moved with some trepidation, but adjusted readily to the culture shock.

A few months later, Steve began to feel unwell. He was becoming more and more winded with even minor exertion and was developing significant cyanosis. For a while, he didn't want to deal with what was obviously a serious pulmonary problem. Eventually, however, he realized it could not be ignored and begged me to take him to UAB hospital for an evaluation.

The date of his epiphany was December 31, 1999.

I spent that famous New Year's Eve in a hospital room holding Steve's hand while we waited for the test results that showed the interstitial lung disease that ultimately killed him two years later.

The process of caring for Steve over those two years, mourning his death, and recovering from my grief, transformed me as a human and as a physician. I developed an innate understanding of the tolls of chronic illness on individuals and family systems that I was able to translate into my clinical practice. My skills and reputation rose. I hadn't ever felt comfortable living in Birmingham. I was a West Coast person, raised in Seattle. I'd lived most of my adult life in Northern California. I had begun to consider pulling up stakes again for a job back west when several things happened serendipitously to keep me grounded where I was.

First, UAB received a significant donation to revamp its Geriatrics Clinic to my design and specifications. Second, I met Tommy, the man who became my second husband. Tommy, who was from Birmingham, had an interesting past with careers as a classical musician (tenor and oboist), professional chef, and pediatric nurse.

When I met Tommy, he was the chief nursing officer of the local federally qualified health center but his heart was still with music and performance. He found out that back in my younger days, I had worked in theater on the semi-pro level, mainly in stage management and as a director, but that I had given it up to develop my medical career. He encouraged me to go back to it and, after seeing me give a number of public lectures, he suggested I try performing.

Within a year, I was playing supporting roles in local musical theater and eventually ended up with leads, and also joining the choruses of Opera Birmingham and the Alabama Symphony Orchestra. Tommy left nursing and went back to school for degrees in Choral Education and Speech Pathology. He ended up as the Company Manager for Opera Birmingham, the Director of the Children's Music Program at our Unitarian Universalist Church, and, through yet another serendipitous turn of events, the wig master for every theater company in town.

In the spring of 2018, Tommy became acutely ill with previously undiagnosed cardiac disease and was hospitalized. He died unexpectedly in the hospital one night, likely from a pulmonary embolism. Once again, I found myself a widower.

I discovered two things right away. The first was that I still had unresolved issues from my first widowerhood; I was really grieving *both* Tommy and Steve. The second was that being a widower at 56, especially in the gay community, was very different than being a widower at 39. It would take a different type of processing to come through to the other side this time around. I started writing to help myself figure things out.

I'm a big Facebooker. I've had an account there since you had to have a .edu email address to sign up. I know all the arguments against it, but I like to think I use it in the right way. Besides, it has become the de facto communications system for those who work in the performing arts in this country. Tommy and I had become an integral part of what I call Bohemian Birmingham, hanging out with musicians, actors, opera singers, composers, theater technicians and the like. I had been writing updates about Tommy and his condition for our friends and, after his sudden death, I started journaling a bit in the same format to process my thoughts and feelings.

I fell into the natural elder role of the storyteller, peppering my entries with anecdotes of mine and Steve's and Tommy's lives, tales that would otherwise die with me if not recorded in some form. More and more people began to read them, and my peer group found that my thoughts on aging, grief, health, and society were helping them understand similar things in their own minds. I received a great deal of encouragement to keep going.

I did some traveling and wrote about that. I returned to performing and wrote about the process of creating theater. I wrote about social foibles and political happenings. Eventually, I realized that Facebook wasn't necessarily the right format, so I started a blog and began cross-posting.

In late 2019-early 2020, I was in rehearsal for a production of Kander and Ebb's *Cabaret* playing the role of Herr Schultz. I had taken on the role once before, back in 2007 and it was interesting to come back to him as a completely different person with a new-found sadness. The production was a smashing success, but I was feeling a certain internal inadequacy at the task of playing the only Jewish character, a symbol for the coming horrors of the Holocaust.

As the show went into production, my 87-year-old mother died. She had been suffering from a genetic dementia for nearly 15 years and had been mute and unable to care for herself for the last five or six. It was a combination of sadness and relief for my family. We don't do funerals, so we planned a memorial service for April when there would be a promise of good weather in Seattle and it would be easy to gather the clan.

From *Cabaret*, I went into rehearsals for Massenet's *Cendrillon* with the opera and Mozart's *Requiem* with the symphony. Fittingly, the *Requiem* would turn out to be my last public performance before America went dark.

On that same New Year's Eve of 2019, when I was pondering Steve's illness and hospitalization of 20 years before, the World Health Organization announced that it had sent a team of scientists to the city of Wuhan, China to investigate the outbreak of an unknown type of viral pneumonia. Through January, while I was busy with work, rehearsing *Cabaret* and mourning my mother, news stories about the spread of a novel coronavirus, related to SARS, began to appear.

I naively believed that this would be handled by CDC and WHO as previous viral outbreaks had been in the past. Resources would be allocated to the region affected, combined with intense screening, testing, and tracing to prevent it taking a foothold here or in other major developed countries.

On January 21, the first US case was identified in the Seattle area. Ten days later, WHO declared a worldwide public health emergency with the US following several days after that. Backstage and at work, everyone began to chatter about what might happen should our public health systems fail.

By the first of March, it was clear that the virus was well seeded in the US with media reports of rapid spread on cruise ships and early spikes in Seattle and New York starting to appear. WHO declared the novel coronavirus a worldwide pandemic on March 11th. I wrote the first piece in what I would come to call *The Accidental Plague Diaries* on March 10th, the day before the pandemic was declared.

Looking back, I wrote very little in the month of February. Some of that was due to being overly busy between work and rehearsal obligations. I had also made the decision to move in January, downsizing from a house to a condo, so I was dealing with the logistics of that. I was likely also processing the recent loss of my mother. But some of my relative silence was due to a sense of foreboding.

Tackling the disease that would come to be known as COVID-19 head-on in my writing would make me acknowledge its reality and the effect it was going to have on my life and the lives of countless others. Eventually, it became the elephant in the room that could not be ignored and I began to write the pieces collected here.

When I wrote the first few, I figured I'd deal with the subject and then move on, but as the upheavals of March and April continued, it became clear that I was living through a momentous time in American history and that my comments and analysis might help others navigate through the same uncharted waters in which I found myself.

About four or five pieces in, I realized that I was writing a plague diary, a literary form with a long history. Much of what we know about prior pandemic disease comes from the observations of private citizens living through a difficult time and recording what they see about the disease and their society's reactions to it. I began referring to my blog posts as *The Accidental Plague Diaries*.

I had never intended to write a plague diary. I didn't even realize I was writing one until I was in the middle of it. However, the title has come to mean something more to me. Not only is my writing here one more serendipitous accident, like so much else in my life, but the whole plague itself is accidental. The progress of the disease and our societal response has laid bare the failures of our federal system at the first task of government: protection of its citizens. Had this disease occurred at most other junctures in our nation's history, it would have been less likely to spread as widely, less likely to have killed as many, less likely to have caused the enormous havoc—cultural, social, political, and economic—that it has.

What follows is the story of one man, coming from the perspective of a healer and a student of humanity, and how his life—past, present, and considerations of the future—intersects with a viral pandemic and the failures of a nation state. Each entry is as I experienced it at the time. The original pieces have been condensed and cleaned up for ease of reading by my invaluable editor, Steve Peha, but the ideas, emotions, and opinions expressed are mine, rendered in real time as I lived through them.

MARCH 2020

Something's Coming

TUESDAY | MARCH 10, 2020

I AM A DOCTOR. It is time to make sense of my existential angst. My brothers and sisters in healthcare professions are feeling it. We're all watching a viral pandemic unroll in real time right in front of us. We all know far too much about the ramifications of where the coronavirus may lead.

It's tough walking the knife-edge of hope and despair: hope that we will weather an infection, despair that a significant minority will suffer and die, and bring our wobbly health infrastructure down with them.

I live in Alabama, a state without reported cases... yet. Does this mean it hasn't reached us? Or is it here and circulating among the untested? What is the correct amount of societal change and social distancing to put in place at this time? Is it better to overreact and cause major disruptions and financial hardship? Or wait until there is proof positive that such measures will have a mitigating effect?

These are the questions people ask me. I'm supposed to know the answers. I don't. All I can say right now is that we can't cure it, but we can support the infected while they heal themselves. And a few other things: Wash your hands, avoid sick people, use common sense.

By some estimates, nearly the whole human race will be infected within the next few years. Most of us will make it. Some will not. Mitigation efforts won't prevent the spread, but may slow it down so that society has the resources to care for the sick while they recover.

I have a number of risks personally. I'm over 50. My health is good, but not perfect. I live with a manageably persistent chronic disease burden which accumulates in all of us over time. As a medical professional, the price I pay for societal respect and a decent salary is the expectation that I will put my body on the line in this sort of situation. I'm used to being coughed at and sneezed on, to catching the viral *crud du jour*. But rarely does this lay me low enough to miss work.

If I get something this winter, do I get tested? Do I self-quarantine and stay home for days, throwing clinical schedules into havoc? When I get viral bronchitis, as I do every few years, does this put me at greater risk? If the virus becomes endemic, and my hospital becomes flooded with patients, and it's all hands on deck, do I brush off my rusty critical care skills and volunteer for extra shifts to spell exhausted colleagues? Will my hospital be able to cope?

Most at risk are my frail elderly patients, many of whom I have cared for over decades, and who trust me implicitly. How do I protect them? This disease may profoundly alter my professional life for the rest of my career. What will that look like? How do I prepare?

THURSDAY | MARCH 12, 2020

THE FEELING OF DREAD IS NO BETTER after 48 hours of unbelievable news from all quarters. I feel like I'm trapped in one of those movie scenes where I'm hurtling toward disaster: Everything switches to super-slo-mo; the next 20 seconds will take 20 hours as I attempt to prevent the gory-accident-crash-murder and the mystery left unsolved by the breaking of the irreplaceable clue.

It is now clear to me, and to most of us in medicine and public health, that our President has abdicated his responsibility to mobilize our government's resources to stop the virus from sweeping the land. Not only is he failing to keep us safe, he is actively and intentionally contributing to public panic by playing down the threat, by making ludicrous promises of a swift return to normal, and by daily attempting to undermine and marginalize the best scientists we have to help us and the best institutions they represent—the CDC and the WHO.

At this moment, I am encouraged by one thing, and one thing only. Some private and public entities are stepping up on their own to stop the mixing of too many people in too little space. Policies and practices of social distancing seem to be the one thing that we as ordinary folk can do to protect ourselves and our fellow citizens by making it harder for the virus to leap from person to person.

This coronavirus is new to humanity. None of us is immune. It's unlikely to cause serious consequences for most. But for a small subset of our people, the consequences will be fatal or at least life-threatening. Even if this number is smaller than the most conservative estimates, if everyone in this subset gets sick at the same time, our healthcare system will be strained to the breaking point.

As a gay man who survived the 1980s, I'm not surprised that the federal government is playing politics while people's lives are at stake. Back when the LGBTQIA+ community realized they were considered a disposable population, they rallied and saved themselves by creating community organizations and services that still endure. Communities are going to have to do this again, looking out for each other, not expecting a federal white knight to come riding to the rescue. This, too, is not surprising. The federal track record over the last couple of decades (at least for Republican administrations) has been dismal. Katrina in New Orleans and Maria in Puerto Rico come to mind.

The closing down of normal life is as painful and difficult for me as it is for everyone else. The distance I feel is more than physical. It's emotional. But spreading ourselves out a bit, and fully isolating if we get sick, are the two things we can all do in this fight. Most of us aren't virologists, and you can't kill this enemy with your stockpile of AR-15s or your weekend warrior zeal.

Viruses don't care about your bank account, your passport, the color of your skin, your religious beliefs, or any of the other elements of privileged protection we seem to argue so much about these days. Viruses care only about one thing: replicating and moving on to the next host. I've heard more than one local official make reference to some sort of godly intervention that has so far kept our caseload down. In my cosmic view, god is the god of viruses as much as of humans. I fear god is on the other side this year.

The closing down of society includes me. Opera Birmingham has canceled both their annual gala, which was to be this Friday evening, and the actual opera itself, Massenet's *Cendrillon,* for which I have spent weeks diligently rehearsing. The plan is to carry the production forward to 2021 and reassemble as many of the cast and staff as possible at that time. It may be a good thing that Birmingham is to be spared the sight of me in full drag as one of *Les Filles D'Altesse* trying on the shoe at the end of Act IV. But there's always next year.

This unwanted change of plans frees up the next two weeks considerably. I suppose I'd better start my downsizing and moving to a new home earlier than I intended. Who am I kidding? I'll binge-watch a couple of things on Netflix, read a few of the books in my *tsundoku* pile, and take some nice walks now that the weather is warming up.

We're open for business at the hospital, of course, but everything is skewed as we prepare for the unknown. A month ago, Italy had a handful of cases. Today, its healthcare system is on the verge of collapse. Will we follow that pattern? The transition, over the last four-to-five decades, of the American healthcare system to the American healthcare industry has demanded of us that we become both leaner and meaner. Healthcare institutions, like hospitals, are required now to operate close to full capacity at all times. The goal for most hospitals is 90% of beds full during normal times to maintain the unrelenting growth of profitability.

The idea of a buffer of some kind for "surge" capacity is a non-starter. It doesn't make sense to the money people to have beds sitting around unused or to pay staff who aren't always on the edge of overwork. If the worst happens and the ventilators all are occupied, I'll be having unconscionable conversations with patients and families. Can I do it? Yes. Do I want to? No. But it will be necessary. I hope I have enough of a reservoir of kindness and compassion from which to draw to be up to the task should I be handed that particular cup.

Be well, eat right, get sleep, steer clear of large crowds and, above all, wash your hands. Holmes and Semmelweis were right.

SATURDAY | MARCH 14, 2020

T'S LATE AT NIGHT. I sit up wondering what's to become of us all over the next few weeks. I'm not worried about my physical health. But I do worry.

I worry about becoming a disease vector for my elderly patients. I worry about getting sick and being put on quarantine, unable to work when I will be most needed. I worry about my ICU skills, rusty and decades out of date, in case I should be needed there. I worry.

I've decided to do the most responsible thing I can think of: Go to work and, when not working, stay home. No eating out. No going out at all other than for walks or briefly into someone's house where no one is sick. (I have to do this anyway; house calls are part of my work.)

It's going to be quiet and lonely in my off hours, and though I don't like it, I know that avoiding human contact is the best thing I can do to help my older friends and those with chronic health issues. If, in coming weeks, we succeed in flattening the curve, I will be less likely to be exposed at work, and less likely as well to be called upon to do things out of my usual scope of practice.

With more time on my hands than I expected and more anxiety rising within me, I'll post more of these writings more regularly. I'm doing this, of course, to process my feelings, better understand the issues, and make sense of it all as I'm all by myself. But the truth is that I need friends, family, and colleagues along for the ride, companions in spirit as I navigate the unknown, even if they come only in the form of likes and brief comments.

As terrified as I am, I am also fascinated. As my heart quickens, my mind digs deeper for news from places like Seattle and Italy. Each day, I race down the rabbit holes afforded by Google and Twitter, digging deeper than I probably should for information from scientists and the CDC, which will calm me and news from places like Seattle and Italy, which won't.

Apocalyptic scenarios whirl up in my overactive imagination. My Taurus stubbornness and library full of books make me feel worse. This doctor's diagnosis? I have a bad case of the heebeejeebies. It probably doesn't help that I've been binge-watching *The Walking Dead*.

No, the virus isn't going to create a world of zombies. Nor is it going to "off" most of the population. But I'm over-identifying with the Dr. Faucis of the world and our healthcare heroes as they try to make sense of life turned upside down. The roller-coaster crash of it all poses a question that haunts me: Would anyone have believed three months ago, amid the joys of the holiday season, that we'd be where we are as we approach Easter?

My family in Seattle are all fine; I'm checking in fairly frequently. Like here, much of the usual life of the city is shut down. Not all is quiet on the western front, however. My sister's tattoo business is booming as college kids on an unexpected break come in for more ink. My brother is learning the quirks of online instruction for high schoolers. My 87-year old father, whose building is on lockdown, is getting a bit bored. We haven't yet made the decision to postpone my mother's memorial, currently scheduled for April 26th, but I think we'll have to.

My sources in the Seattle medical community tell me that things are holding up so far. The biggest issue is lack of gowns and gloves and other forms of personal protective equipment. Some hospitals are down to less than a week's supply, and with all of the problems in the world, the usual supply chains are disrupted. I keep my ear to the ground so I can pass things along which I hope will be helpful when the virus arrives at both UAB and the Birmingham VA.

The day I am most reminded of at the moment is late October of 1999. My husband Steve and I were on St. Martin at a resort with several hundred other gay men when hurricane José came barreling down on us.

There was an incredible sense of anticipation in the air. Everything had been canceled (which didn't stop a couple of hundred queens from drinking every drop of liquor in the resort) and by afternoon the wind started to pick up, getting stronger and stronger.

The deep sea birds, albatrosses and the like, appeared out of nowhere, hovering over the beach and looking out to sea in the direction of the storm. The land birds fell quiet. It was an eerie calm.

Steve and I went back to our room as darkness fell, the electricity went out, and the rains began to pour around 10 PM. We were in a cheap room, not ocean view, and were spared most of the weather. We did not have to spend the night hungover in a bathtub while the roof peeled off like two of our acquaintances.

This weekend has that same anticipatory feel. I hope everything's lashed down tight when the storm hits.

MONDAY | MARCH 16, 2020

THIS IS MY FIRST WORLD-WIDE VIRAL PANDEMIC. I'm not sure how I'm supposed to feel or to react. If anyone knows, please send me a message. In the meantime, let's all continue to muddle through together and make it up as we go along.

Our nation has narrowly but successfully avoided Big Bad for 75 years. Bad was the polio epidemic; bad was 9/11; bad was the 2007-08 financial crisis. The Great Depression followed by World War II? That was Big Bad.

However, those of us with fewer than four score years on the planet are learning the terror of Big Bad as it rolls over us thicker and faster than we can absorb. This might explain some of the stranger posts I've been seeing on social media over the last couple of days.

I have great faith in America and Americans. Historically, when tested, we have risen to the occasion. I have great hope for Millennials, in particular. If you believe in the four-generation cycle of American history, they occupy the same place as the World War II generation. Perhaps they will grow to become our next Greatest Generation.

I feel, at age 57, like I've been drafted and am preparing to ship off to war. The enemy is coming, implacably and inexorably. But this is asymmetric warfare, the kind that won us our independence from England and lost us our moral authority (and so much more) in Vietnam.

Our enemy is microscopic; impervious to the usual weaponry. No amount of drilling or stripping of field rifles is going to help. Our best defenses are functioning supply chains, good hygiene, availability of medical care, necessary equipment, accurate information, and national leadership. The home front can contribute by staying home. This will all rip a giant hole in the economy, but we're all in this together.

I don't trust the gerontocracy of the federal government to handle the post-pandemic well. They're not flexible thinkers who adapt to new norms. I think, as communities, we're going to be more on our own than we're used to being. Accordingly, we must commit ourselves to this. It will be new and hard. The new normal will be a not normal. But we must achieve normalcy again, and I believe we will.

Today, work was mainly about planning. How do we reimagine our clinic work from face-to-face visits to telephonic visits? Who can be pulled from outpatient to inpatient duty to cover all the usual medical issues if the inpatient docs are either busy with COVID-19 patients, under quarantine, or ill themselves? I last did inpatient ward duty in a previous millennium. I hope to be low on the list of draftees to COVID-19 wards, less for my own sake than for those who will not necessarily get top notch care from a guy operating way outside of his usual practice patterns.

Same thing for me tomorrow at the VA. Then on to Wednesday, when we confront the hospice piece. One of the most interesting problems is how to deal with the myriad rules of Medicare and HIPAA. They aren't suspended until they're suspended, and working within these constraints makes things even more difficult.

We're all stepping up to do our part without complaining. It's what we signed up for when we decided to go to medical school and took all those loans out to do it. But now a new bill is coming due, a bill we will pay beyond the immediate crisis, a series, actually, of unending and inexorable dunning notices, year after year, as the Baby Boomers crest gracefully and less-so, into their 80s and 90s and require more health care as a result.

Having received responsive health care for most of their lives, they will feel entitled to continue receiving it. And who can blame them? We celebrate long lives in our society. But, in this case at least, demography is destiny. An aging generation that does not believe that aging applies to them, or that the healthcare system cannot somehow magically cure the chronic illnesses that are the price of a long life, is in the crosshairs of this particular pandemic and may bear the brunt of unknown medical sequelae.

Baby Boomers, due to their numbers and attitudes of demand, have unintentionally ravaged social institutions as they have moved through them with each stage of life. Health care and senior living, the provinces of older age, are next. Without radical change to our healthcare system in the coming decade, we will have no healthcare system to change. With each day that passes, each day the body counts rise, the virus is tapping us on the shoulder, telling us that this is not as bad as it can get. "As bad as it can get" is yet to come.

My much older patients, those over 90 who survived the Depression and World War II and have clear memories of hard times, are philosophical about things. They've seen the past, they see the present, they infer the future, and embrace all with equanimity for they know that death lies in wait for them just outside their field of vision.

My younger patients, those on the cusp of the Boom, are struggling most. They believe in eternal youth and immortality. They don't fully grasp that this is not something they can wish away, that neither affluence nor influence are prophylactic. For the most part, they are following my advice about hygiene and staying home. No matter how vigilant they are, however, I'm sure I'm going to lose a few familiar faces, people I've been taking care of for decades, patients I've had since I first arrived in Alabama, in their 70s then, their 90s now.

Together we've seen social changes, health catastrophes, major improvements in function, widowhoods, and other triumphs and tragedies. I learned how to say goodbye in the 80s with HIV. I'll make it through this.

Be well everyone. Use your downtime to clear your heads. Practice a little Zen. Let these times carry you along instead of fighting against them. Keep a vigilant eye on your politicians. Some are itching to use this as their Reichstag Fire moment to rush new policies through while we're distracted and prevented from protesting en masse. But mostly, watch out for your neighbors, your friends, your communities.

WEDNESDAY | MARCH 18, 2020

WE'VE ALL BEEN SLAPPED UPSIDE THE HEAD these last few weeks with two basic truths.

First, humans aren't special. We're just one of many species struggling to exist on this blue ball teeming with life, and Mother Nature is in charge. We may like to think we're exempt from the natural processes of the way the world works, but we're not.

Second, Americans aren't special among humans. As the stress of the pandemic and societal shut down grinds inexorably on, we're starting to recognize that 40 years of hollowing out public good for private profit might not have been the best of ideas and that our tools for responding to this situation aren't anywhere near as robust as they are elsewhere in the world.

This past week seemed surreal, but it's only the beginning. This is not something that's just going to go away in a week or two. We'll survive. We always do. Humans are a hardy species. We're pretty darn ingenious when we put our minds to it, and this isn't the first (nor will it be the last) tough spot we've been in.

I read somewhere that sometime during the Cro-Magnon era, the human race was down to eight breeding females. (This was determined from sequencing mitochondrial DNA.) We made it out of that tight spot. We can make it out of this one. But at what cost?

The looming economic catastrophe is worse than the health catastrophe. That's probably what finally woke up the federal government. They're not terribly concerned about the safety of their citizens (a failure of the first magnitude as this is the most basic job of government), but they do care deeply about the preservation of wealth, especially in the hands of those who run our most important institutions and largest corporations.

I foresee many changes coming because of this, but whether those will be in the direction of an authoritarian crackdown by the power-holders, or a more equitable future for ordinary citizens, is impossible to predict. Perhaps both of these movements will expand. Perhaps neither. Perhaps some now-unknowable third way will emerge. I read a meme somewhere that we're back in the roaring 20s, starting off with a pandemic, the bars are closed, and Wall Street is crashing.

If nothing else, I think we're starting to recognize who's really important in our society. As a doctor, I signed up for a job that I knew might include a time like this where I might have to take on personal risk to benefit patients. It doesn't bother me. It's part of the calling. If you don't have that ethos, you don't belong in medicine. But people like grocery store clerks didn't sign up to risk their health keeping shelves stocked for a populace that seems to have lost its collective mind over toilet paper.

Think of the people who truly are helping us get through this crisis, day by day. Think of the millions of people involved in the global supply chain: clerks, truckers, railroaders, port workers, warehouse workers. Think of the people we turn to when we're cooped up at home: the writers who give us good books to read; the actors, directors, and technicians who create movies and television; the musicians who lighten our hearts with song.

We've under-funded the arts for decades. It's time we stop that because artists are the tender keepers of our souls, especially in times of trouble. And don't get me started on the teachers: underpaid, under-appreciated, and with each year that passes, seemingly more sad. With most of the country being thrust into homeschooling, when the schools reopen, I hope to see mobs of angry parents marching on the local school district demanding better salaries and working conditions for teachers now that they've figured out what teachers actually do—and that it isn't child's play.

At my job, the people I'm saluting are the behind-the-scenes folk. The cooks and serving-line people who make sure there's a hot lunch in the cafeteria so I can keep going. The custodial staff who are doing double duty disinfecting. The IT people who make sure the computer systems work the way they need to. My receptionists who are fielding with a smile calls from frightened and confused people. My nursing staff who give a damn on a very personal level about the well-being of our patients. It's easy to put a doctor up on a pedestal, but there's a whole team of unsung heroes who enable the job to be done.

With three days of work, we've managed to get ambulatory care in geriatrics shifted away from bringing people into a clinic in a hospital environment over to a telephone-based system where we can still provide care. We're open for business. We will see people in person to keep them away from the emergency department, but most routine care will be done via phone or video chat for the next few months to try and keep our patients safe and out of harm's way. I can't say I like it because I'm a toucher and a hugger with patients (sometimes it does more good than any pill I can come up with), but desperate times call for desperate measures. Anything we can do to keep my people from falling ill is fine with me.

I'm fried when I get home in the evening. It would be nice to have someone to unwind with other than the cats, but I'm still being rigorous with my social distancing and will likely be so for a while as I don't want to be a vector carrying disease to vulnerable populations.

I had my first outing outside work in nearly a week this evening when I stopped by the Piggly Wiggly on my way home to pick up a couple of things for the fridge. Sanitize hands before going in. Don't touch the face. Try not to touch anything other than products I'm buying and the basket I'm putting them in.

Most things were well stocked other than bread, and I wanted a loaf. The bread aisle was completely cleaned out, but I wandered over to the deli and found a few loaves of special brioche bread in an out of the way corner that had been overlooked. Score! (I love brioche.)

Sanitize hands again in the car. Get home and scrub. My current wash-hands song is *The Ladies Who Lunch*, last verse. May Elaine Stritch forgive me.

FRIDAY | MARCH 20, 2020

N A DIFFERENT LIFE, I'D BE ON STAGE, roughly half way through the opening night of Massenet's *Cendrillion* at Samford University's Wright Center. But a burgeoning viral pandemic has other ideas, and the production came to a crashing halt ten days ago.

I've now spent more than a week either at work or sequestered away from the world hoping I don't get infected. I don't want to become a disease vector for the frail elders for whom I care, and I may have to serve as part of a reserve unit for the hospital doctors who are more likely to fall ill from their frontline duties. Those of us who normally do ambulatory care are transferring the majority of our work to telephonic, trying to minimize our contact with others and stay healthy for the time when we will be needed.

When I began these writings several years ago at the time of my second widowhood, a tragedy of a more personal nature, I had no idea I was going to end up as some sort of 21st century plague diarist. Like the rest of the world, many of my assumptions about life have come crashing down around me in the last few weeks. I feel relatively optimistic about the ultimate outcome (history shows we tend to do rather well after a major crisis passes), but I am concerned about the near-term issue of how we hold our institutions together under incredible strain, especially in this country when half of it seems to be living in one reality and the other half in another.

Alabama entered the triple digits of diagnosed cases today (up from single digits last weekend). Sick people are beginning to turn up at the hospitals. A lot of planning by a whole lot of very bright people has happened over the last two weeks, so we should weather the initial surge well. The biggest immediate issue is a shortage of PPE (Personal Protective Equipment) for the frontline doctors, nurses, techs, respiratory therapists, etc. who are going to be exposed over and over again.

Our societal decision to treat health care as an industry like any other (one which manufactures patient/provider "encounters") has led to a business model where we keep no excess inventory and order "just in time" so we don't have to pay to store items, discard outdated supplies, or staff unneeded hospital beds. The side effect of this, of course, is that when there's an instantaneous nationwide demand, it's not possible to ramp up quickly. The beds don't exist. The supply chain buckles. There's a shortage of trained staff. Some of my craftier friends who sew have already started making cloth masks to donate when the stocks are depleted. It's better than nothing.

The local authorities have become more serious as the week has gone on. We're not on full lockdown, but most shops are closed. All food establishments are carryout only. Gatherings of more than ten people are strongly discouraged. I have a couple of friends working as

37

grocery clerks who are just about to call it quits on the human race as they try to deal with panic buying. Fortunately, my local Piggly Wiggly has been sane and relatively well-stocked.

For those of my friends who have suddenly found themselves unemployed, most grocery stores are hiring. Not the most glamorous of jobs, but essential and likely to provide steady employment for the duration. I shouldn't need to go to the store for about a week. I'm pretty well stocked and, as one person, I don't eat that much. I did have a major score today when I found a liter jug of hand sanitizer in Tommy's wig studio, so now I'm stocked up on that.

I've been looking at the differences between Western and Asian societies and their approach to containment. China has nearly stamped out its original epidemic. South Korea's is beginning to come under control. The virus never really took off in most of the other Asian countries despite early transmission through travel routes. Meanwhile, we and Western Europe continue to rocket along.

Part of this comes from a difference in our conceptions of who we are. Western thought, starting in the post-Renaissance period with Cartesian dualism and then expanded by the Enlightenment thinkers, places all emphasis on the self. I am who I am, you are who you are. We are individualists at heart. We come together for the common good, but we do so as individuals. Many Asian cultures, which developed without those changes in philosophy, still use the community, the tribe, the family as the unit of existence rather than the individual.

If one conceives of oneself as being part of a larger collective, collective action for the good of the group is easier. I think they understood the need for individual behavior change in a deeper and more logical way than we can with our "no one can tell me what to do" ethos. I hate making these kinds of generalizations because I'm always afraid I'll end up stereotyping people. If I've offended anyone, it's unintentional. I'm processing big ideas with inadequate words.

I figure our next hot spot will be Florida, thanks to young people refusing to give up the beaches and crowded theme parks that were relatively late to close. It takes about two weeks from the introduction of the virus in an area for the rate of cases to become significant, so I'm thinking next weekend should see a surge in the Sunshine State.

I saw an interesting article today on the manufacturers of a smart Bluetooth thermometer that can upload your temperature to your home computer or to a hospital information system. Apparently, all those temperature readings, stripped of any identifying data, go to a central data bank so the company can look for trends. They usually see a hot spot of increased temps a couple of days before a flu or other viral outbreak and are better at predicting where flu is circulating than the CDC. According to this report, Florida is starting to light up like crazy, far more than most of the rest of the country.

I wonder what Steve or Tommy would have made of all this. Steve would likely have alternated between mild hysteria and laughing over YouTube videos of middle America emulating WWF smackdowns in the toilet paper aisle. Tommy would have been miffed at the shutting down of the music and theater world, gotten out some new music to learn, gone to work in the garden, gotten out the sewing machine and a mask pattern, and started in to work, all the while with a big "I told you so" on his lips.

Tommy had a keen eye for the fissures and fallacies of American society and was very much a realist about the rot at the top. If Tommy were still alive, we'd be arguing about the politics of it all, but after that was done, we'd still love each other and head off to bed to watch Star Trek with a bowl of ice cream. That's the hardest thing at the moment for me; having to be on soft lockdown by myself. I'd go stir crazy if it wasn't for the age of social media which allows me to feel somewhat connected to my communities.

SUNDAY | MARCH 22, 2020

WENT FOR A FIVE MILE WALK TODAY. The weather was lovely. Cloudy, a hint of mist in the air, cool without being cold. The relatively mild winter we've had means that the pastel season is in full swing: fresh spring green leaves on the trees, azaleas, forsythia, red buds in bloom. Daffodils, grape hyacinths, violets, spiderwort, all are coming up in profusion. There was also more bird song than I'm used to. I don't know if that's due to more birds, a reduction in ambient noise as we all stay in, or if I, in my current situation, am more conscious of the simple things. I've always been a big walker, from childhood on. It's one of the things I can still enjoy in my semi-isolationist state. I just have to be careful not to touch things like park benches.

It's been an uneventful weekend, and today is day eleven of my new life patterns. Lather, rinse, repeat. Cut out most usual activities in an attempt to stay healthy until such time as I am really needed by the medical system. I'm apprehensive, but not particularly worried about myself. I'm far more worried about patients, friends, and family. Assuming I don't get sick and die (a small, but real chance), I'll come through all of this all right, but the early retirement with lots of travel is unlikely to happen the way I was planning. Those who enjoy my travel diaries may have to wait a while.

I did get in one piece of theatrical fun: *The Politically Incorrect Cabaret*, now in its 16th year, made a PSA about staying home, and I provided the tag at the end. (They shot it from my front lawn without my having to get close to anyone.) It's fun slipping into the Ansager, my Emcee character, even for a couple of minutes, but I can't do the makeup like Tommy could, and it's harder to get my eyeliner and eyebrows right now that I'm getting blind as a bat without glasses.

I talked to my father in Seattle this afternoon. He was interested in the concept of "flattening the curve." He has, quite rightly, noticed that the area under the two curves in the standard diagram that is being shared around is roughly the same (meaning the same number of people become ill in both trajectories), and that the flatter curve means that the disease is present over a longer period of time. This led to a discussion of lies, damned lies, and statistics.

I had two takeaways for him. First, the flatter curve may last longer but is less likely to overwhelm the medical system, meaning that those who can be saved will have the resources to save them.

Second, the usual medical issues we cope with are going to happen whether COVID-19 is here or not. If the system is swamped, there's no way to care for them and the death rates for other medical conditions such as heart attack and stroke will start to increase.

Therefore, the flatter the curve, the better, at least as far as my brothers and sisters in health care are concerned. However, those curves suppose normal distribution and, with a new disease process, it's impossible to say if that will hold up or not. There are a whole lot of variables, most of them unknown.

The people I am most worried about are the healthcare providers. The health system, with its just-in-time ordering mantra and financial disincentives against stockpiling, is incredibly low on protective equipment and, as most of these products come from outside the US, N-95 masks, gloves, clean protective gowns and the like are in short supply.

Within days, my frontline friends are going to be sent in to care for the ill without the necessary protective gear. Many will catch the virus and fall ill; some will die, completely unnecessarily on the altar of short-term profit. It's the moral equivalent of the World War I commanders ordering the young men of Europe out of the trenches and into charges against machine gun emplacements. It makes me incredibly angry and incredibly sad to know I will soon be hearing about the deaths of cherished colleagues, done in by the political and economic failure of a system that should be there to protect them.

It's back to work in the morning. No clue what the day will bring. Two weeks ago, there were no cases in Alabama, I had just finished successful performances of Mozart's *Requiem* (how ironic), and I was looking forward to opera staging rehearsals. Much has changed; more is about to change. Where do we end up? I don't know. Looking at the history of various disasters, societies usually end up transforming themselves for the better. Perhaps this is nature's way of reminding us not to get too fossilized in our thinking or in our institutions.

TUESDAY | MARCH 24, 2020

REMAIN HEALTHY. My social isolation/soft quarantine confining me to work and home continues and trepidation mounts as Birmingham alternates between thunderstorm and warm and steamy.

It's as if it were late May already. The weeds in the garden are having a field day, but it's been too wet to go out and do anything about them. Maybe it will dry off some by the weekend. My yard people are still showing up, but I have told them they needn't come by if they need to be off to take care of kids out of school. Same with my housekeeper. And I am continuing to pay them both. I'm not that guy.

The first lappings of the COVID-19 tsunami have hit the foundations of UAB. On Friday, there were three cases in the hospital. Today there are 45, with more coming in. If the social distancing and other measures that have been put in place locally are effective, we should start to see a leveling off in another week or so. What's happening today reflects the social behaviors of roughly two weeks ago, just as it was recognized that the virus was here and starting to spread in the community.

The city of Birmingham and Jefferson County have been fairly proactive. The state has not. What I fear most at this moment is that the exurbs and rural areas, filled with people who get all of their news from "conservative" media outlets, have no idea what's coming for them. When things get rough, they'll turn to the Birmingham medical system for help. Alabama, for political reasons, did not take the Medicaid expansion offered by the PPACA. As a result, over the last decade, a number of rural hospitals have closed and services outside the urban cores are tight, at best. I'm already hearing stories that the emergency departments in the rural hospitals are starting to look like war zones.

I cannot save the world nor can I save people from the macro forces of politics and economics. I learned that lesson a long time ago. All I can do is work as best I can to try and protect my patients any way I know how. My whole career has been about saving one person at a time—the person in front of me. That's all I've ever been able to do. At the moment, this is happening by taking most of our work telephonic in order to keep people with the chronic disease burdens of age away from a hospital or clinic building where the acutely ill will be also. It's working so far, and we can temporize in this way for a month or so, but eventually we're going to have to work out a way to see and examine people safely. We have some ideas, but we can only tackle one major set of problems at a time. It's a good thing I'm relatively creative and used to thinking outside the box.

A friend asked me about dealing with very frail and demented elders in this current situation. Many reside in senior living. The managers of such institutions have, quite rightly, locked the buildings down to keep traffic to a minimum and the virus from spreading within their vulnerable populations. When such measures are not taken, you get what happened at Lifecare of Kirkland, outside of Seattle, which rapidly became the ground zero center of the outbreak.

The approach to one's elders depends on their cognition. Those over the age of 80 or so who are relatively intact have living memories of the Depression and World War II. They will have an innate understanding of what bad is and of the kinds of rapid changes a society must sometimes undergo in order to protect itself. My father is 87. The Depression and World War II formed the backdrop of his childhood. Germany invaded Poland when he was six. Pearl Harbor was the week of his ninth birthday. The war ended when he was twelve. He's philosophical about where things are. He's a bit bored being stuck in his apartment in his senior living facility in Seattle as he's a naturally gregarious sort, but he gets it. His generation has a few things to teach us about surviving bad times. Ask and listen.

If you have a cognitively intact parent or grandparent stuck in senior living, call them. Get them to tell you stories of their lives. The role of the elder is the role of the storyteller and the keeper of collective wisdom. Let them pass it on. If they have problems hearing, try FaceTime or Skype. If they don't have a smartphone, see if one of the staff will lend his or hers for a conversation. Many older people don't do well on the phone because they need the visual cues from the shape of the face in order for the brain to process language correctly. Video chat can help.

Working with the cognitively impaired is harder. They can't process the changes happening around them. All they know is that spouses or children have suddenly stopped visiting. Their realities are different than ours, but they don't have to be made to inhabit a world they don't understand. If you're talking to them on the phone, ask them to explain what's going on. Their brains will create a narrative that makes sense to them, even if it's far from reality. It's OK to go with it. It's OK to tell white lies. It's OK to shine them on and change the subject.

The best thing to do if they start perseverating and getting repetitive is to get a different brain pattern going, kind of like pushing the needle on a stuck record (a metaphor that I know has just gone right over the heads of everyone under 35). If they have a snack nearby, tell them to eat it (taste bud stimulation is good). Have them turn on the TV (visual stimulation is also good). Start singing something or reciting a familiar hymn or childhood poem—lyric and melody are stored differently in the brain and can sometimes push people into a new pattern quickly.

I've seen some heartwarming and heart-wrenching displays of love amid lockdowns. Spouses of decades visiting by coming up to the window of a room. Children singing in the garden to their great grandmother. Don't forget your friends and family members, just as frightened as you, just as unable to move freely as you, but with a much bigger concern regarding mortality than you.

THURSDAY | MARCH 26, 2020

FOR SOME REASON, I'M HEARING *REVOLUTION #9* from the Beatles' White Album in the back of my mind as I write this. (Younger readers, ask your parents.) Cacophony and chaos and an attempt to capture in sound the devolution of a society. Maybe it was some sort of foreknowledge of events 50+ years in the future.

The weather has been glorious the last few days. After work, I have been taking lengthy walks. My pedometer is happy and glowing green at my number of steps. I like walking. One of my thoughts about the new condo, assuming I ever move into it, is that it's within walking distance of work and more days than not, I can leave the car at home.

When I was in medical school, my apartment was about a mile away from the University of Washington campus and a straight shot on the Burke-Gilman trail, so I walked back and forth to class most days and had half an hour each way to clear my head, thinking about nothing. It was one of the things that helped me make it through medical school.

Being a true Seattlite, rain never stopped me, but I did get a bit grumpy during my surgery rotation when I had to leave the house at 4AM in order to make it in time for pre-rounds. (I have a coffee cup somewhere that says "Not-a-morning-person doesn't even begin to cover it".) The hours were not the only issue on which surgeons and I did not see eye to eye. I removed that possible career path from my future very early on.

I feel like I'm in a state of suspended animation. The reality of the situation with the coronavirus seems dreamlike. Because I do not do inpatient work, I have not yet come face-to-face with it. I know I will shortly. My aggressive social distancing is all about keeping myself healthy as a reserve unit, so I can spell my colleagues in the hospital later. I hear stories through the usual channels. I have friends who have been diagnosed. I see the mounting statistics. I know what the numbers are for UAB and the Birmingham VA as part of briefings for the medical staff.

Health professionals in this country, especially in smaller specialties like mine, are a tight knit group. We all have friends and colleagues who are telling us exactly what's going on in New York, Los Angeles, New Orleans, Atlanta. We're all taking this very seriously, regardless of our political leanings.

The anger from colleagues at politicians who continue to downplay what we are facing, and who do not take seriously the tools we have to fight pandemic illness such as quarantine and social distancing, is palpable. We all know that many of us are going to get sick and that some of us are going to die because of catastrophic societal and political failures far outside of our control. We want those sacrifices to have meaning beyond partisan tit-for-tat. The poem, *In Flanders Fields,* keeps running through my mind.

As for me, I'm fine. I'm healthy. I have resources, and my life experience—which includes a career in geriatric health care, two widower-hoods, and surviving a previous viral pandemic—have given me a strong and resilient psychic armor which allows me to deal with most crises with a certain level of equanimity. I'm also keenly aware of my own mortality and have been spending the last year or so putting things in order so, if I should die prematurely, my family won't have a huge mess to clean up.

The last piece of the puzzle was selling the house and downsizing to a condo. I find it very inconsiderate of COVID-19 not to have held off for a few more months while that was finishing up. I do appreciate the calls and the texts and such from friends checking up on me, especially in the evenings which are suddenly empty without rehearsals and performances and nights out to dinner.

I was talking with a friend on the phone last night about the plague bridge in Lucerne and the moral of those paintings. Death and disease are implacable, cannot be reasoned with, and have no interest in human concerns. If you ever wanted to know what it was like to live in 14th century Europe, you're finding out. I reread *The Masque of the Red Death* earlier this week. It's a short story, easily finished up in half an hour. The wealthy and well-connected, busy fleeing to Vail, Nantucket, The Hamptons, and other enclaves seem to be trying to recreate it. I haven't read Camus' *The Plague* yet, but I think I ought to.

I posted a Washington Post article yesterday about decisions regarding DNR orders in the time of COVID-19. The article got some of its facts wrong when reporting on discussions at Northwestern in Chicago. While the article stated a blanket DNR order for COVID-19 sufferers was on the table, this is in error. What is on the table, is an automatic DNR for those with COVID-19 whose course suggests no hope of recovery and that those who wish to be resuscitated and have the possibility of surviving will be coded, but only if staff have appropriate PPE on to prevent them from getting infected by blood and body fluids during the procedure.

There's a lot of misunderstanding about CPR, what it can and cannot do. It's a medical procedure like any other, although it can be administered by trained lay people in the community. It was originally invented by the Norwegians to help fishermen who fell off boats in the North Sea and had cold water drownings in sub-freezing ocean waters. In these young, healthy men with profound hypothermia as well as cardiac arrest, it was somewhat successful. From there, it spread from this very specific use to general use in any sort of cardiac arrest.

Currently, if you have sudden cardiac arrest outside of the hospital and you are found down and CPR is started, your chance of survival to leave the hospital is about 4%. If your arrest is witnessed and CPR is started right away, your chances increase to about 10% (which is why we train the population; it makes a difference).

If a defibrillator is available, and is applied within a couple of minutes, your chances go way up to about 35% which is why defibrillators are now so widespread. If you are in the hospital and arrest with trained medical personnel nearby, your chance of surviving a code blue is about 10% if you're under 60 even with the presence of a defibrillator. (It's so much lower because the population arresting in hospitals is so much sicker). Your chance of survival is about 7% if you're between 60-80, under 3% if you're over 80.

That's surviving the procedure. Your odds of surviving and returning to baseline health are much lower. CPR doesn't work anywhere near as well as the public believes, raised as we are on a steady diet of television medical dramas. Healthcare providers know this which is why most of them, once they turn sixty or so, make their advance directives DNR ("Do not resuscitate".)

I get death. I've seen too much of it over the years. All the gay men of my generation did. When the acute phase of the HIV pandemic was over, we came back stronger than ever and much more integrated into society. Here's hoping that all of our experience with COVID-19 delivers similarly positive results on the other side. I'm optimistic about the human race. I think we're going to reprioritize what's actually important in life and that those new priorities are going to launch a new creativity and a new worldview that we, with our inside-the-box ways of thinking, can't yet imagine.

SATURDAY | MARCH 28, 2020

ANOTHER SATURDAY NIGHT AND I AIN'T GOT NOBODY. I've eaten my gumbo and am now finishing up a glass of red wine and eating some cookies I found at the back of the freezer that Tommy and I baked together for our last holiday open house.

We were an unstoppable tag team in the kitchen when it came to holiday baking. He made the dough, we portioned it out together onto the baking sheets, and then I was responsible for rotating the sheets through the oven and getting them out onto the cooling racks. After fifteen of those parties over the years, we had it down to a science and were able to do most of the baking in one long evening with some favorite music on the stereo, each with a glass of wine. Neither of us could foresee that some of those last batches would help sustain me through a viral pandemic after his untimely death. Life's funny sometimes.

It's the weekend. I don't have much work to do. The little projects left over from the week I completed this morning without difficulty, then I cleaned out all the cabinets in the dining room. I felt very accomplished.

Most of the first floor, with the exception of the kitchen, has been de-junked and is ready for packing. Much of the kitchen stuff won't go. I don't have the talent to cook for 100 at a time, so I don't see the sense of holding on to huge amounts of cookware. I can cook; I was the cook for me and Steve. But I've never enjoyed cooking for one. Once I get moved, perhaps I'll have a dinner party or two, but I doubt I'll have any of the huge soirées Tommy and I used to throw.

The number of COVID-19 cases continues to climb, both locally and nationally. Locally, we seem to be weathering the surge from what I can tell. Perhaps the relatively early closing down of things is starting to pay some dividends. Fingers crossed and all that. We should know by the middle of April if local health systems will hold up or buckle at the strain. I think Birmingham will be fine. I am afraid the combination of poverty and reliance on information systems that are primarily propaganda in more rural parts of the state may lead to serious issues.

Today, I've been thinking about what comes after. Eventually, even this, too, shall pass, and we'll come out of our isolation to confront the changes in our lives: social, political, economic.

I read somewhere about the choices one can make after upheaval. Imagine two tribes on opposite sides of a river after some great calamity. The first tribe, comprised of strong individualists, adopts an every-person-for-him-or-herself mode of survival, each member hoarding as many resources as possible. Those in the second tribe, being more cooperative, come together to share resources and skills and to reinforce the group as a whole. Which tribe positions itself better for long-term success? I think most of us would agree that the latter is more likely to flourish over time. We must begin now, laying the groundwork for this cooperation, sharing now so we can hit the ground running when we emerge into the new world.

Many people I've been talking to have been complaining of excess fatigue and needing naps, even though they haven't been doing all that much. There's a basic biological reason for this. We're all marinating in a high-stress, high-anxiety environment, and our sympathetic nervous systems are working overtime getting us ready for fight or flight. However, the current situation is neither conducive to fighting (How do you punch out a virus?) nor fleeing (Where ya gonna run? Where ya gonna hide?) Therefore, our bodies are switching over to the only other alternative: Play dead and hoard energy for later. We have to remember, we've all got that little lizard brain ticking away deep inside our cerebra and no matter how intelligent or witty we may be, it still holds sway in its primitive fashion.

I've been falling down rabbit holes of reading about new antivirals, large numbers of cell service cancellations in China that belie their official numbers, the conditions of hospitals in NYC, trying to separate wheat from chaff and add to my knowledge base and armamentarium, so that when I get calls from patients next week, I can sound somewhat authoritative and reassuring. I may not be able to visit with them face-to-face at the moment, but I remain their doctor and will continue to fight for anything they need to be as healthy and functional as possible. This has been my calling for decades; I'm not backing out now.

MONDAY | MARCH 30, 2020

ACCORDING TO THE HANDY-DANDY coronavirus counter maintained by Johns Hopkins, we're up to nearly 1,000 cases in Alabama, half of those in the greater Birmingham area. UAB continues to weather the storm, but folk are getting tired and we're still on the upswing.

My professional life is peripheral to the main hospital where the majority of cases are being treated. Currently, it's my job to look after my own patient population and try to keep them healthy enough so that they don't need to come into the emergency department or the hospital for any reason. I'm making many phone calls, checking on medications and refills, making sure people aren't falling, that fluid status is OK, and nipping UTIs and bronchitis in the bud. Anything I and my colleagues can do to reduce pressure on the hospital system in the next few weeks will be for the better.

The rhythm of my work week is out of whack. It doesn't feel right to be a doctor and not be able to see my patients other than via the occasional video chat. When you've done this job as long as I have (32 years now), you get this spidey sense about who is sick and who is not, what is normal, what can be safely ignored, and what needs to be investigated further. This just doesn't work without the physical presence of the patient.

I'm pretty good at what I do, and I'm afraid that the current strained circumstances will lead me into missing something significant. We can still see people in the office, we're just trying to avoid it as much as possible as we are just down the hall from the emergency department, and we want to minimize the risk of exposure to COVID-19 in my patient population.

For various reasons, I've had to cancel the time off I had scheduled for moving. It's just as well. I still haven't figured out how to move furniture when one lives alone in a time of quarantine and social distancing. If Tommy were still here, we could make it work (aside from the piano), but he's not here, and I am not as young as I once was.

Even when I was in my prime, I could not move a couch by myself. Steve and I moved ourselves a number of times over the years. We were young and energetic, and we were always moving within the same neighborhood, so a pickup truck and a few boxes usually sufficed.

Steve moved in with me towards the end of my internship year in early 1989. I didn't ask him to. I just came home one day to find his living room set in my apartment. When I said we should talk about this first, he got upset and, when I came home from my next call night, the furniture was gone. I think he drove his living room furniture up and down Highway 99 between Sacramento and Lodi, where he was living with his mother, three or four times. It became a standing joke between us. Whenever the couch disappeared, I could tell that he was mad at me.

Our first move together was upstairs in the same apartment building to a slightly bigger unit. About a year and a half later, in mid-1990, we found a condo in the upper story of an old Victorian house a few blocks away, so we hauled everything over there where we settled in for the next few years.

Timothy Busfield's brother, Buck, and his family lived next door. He and Tim were in the process of starting The B-Street Theatre in Sacramento at the time, so I got a little vicarious theater interaction when we would run into them. For the most part, however, it was buckle down, finish residency and fellowship, and get my career underway.

Our last self-move, in the summer of 1993, was to a lovely little place a few blocks further uptown as I had finished all of my training and finally started making a real paycheck. Steve had gotten a deal on some furniture through a friend, and we had stashed it in various neighbors' basements until we took possession and found a long weekend when we could retrieve it.

The house, a craftsman bungalow-style from 1912, had been designed for single-level living with an unfinished second floor. A previous owner had finished out the second floor and then our friends from whom we bought had later redone it with a grand master suite (including a shower to die for), but the interior stairwell remained small as it had only ever been intended to be attic stairs.

One of the pieces of furniture we had bought was a large white wood desk. Steve had picked it out. He thought a doctor should have an impressive desk in the home office (the old sleeping porch). That sucker weighed a ton and was large enough to be impractical. Steve and I struggled it up to the house and into the stairwell where we managed to get it wedged tightly between wall and banister. We couldn't get it up, we couldn't get it down, we couldn't back it out. We asked one of our body-building neighbors for help. He couldn't budge it either. We finally had to get out a skill saw and cut the legs off (the desk, not the body-builder) in order to free it. We then reassembled the whole thing in the office with a little wood glue. And never did it budge again. When it came time to move to Alabama, we left it in the house. For all I know, it's still there.

I'll figure out the moving thing eventually. Truth be told, it's not high on my list of worries right now. But I remain amazed at my long track record of poor timing in real estate transactions. If COVID-19 had hit six weeks earlier, I wouldn't have been out looking. Had it hit six weeks later, I would already have moved.

APRIL 2020

With So Little To Be Sure Of

WEDNESDAY | APRIL 1, 2020

T'S HUMP DAY EVENING. I've eaten my leftover chicken massaman from the local Nepalese takeout accompanied by a glass of Côtes du Rhône (Tommy's favorite); and I finished sorting the movie collection and pulling the obvious discards.

I've never been one to drink alone, but as day drags on into yet another of the same day, by myself in the house, I'm opening a bottle of wine a week and enjoying the occasional glass. One less thing to have to move. I still haven't quite figured out how I'm going to do that in the middle of a societal lockdown, but that's a problem for another drag-on day.

The coronavirus counter I check every evening shows that we're now at roughly a million cases reported worldwide (likely a huge under count as the statistics from a number of countries are not to be trusted). That's including twice as many cases in the USA as in Italy over the last two weeks, and the Alabama number is entering four figure territory for the first time.

We continue to cope with local needs at UAB and at the Birmingham VA. But two weeks in, there is already a feeling of fatigue amid the certainty that this is going to get a whole lot worse before it gets better. I figure we're going to have a better sense of the local parameters of the pandemic in about two more weeks when we see what the behaviors that we choose today are doing tomorrow in terms of either controlling or promoting spread.

I tend to hang out with relatively compassionate and socially minded people, so we're all practicing our social distancing and isolation with reasonable success, but I can tell from the social media feeds of my friends that there's a longing for a return to a world of rehearsals, neighborhood restaurant nights, theater parties, and the simple joy of hanging out with one's usual crowd and not feeling a need to do much of anything. A friend of mine is trying to work out an online version of Cards Against Humanity but it's just not going to be the same.

Today's musings have to do with trying to battle instinctual behaviors. We all have them. They're buried deep in the limbic system and tend to make themselves known at times of stress. Social animals that we are, in times of fear and uncertainty we seek solace in the group. I absolutely understand why some communities are still trying to come together in religious rituals. It's a deep and innate longing and a true need in unsettling times.

Unfortunately, our intellectual selves, having mastered an understanding of biology and basic virology, know that this is one of the worst things we can do from an epidemiologic point of view. It leads to primitive conflict playing out, especially here in the South, between militant church goers and other members of society who recognize that this behavior will endanger others.

Where do I stand on this? I believe that god will understand if church is in abeyance for a while and also that god is helping me through this; god gave me a brain smart enough to not put myself in a position of danger.

I think I learned the most about battling my own instincts when I took trapeze lessons for a year a couple decades ago. I'm not going back to it. At my age I'd likely dislocate a shoulder or fracture a hip or some such.

I started at a resort in Mexico. Steve and I had booked a vacation there in the spring of 1998 and, the week before we left, UC Davis decided to disband its clinical geriatrics program and handed me a 60-day pink slip. Needless to say, by the time we arrived at the Blue Bay Los Angeles Locos resort North of Manzanillo along with a couple hundred other gay men, I was fit to be tied and needed something to make me feel like I still had some mettle left in me. They were offering beginner trapeze lessons, so I signed up thinking that if I could face my acrophobia, I could take on upcoming work challenges.

Trapeze is all about physics. At the peaks of the arc, you're basically weightless and can do your maneuvering without too much difficulty. Some of the tricks that look spectacular from the ground are relatively easy. The hard part occurs, after being caught, in returning back to the original fly bar. I never did quite get the hang of that.

When you're standing on the platform with the fly bar in your hands, everything in your brain is trying to make your body thrust its center of gravity backwards onto the platform so you won't fall 25 feet or so. However, to successfully launch, you must do the opposite and puff out your chest, draw your hips in and keep your center of gravity forward towards the bar. It's difficult to get yourself to do that. It requires a sort of zen tranquility to override the lizard brain that's in full flight or fight mode.

I took several series of lessons at that resort the next few years, and then continued with a flying school in Atlanta for a time. I stopped when I met Tommy and got interested in other sorts of performing. Running off to join the circus in my forties wasn't in the cards.

The apprehensiveness that I feel, that we probably all feel as we experience this global event, has me feeling like I'm standing on a trapeze platform. I want to bend backwards and hold myself in a completely wrong position because it feels like a place of safety. But I know I must stand tall, stick my chest out, and launch myself into a new and unknown world. It's scary as hell but I've done it before in all sorts of ways. I have to trust that the safety lines and the net of my intelligence, my education, my family, my friends, my career, my performing instincts, and all the rest, will lead to a successful trick and dismount. Even if I fall, I have learned how to do so safely and gracefully; falling is the first thing you learn in trapeze because you're going to do it again and again.

FRIDAY | APRIL 3, 2020

AND SO WE COME TO THE END of another work week. My patients are as tucked away as I can make them from a distance, the staff are free for another weekend of social distancing, the reports of more and more cases overwhelming the greater NYC area roll in.

Birmingham has remained stable this past week due to the early adoption of closures and social distancing. The state of Alabama finally followed suit today, but I'm afraid it's going to be too late for many of the smaller towns that have assumed they're safe outside of an urban core. The numbers for many of the rural counties are starting to spike. I figure we will know where we are locally in another two weeks.

I do not watch the executive branch daily news conferences. From what I can tell, they consist mainly of contradictions and word salad. The election of someone who promised to take a wrecking ball to government institutions means those institutions are non-functional or non-existent when we need them. It's every state for itself in terms of pandemic response; some have been more proactive than others and you can see that in the numbers.

Numbers on the West Coast grow but at a slower proportional rate than the Deep South. I'm hoping we're all learning a painful, but necessary lesson in the role of the federal government in times of crises that affect the whole country equally.

My housekeeper is on furlough with four children suddenly out of school. I came home from work intending to vacuum and dust and make the house presentable, but the only person who sees it is me. So what if there's cat hair on the living room rug? It adds to that lived-in look. I played Xbox for a few hours instead, then made myself a gourmet meal of Kraft macaroni and cheese, hot dogs, and salad in a bag.

In the freezer, I found some of Tommy's famous chili left over from our last holiday open house on New Year's Eve 2017 and some butternut squash soup he made of more uncertain date. I've put all that in the fridge to thaw for dinners this weekend.

I am continuing my slow sort and clean-out of junk. I still have to tackle the kitchen and the closet in the spare bedroom. Then I'll have made a first pass on the main living areas. I'm leaving the basement and the garage for later. They are the Big Bad Boys.

I'm trying to think what to write about tonight and absolutely nothing is coming to mind. Perhaps it's the glass of wine with the mac and cheese robbing me of creative thought. Perhaps I'm just carrying too much psychic weight. Perhaps I've told all my good stories already.

For some reason, I've been thinking about early childhood. I flashed on my first day of kindergarten. The neighborhood where I grew up in Seattle was the faculty ghetto for the University of Washington back in the mid-1960s when we moved into the house in which I grew up. I started kindergarten in the fall of 1967, right after the Summer of Love. It was a half-day program. I was in the morning class with Mrs. Easterwood. I quickly learned how to walk to school, about twelve blocks for me each way, but on that first day, my mother brought me. I had been in pre-school at Acorn Academy (from little acorns, mighty oaks grow), so going to school was nothing new.

I came in, marched around the room, and read all the signs on the walls aloud. Mrs. Easterwood looked at my mother and said something like "So, he can read," and my mother looked somewhat abashed. My parents hadn't formally taught me; I more or less taught myself from picture books, being read to, and marching up to my parents, book in hand, demanding to be told what this or that word was.

It was decided that I would be sent next door to the first grade classroom during reading time as I would be bored silly by the elementary exercises happening in the kindergarten room.

I loved school, still do, although my mother chuckled for years about the time I came home, stomped in the house, and started complaining about how one girl told me what color to color my balloons. I also remember another being much better at cutting circles than I was.

My first years of elementary school were run on the precepts of the 1940s and 50s. Boys and girls had recess on separate playgrounds. Everything was very formal. Girls were expected to wear dresses. Boys were expected to be assertive and unemotional.

Seattle Public Schools didn't have its act together yet on arts education, so big black and white televisions were brought in for broadcasting music and visual art class from the local PBS studio at the University of Washington, before it was actually PBS. I still remember chanting the universal tah-tah tee-tee-tah music class rhythm along with the other 5-year olds. That all returned again much later in life when Tommy went off to the University of Montevallo and got his degree in choral music education.

Mrs. Easterwood seemed incredibly ancient to me, but was in her mid-40s. I Googled her several years ago and found her obituary. She made it well into the new century before dying at age 98, having taught several generations of kindergarteners. More than 50 years later I still recall her voice.

I seem to have a good ear for voices even after many years. At a public lecture I gave in Seattle a few years ago, a lovely older woman came up to me to thank me and to ask me if I remembered her. I didn't recognize her at all, but as she spoke, I knew exactly who she was: my fourth grade teacher. I don't run into too many people from my distant past these days, but when I do, the voice tells me who it is.

Today's children will have a vastly different growing up. One thing I am hoping happens with the current crisis is that families spend more time together as they stay home and focus on each other. I hope the kids, when they are my age, look back on this time as a time of togetherness, silliness in the backyard, family games, projects with siblings, and a break from the overly scheduled lives we've tended to foist upon them in our quest to mold them into competent, competitive adults. I hope we all take the small joys that this time has to offer and that we treasure them.

In the meantime, be well.

SUNDAY | APRIL 5, 2020

LAST TIME I WROTE AN ENTRY in the plague diaries, it was the end of the work week. This time, it's the end of the weekend. Was it an exciting and action-packed weekend? Hardly. Those are in abeyance for the duration, but I had a few minor triumphs.

In the harsh light of day, I decided the cat hair on the rug was not a lived-in, but a slovenly look, so I broke out the vacuum cleaner and the duster and cleaned the main floor of the house. I also finished sorting the DVD collection for discards and entered all the ones I'm keeping into an app database, so I'll know what I've got the next time I look for a physical copy of something. I played three very long games of Civilization VI on the Xbox, losing every time to my AI opponents.

I've always enjoyed games of all sorts and I don't have a live person to play with at the moment, so I have to make do with the computer. I read a dozen chapters in the book my sister gave me for Christmas, a zombie apocalypse tale in Seattle told from the point of view of a tame crow and the pets left behind. I took two long neighborhood walks. And I "attended" online church with a sermon on the non-canonical gospels entitled *The Heretic in the Pulpit.* Let it not be said that we Unitarian Universalists have no sense of humor.

On one of my walks I encountered an old friend and neighbor and we called a few pleasantries to each other across the street, practicing the new normal of social distancing rather than standing toe to toe and giving each other a friendly hug. While we were talking I had a flash about what to write this evening.

One of the themes I've seen as friends have been posting about the coronavirus is the common fear of being stranded without health insurance due to job loss. We are the only advanced society that ties health care and employment together. As most of us grow up in this system, it seems normal to us while most of the rest of the world considers it bizarre, inhumane, and unworthy of an advanced democracy. How did we get here? Why do we do it?

To answer these questions, we have to go back to the 1920s and 30s. In the 1920s, the average American family spent a greater portion of their wealth on cosmetics than on health care. For the most part, you didn't access the system. Doctoring was done by mom or granny, and the vast majority of illnesses were handled at home. Doctors, almost exclusively men, were mainly general practitioners who were part of a community that supported them in a symbiotic relationship. This is where all the stories about paying the doctor in chickens came from.

If the doctor had an office, it was often part of his house and he spent most of his time making the rounds in the donkey cart or the Model T calling on the sick at their homes, providing service and succor as he could. There were hospitals, but they were small and generally used for a few specific purposes: surgery, separation of those who might be dangerous to the greater community (via the asylum and the sanitarium), teaching, and as a carer of last resort for those without intact family structures who were medically ill. These hospitals were owned predominantly by public or religious institutions with a charitable mission to provide care for the ill and were non-profit in nature.

Health insurance, as we understand it, was invented in 1929 in Dallas, Texas. Baylor University had constructed a large new hospital and was having difficulty filling beds. The vice president for health services at Baylor, Justin Kimball, had connections with the Dallas school teachers union and hit upon a plan. If the teachers would pay Baylor fifty cents a month, they would then be eligible, should they require hospital treatment, to enter Baylor's hospital free of charge for up to 21 days. This ensured Baylor a steady stream of income via a steady stream of patients over the next decade or so.

This original plan morphed over time, as it grew, into Blue Cross: an amalgam of local plans which over the next couple of decades became the organization that those of my generation remember from childhood. Blue Shield, which eventually merged with it, had a different origin. It came from a banding together of workers in the logging and mining camps of the Pacific Northwest into fraternal organizations that paid doctors fees if one of their number became ill. Blue Cross and Blue Shield grew piecemeal throughout the 1930s due to the state of the economy wrought by The Great Depression.

In the early 1940s, with the United States now at war, many of the heavy construction jobs, especially in the shipyards and airplane factories, were taken by women as the men were fighting overseas. (These were the days of Rosie the Riveter). It didn't take long for the titans of industry to figure out that if these women fell ill, or if their children fell ill, they could not come to work, and productivity would be hindered. It started to become the smart business decision for a company to begin thinking about the health of its employees and their families in order to keep the line, and its profits, running at peak efficiency. The leader among the heavy industry types was Charles Kaiser, head of Kaiser Aluminum. He led the way in making sure his employees had access to good and timely health care and that the bills would be paid.

In the latter half of the 1940s, after the end of the war and the return of the men to the workforce, heavy industry faced another problem. While the economy was gearing up to meet 15 years of pent-up US consumer demand, not to mention helping the rest of the world rebuild its shattered infrastructure, there were still laws on the books left over from The Great Depression, which controlled wages. As such, it wasn't possible for company A to offer potential employees more money than company B for the same job. So corporate America found something else to make up the gap: the benefits package, which did not fall under these rules.

Health insurance, as it had already taken root in heavy industry, quickly became a carrot for getting employees to sign on the dotted line. By the late 1940s, industrial America lobbied congress to change the tax code so that it became advantageous to the owners of industry to offer a health benefit. So, like many other American social changes, employer-sponsored health insurance has its roots in American tax policy. Nobody really thought about the long-term ramifications as employer-tied health insurance was born. Nor was much thought given to the marginalized groups that would be left out of such a scheme.

Through the 1950s and 60s, the system worked relatively well. Hospitals were not-for-profit by both custom and law. Physicians were small independent businesses. There wasn't much money in the health sector of the economy and, as employment was relatively easy to get in the booming post-war economy, everyone was happy.

Things started to change with the introduction of Medicare and Medicaid in 1965, created by President Lyndon Johnson and congress in the wake of the Kennedy assassination as part of his Great Society initiative and his war on poverty. The thought was to give populations who were not employed or employable access to the healthcare system: Medicare for the elderly and disabled, Medicaid for the impoverished. This caused a sudden influx of federal dollars. The initial 1965 budget for Medicare was $3 billion (about $25 billion in current dollars) and the healthcare sector as a percentage of GDP began to mushroom from 6% in 1965 to 8% in 1975 to 10% in 1985 to nearly 18% today. Money always catches the eye of the businessperson, and this was no exception.

It was Charles Kaiser who went to his old friend Richard Nixon in 1973 and persuaded him to sign a piece of legislation known as the HMO (Health Maintenance Organization) Act in order to allow him to spin off his health organization into a free-standing company (Kaiser Permanente). The consequence of this, intended or not, was that the language of the act made health care, up to then a not-for-profit enterprise, into a for-profit industry.

Wall Street took notice, and corporate America arrived in health care in the late 1970s, determined to turn medicine into a business, one that manufactured hospitalizations and patient encounters, using the same business principles that had served it well in other sectors of the economy. By the mid-1980s, the field of medicine was very different than it had been just a decade earlier as we evolved from a healthcare system, whose goal was to heal the sick and injured, into a healthcare industry whose goal was then, and has been ever since, to create profit for those who control it.

These trends have continued over the intervening decades (coinciding with my time in medicine; I entered medical school in 1984), and now there is an enormous stress on the system wrought by COVID-19. What will the ultimate outcome be? I don't know, but I don't think the health system will look the same or operate the same when we emerge on the other side. I'm hoping that it will push the American population to begin demanding that our healthcare system put health above profit again, but it's going to be a long tough road.

Stay well.

WEDNESDAY | APRIL 8, 2020

'VE TRIED TO BE DISCIPLINED and keep posting every other evening, but last night I felt like a balloon after all the air had been let out. I crawled into bed at 9 and slept until the alarm went off at 7 this morning.

I feel fine. I think my brain just needed some off time from the toxic stew of life stresses we're all marinating in at the moment. At least the new work patterns are becoming slightly more predictable. I've been able to stay on top of the crises in three different systems: UAB Geriatrics Clinic, Birmingham VA Home-Based Primary Care, and Comfort Care Hospice. One day, one patient, one problem at a time—plus the regular dinging of my phone with incoming texts from whichever two sites I'm not currently at.

The number of Facebook friend requests I'm getting and my blog readership are going up astronomically since I've begun with these diary entries. I'd much rather be doing travel diaries, but one writes about what one knows. Journaling comes out of the mundane and the minutiae of everyday life, and all of our everyday lives have become about COVID-19 whether we want them to be or not.

In my last entry, I briefly explored why the US has health insurance tied to employment while such a system happened nowhere else in the industrialized world. Tonight I want to say a few words about another aspect of the US healthcare system that is unique and uniquely tragic to our country because it causes a significant amount of trouble. I'm not going to pass judgment on why this is or the ethics or social trends behind it. I'm just going to put it out there.

The majority of world health systems, especially those of the developed world, are morbidity-driven health systems, systems driven by the need to reduce the suffering and dysfunction of illness. The aim of these systems is to keep their people well. These countries in Scandinavia, Western Europe, and East Asia, among others, understand that health is much cheaper than disease, and that resources are best deployed to keep the majority of the population as healthy as possible. Healthy adults come from healthy children who come from healthy infants who in turn come from healthy adults.

These countries put enormous resources into making sure all of their population has easy access to high quality care, that primary care is well funded and readily available, that there is adequate prenatal and child care, that pediatric care will not stress a family unit, and that preventive services that catch disease early are easy to obtain. What's the result? Their populations have higher life expectancies than we do, their systems cost much less (usually 9-11% of GDP while ours is about 18% of GDP), no one worries about medical bills, and the possibility of bankruptcy from a health condition is so alien as to be unfathomable.

In contrast, the US healthcare system is a mortality-based system, a system concerned with the prevention of death, but not of disease. We worry about why people die and do everything we can to prevent that occurrence. A death is considered a failure of the system to provide adequate care in some way (and our legal system is always looking to find someone at fault). We view life as linear with death as an endpoint and, if our health system is applied properly, we should never actually allow anyone to get to the end.

There are some generational differences in these ideas, but it is most clearly seen in the early Baby Boomers, those now heading into their early 70s who were born in the late 1940s and early 1950s, and who still view themselves as being forever young. There's a line from a film which, paraphrased, goes something like this: "How can I be old? I was at Woodstock!"

Our cultural need to prevent death leads us to pour huge resources into individuals who are obviously in a dying process. For most people, death is a process, a quick one for some (almost instantaneous in some cases), a slow one for others. Most health professionals know when someone is in the dying process, but we are taught from early in our training how not to take away hope and are immersed in the ethics of doing everything in our power to preserve life if that is the wish of a patient and family. But, deep inside, we often recognize when continued treatment is doing no good.

The specialty of palliative care, which has arisen over the last few decades, is capitalizing on this mismatch, showing that there is another way of not being aggressive with treatments during the dying process. It has even been shown scientifically that, in many cases, people actually live longer just having their symptoms treated than they do when someone is trying to cure their incurable underlying disease process.

Other countries look at us somewhat amused: "Those crazy Americans! They see death rates ticking up from cardiac disease and put everyone on aspirin, everyone on a statin, train more cardiologists. Then cancer rates start to climb, so they open more cancer centers, create new chemo regimens, invent new biologic tumor annihilators. Now it's an increase in dementia they worry about, so they're putting in more work on new drugs to prevent it (so far, unsuccessfully). Don't they realize that the numbers always add up to 100%, and that all anyone can do is move people from one category to another?"

The problem is that we don't realize this when it comes to how our health system operates. I am fond of reminding Medicare insurance executives in meetings, when they're touting how wonderful their product is at keeping people alive, of the fact that everybody dies. It has not endeared me to them, but I don't mind.

This issue of morbidity versus mortality is going to play out during the current pandemic. I don't know how just yet, but it will be interesting to keep comparing the response in other countries to our response here. I remain afraid that we're still in the early days of all this, no matter how tired we may be of our disrupted lives.

Stay well.

SATURDAY | APRIL 11, 2020

SHOULD HAVE WRITTEN a long post last night, but I was feeling a bit down. It was Tommy's birthday (he would be 55 were he still here), and that took me back to memories of the last birthday we spent together.

He was in the Cardiac Care Unit at UAB recovering from an infected central venous catheter. That had to be cleaned up so he could have cardiac stents placed in what would ultimately be a fruitless attempt to preserve his cardiac function, and his life.

Tommy hated what he called Hallmark holidays and didn't like his birthday commemorated. (Heaven forbid I should give him a birthday present.) He eagerly accepted presents on all non-holidays however, part of his contrarian nature. I did ask him that day if he would like anything for his birthday. He surprised me by saying yes. He wanted carrot cake from Continental Bakery where he had worked at some point in the 90s. So off I went to get a small one for dessert that night. I don't think the nurses were happy. It wasn't on his diet plan. But he had let them know early on that he was going to eat as he pleased, diet plan be damned.

Last year on his birthday, I decided to keep up the tradition and went and got myself a carrot cake at the same bakery. This year, trying to minimize community contact as I am, I didn't go to the Continental, but I did do my once-every-three-week grocery run and, while my local Piggly Wiggly didn't have carrot cake, they had a package of carrot cake Oreos, so I bought that instead. I don't think Tommy would mind; he'd probably find it funny.

This week in April is always hard. Steve's birthday is this coming Monday. What is it about me and Aries men? I suppose to continue the pattern, if I have a third husband, his birthday will have to be April 7th. Also, he will have to have a first name he doesn't use and alliterative middle and last names he does just like Jon Steven Spivey and Louie Tommy Thompson, Jr. This may be a tall order.

Another work week has ended. UAB and the Birmingham VA continue to handle coronavirus cases without too much difficulty, but I am concerned about how we will fare a few weeks from now when small town Alabamians who have not been embracing social distancing start to manifest infections. A few people of my acquaintance have been infected and recovered. One has died. Most of us have remained healthy due to the Birmingham area's early embracing of shut downs. It helps when the biggest economic engine of the community is a major research university with a huge medical school. I've got the new work patterns down pretty well, and we're holding the geriatrics program together via the brave new world of tele-medicine, home health agencies, and creative problem solving.

I checked my official coronavirus counter: Today we surpassed 500,000 cases in the United States (almost certainly a huge undercount as testing remains spotty), 3,000 cases in Alabama, and we're relentlessly creeping up on 1,000 cases in Metro Birmingham. Despite indifferent political leadership, the medical community has rallied, pooled information, pooled resources and, even in the greater New York area, seems to be plowing forward with what must be done.

Of course, the pundit class, thriving as they do on the 24-hour news cycle, has grown weary of social distancing, quarantine, and isolation and wants this all to be over so they can move on to the next sensation which will distract us all and make their advertisers happy. Unfortunately, viruses have no interest in human concerns, their only concern being propagation. They cannot be reasoned with, bribed, or otherwise made to do human bidding—even for better television ratings or higher Q-scores. There is a well-known series of steps necessary to bring pandemic illness under control but, from what I can see, no one's that interested in following them as they are difficult to sensationalize or monetize. But, until we start accepting this biologic reality, we're going to have trouble.

No big plans for the weekend. Nowhere to go. My usual distractions of rehearsal and performance are on indefinite hiatus. It does look like the condo sale will close next week as scheduled and that I will take possession by the end of the following week. I still haven't figured out how I'm supposed to move while we're shut down and in isolation. In the meantime, I am slowly de-junking the house, finding some rather surprising things tucked away in corners.

As I've only been here four years, there hasn't been too much time for accumulation, but there are still moments of "What the hell is this and why do I own it?" I think many of the odder things are the result of Tommy's late night online shopping addiction. He would order the strangest things at 3 AM. There were many times when he would show me his latest gadget, and all I could think was "Garage sale in

73

five years." But it kept him happy. Wherever he is now, I hope he's just as happy.

Stay well.

MONDAY | APRIL 13, 2020

THE DATE TODAY BOOKENDS THE DATE at the start of the weekend. Friday, the 10th, was Tommy's birthday; today, the 13th, was Steve's.

If Steve had lived, he would be 72 years old. I have a hard time envisioning a septuagenarian Steve. I don't think he would have enjoyed that age much. Perhaps it's best he left the party a bit early. If someone had told my younger self that by the age of 55 I would be widowed twice and living in Birmingham, Alabama, I would inquire just what drugs they were ingesting. Funny how life turns out sometimes.

The coronavirus caseload locally continues to remain steady. The health system has been able to absorb it and cope with the needs of the ill. From what I can tell, people in rural areas are starting to understand that they are not immune and are beginning to take social distancing more seriously, doing such things as drive-up church, where everyone stays in their cars in the parking lot while the pastor on the porch uses a PA system. Whatever it takes.

When you're in more rural parts of the state, there's not much Wi-Fi or Zoom conferencing available. A decade or so ago, when I was working with mine workers in rural West Virginia and one of the nurses was having database problems, she called into tech support (in Minneapolis, if I recall), and the tech just wanted her to go down to the local Starbucks and hop on the Wi-Fi. She had to educate him as to just how rural the hollers of West Virginia actually are: Starbucks was a three-hour trip to Charleston.

I now have a proper video conferencing station set up at my UAB clinic office, so I can connect face-to-face with patients and families with smartphones. It's not the same as being in the same room, but it's better than trying to hazard guesses about certain issues over the telephone. Now I just have to get the over-80-set to trust their smartphone capabilities. Most of them are still tied to their landlines.

I've considered finally leaving my landline behind when I move to the condo. The problem is that it's the only thing loud enough to wake me up at night when I'm on call. The cell phone just doesn't do it. Perhaps I'll find a nice klaxon ringtone for it. Tommy was always an early adopter of new technology. He got an iPhone about a year before I made the switch. He would get the latest and the greatest, I would watch him use it for a while, then he would trade up, and I would get his old one, having finally figured it out. It worked as a system.

Yesterday was Easter Sunday. The Deep South was wracked with thunderstorms and tornadoes, a good day for me to stay indoors under a blanket with a book and the Xbox. Birmingham proper was fine, just a lot of noise, flash, and torrential rains that led to some spot-flooding, including the basement of the theater where I do most of my performing. There were tornadoes in outlying areas but, at last report, no one in Alabama was killed. Mississippi wasn't so lucky. More storms are due to come through tonight.

I was in need of comfort food, and in digging through the freezer, I found more of Tommy's famous chili. I thawed it out and had it for Easter dinner. It had lost none of its heat for being in the freezer for a couple of years and, per usual, I had to cut it with a bunch of sour cream. Tommy cared immensely for people. He didn't always show it and could be a little rough around the edges, but he did, and the way he showed it best was in cooking for them. He always took great pride in our parties where he made everything on the table himself—from scratch.

As I've been haunted by the ghosts of husbands past this weekend, and this haunting has coincided with Easter, I've been pondering life and death. I can't open social media without seeing a story of some promising life cut short by COVID-19, trapped in a miasma of worry, wondering whether we or those we love will be next.

What do I think about death? I've been around long enough and seen enough people die not to be frightened of it. I don't have any intentions of dying myself in the near future. I don't think I'm done yet.

I've barely scratched the surface of my bucket list but, if my number comes up, I won't be able to complain too much. I've had an interesting life and accomplished a lot more than most with the time I've been allotted so far. If I do get carried off by COVID-19, I have one request. Whoever puts my obituary together is to call out a certain US president and a certain Alabama governor by name, suggest that my premature demise was unnecessary, and was directly linked to their inability to follow proper public health protocols in a timely fashion.

Matter is essentially indestructible, just transformable. The matter that makes up our bodies was forged in stars billions of years ago, billions of miles away. We are, literally, made of stardust. We're allowed to borrow it for a time and then we return it back to the universe where it is recycled in unknowable cosmic plans. What happens to our self, our consciousness, our soul? I have no idea, only that whatever it is it's the same for everyone. The dichotomous afterlife so popular in certain religious traditions makes no sense to me. Each new baby brings light and hope and salvation to the world and, no matter what circumstance or bad choices may bring, that original promise remains within. As we all enter the world in the same way, I think we must leave in the same way as well. I do hope to see both

Steve and Tommy again after. It'll be interesting to see what they've made of each other and what they'll think of what I've done with the remainder of my life.

Stay well. Stay home. Wash your hands.

WEDNESDAY | APRIL 15, 2020

ND JUST LIKE THAT, IT'S APRIL 15TH. In an ordinary year, people would be pounding their heads into their laptops trying to make TurboTax spit out comprehensible numbers and a refund. This is not an ordinary year, however. Taxes aren't due until July.

I had everything complete and to my accountant in early February this year, figuring that a late March or early April refund would help fill my coffers for moving expenses. More fool I. I called my accountant late last week and he, like every other CPA, is snowed under with stimulus program havoc. Routine tax returns will have to wait. He's done my taxes since I moved here during the last millennium, so I trust him to do what he knows how to do.

The great shut down of 2020 is, of course, playing financial havoc in more ways than just accountants trying to figure out the byzantine rules of hastily passed small business loan assistance programs. As money makes the world go round, the lack of it flowing through the system as everyone retrenches for a more sedentary and less consumerist life, is shaking the powers that be. Conservative "grassroots" protests against shut downs and social distancing are sprouting up. The most visible one today was in Michigan at the state capitol in Lansing.

What most of the media reports are leaving out is that these are orchestrated by the usual big money conservative families with a hidden agenda: The Lansing rally was paid for by groups tied to the DeVos family of Amway which includes Betsy DeVos of Secretary of Education fame. I don't think there's been much protest on the right wing in decades that hasn't been paid for out of someone's deep pocket. There are, of course, some economic winners in all of this. The Ravensburger jigsaw puzzle company is having its best year in all 138 years of its existence.

The number of cases keeps going up. There are some interesting social epidemiological trends happening with 50 states responding in 50 different ways due to a lack of centralized federal leadership. The one I was most interested in today was South Dakota, a relatively small state population-wise, where cases have increased nearly tenfold over the last ten days from about 100 to nearly 1,000. The culprit? The conservative governor's steadfast refusal to employ any social distancing or shut down orders of any kind.

I imagine we've only seen the tip of this iceberg, epidemiologically and politically. The pattern will be similar in much of rural America, a population that has been fed a diet of misinformation about how COVID-19 is no worse than the typical flu. We won't hear about most of the deaths in small town and rural America as it's outside the ken of most media figures.

Tonight's subject seems to be money. There's an odd thing going on which at first seems counterintuitive but, on closer examination, makes perfect sense given that we're operating in a healthcare industry and not in a healthcare system. At a time when doctors, nurses, and other healthcare workers are being called upon to put themselves in harm's way, and to sacrifice much, including possibly their lives for the good of American society, they are being faced with pay cuts of 10%-20%. I have even heard some reports of 50%. Why on the one hand are they being lauded as courageous heroes and on the other hand being punished as though they were greedy villains? Because healthcare is big business, big for-profit business. And the unforgiving capitalist truth of supply and demand is calling the tune. COVID-19 is keeping people with other illnesses away from the healthcare system as they start to realize that whatever is going on with them is not so serious as to risk exposure in a crowded emergency room or urgent care clinic. Visits to healthcare providers are plummeting. Doctors are wisely keeping those with chronic illnesses out of hospitals and large clinic buildings where sick people congregate. The result is that outpatient volumes are down 50%-75% nationwide.

Hospital bed occupancy is also way down in order to free up more frontline staff for COVID-19 cases, and to keep other ill people away from active cases as much as possible. Those coming in with COVID-19 are, of course, sicker than snot, but the numbers are small compared to the numbers of patients who usually show up over the course of the average workday. Without elective surgeries, lab tests, routine check-ups, monitoring of diabetes, hypertension, the administering of chemo, and all the thousand-and-one other things that happen every day in predictable volume, collections are down. If a business isn't bringing in sufficient funds, expenses must be trimmed.

Thankfully, I don't have to worry much. As personally alarmed as I am, I'm a pretty cheap date. I work in a specialty where we all support each other and are decidedly socialistic about such things as compensation. It's going to be different for the young 'uns, however, who gave up their youth, buried themselves in debt to complete their educations, and now won't be able to manage the loan payments, the mortgage payments, the college funds of their children, and so many of the little things that chip away relentlessly at their pride and security. The days of the rich doctor were over before I ever entered the profession, and primary care and cognitive specialties have never paid terribly well. As a result, we have had a terrible time recruiting students over the last few decades.

My specialty of geriatric medicine is especially underserved. It peaked at around 9,000 board certified geriatricians in the 90s and, since then, has descended to around 6,000. At the same time, 10,000 Baby Boomers a day have been crossing the line of their 65th birthday over a period of roughly two decades. Those individuals are going to continue living into their seventies, eighties, and nineties.

Selling trainees on geriatrics or other low-paying cognitive specialties is going to become harder than ever. I think a number of mid-career physicians, when this dies down, are going to look at these trends, get themselves out of medicine altogether, and do something else with their lives. I'll keep at what I'm doing; I'm too old to change. And I've made commitments to my patients and to myself to continue seeing things through.

Speaking of money, as of today I have two mortgages, at least until I sell the house. As of 2 PM this afternoon, I am now the proud owner of a new condo. The next couple of weeks will be spent getting it ready for move-in and then I'll figure out some way to execute a move in a time of social distancing and coronavirus. I'm going to have it painted. I don't think I'll go for the wild palette Tommy used in the old house, but it's going to have color and reflect my eccentric personality. My favorite style is Regency-Empire but, of course, I don't have much in the way of furniture that fits this. Someday perhaps. And I can't go too far that direction in a mid-90s condo block. It would look a bit silly.

Be well, be safe, and wash your hands.

SATURDAY | APRIL 18, 2020

W E'RE UP TO ABOUT 730,000 CASES in the US and 4,300 in the state of Alabama. Greater Birmingham is leveling off between 1000-1200 due to our early adoption of shut downs and social distancing.

Unfortunately, those in charge of the economic life of this country, and those who profit most by their policies, seem to have decided that an increased mortality rate is worth it as long as the next quarter's profit margins increase, so they are getting their minions to agitate for opening things up prematurely. It's the old tension of profits versus people that has underlain capitalist economics for the last few centuries and which has been described in detail by far better writers than I.

All opening up at this point is going to do is cause flare-ups and increased infections. Fortunately, Alabama is not yet among the states where a Trump rally sans Trump is happening on the steps of the state house. I see pictures of those people rushing and roaring at buildings, or of Alex Jones who seems to have been strapped in a Barcalounger on top of an SUV, and all I can think of are the zombie hordes in *The Walking Dead*.

I never thought my job as a physician was going to become part call center employee and part tech support engineer. But so it has. We're transferring visits to video conferencing software as much as we can. You haven't lived until you've tried to get 90-year olds to download and connect over a video app when neither their cognition nor their hearing is what it once was:

"I'm sorry you're having trouble hearing me. Let me use my opera voice."

"No, you need the app store."

"No, don't open the app, it will run in the background. I'm going to send you a text."

"No, don't text me back. You see that link in the text? Just click on it."

"No, we can't do this through Facebook."

"Is your daughter there? Could you give her the phone? Perhaps she can help you."

"Can you turn the camera around? The breakfast table doesn't help me."

"Yes, I'll look at your legs, but let's not point the camera up your dress."

And on it goes. Every time I successfully complete a video visit, I feel like I've won a small victory.

On the home front, I was somewhat constructive today. I'd been at a loss after Tommy's death regarding what to do with his home-based studio businesses: teaching children's music, theatrical production, and most importantly theatrical wig-making and styling. One of the reasons we chose this house was the craft room attached to the garage which was fully plumbed, had its own HVAC, and which made a perfect wig studio. Over the last few years of his life, Tommy turned out wigs for show after show after show from *The Little Mermaid* to *Fiddler on the Roof* to *The Color Purple*. Our theatrical endeavors being many, and the remnants voluminous, even the studio and our basement were not enough to contain it all, necessitating a storage space crammed with costumes, props, set pieces, and various other bits of theatrical miscellany.

I have at least figured out what to do with the wigs. I'm donating all of them and all of Tommy's wig-making and styling equipment to the Red Mountain Theater Company in order to furnish out the wig room in the new theatrical complex they are building. In return, the room is being named after him. And so I went down to our storage space and retrieved all of the remaining wigs I could find and put them in the studio so everything would be together when the good folk from Red Mountain come to pack it all up and take it away this next week.

Once the studio is empty, I'll have a staging area for my de-junking of the house. I'm hiring Tommy's wig assistant to be my move coordinator and help make this all go well. As a military wife, she's moved her family multiple times and knows how to make it all work. I also met the contractor at the new condo and went over all of the minor repairs that need to be done prior to moving. We both agreed that the bathrooms ultimately need updating, but that's another problem for another day. They're perfectly functional for now. I'm starting to think about colors for the paint job. I keep changing my mind about them. One of my friends has volunteered to come over with her decorator daughter and kibitz next week.

Someone brought up in a comment on a previous entry that most of the doctors of his acquaintance were quite conservative in their politics. I am definitely not, and he was wondering why that was. First of all, I'm not that far left. I'm a bit left of center for the Pacific Coast. This, of course, makes me somewhere to the left of Vladimir Lenin in the state of Alabama. Second, not all doctors are the same. We're as varied as any other profession. I believe some of these traits, their expression, and the self-sorting of personality types in American medicine comes from the structure of the training.

The US medical education system works as follows. In order to get into medical school in this country, there are a number of requirements, most having to do with college-level science classes plus reasonable scores on the MCAT (Medical College Aptitude Test) entry exam. This tends to push most pre-med students into majors like biology or chemistry. (I majored in both; more fool I). In the 60s and

70s, top grades in science and high MCAT scores were all that were necessary. As a result, the system churned out great clinicians who were not terribly well-rounded people and often had problems with the humanistic aspects of medicine.

There was a shift in the 80s (when I was a med student) to admitting people who had something else going for them, a well-roundedness in addition to good grades and high test scores. The admissions committees wanted evidence of some sort of non-science interest, something that made you stand out from the pack. They also, for the first time, started considering non-science majors seriously as long as applicants had the science credits in place.

For me, it was my technical theater background and my wide-ranging interests. By the time I graduated from Stanford, I had courses in 19 different departments. My medical school class included a professional kayaker, a modern dance major, and a table dancer from one of the more notorious bars in Fairbanks, Alaska. Of course, the education hadn't changed: Most of us round pegs were still being pounded into the same square holes and were pretty miserable.

In your fourth year of medical school, you apply for a residency position. This determines your specialty. Residencies range from three years for most primary care specialties such as family practice and internal medicine up to six or seven years for the more technical surgical specialties such as cardiac surgery or plastic surgery. Your education will be very different and the demands on you will vary widely depending on what you select.

The number of residency slots per specialty is fixed at each institution, and the choice of which one to apply for is up to the student. For certain specialties with limited slots and the possibility of a very lucrative career on the far side, there is enormous competition (dermatology and ophthalmology, in particular) while others go begging due to the high numbers of slots and the low prestige and reimbursement (family practice). I chose internal medicine because I didn't know what I wanted to be when I grew up. The same process happens again after residency for fellowship (subspecialty training), anything from another additional one to four years, depending on what you're learning. For me, it was two years of geriatric medicine. Geriatric medicine is the second-least popular specialty in the country. The least popular is geriatric psychiatry.

Why is this? Because everything about medical training is about diagnosis and cure. In geriatrics, we don't worry so much about that as we do about how people function and feel. That's antithetical to the medical mind and makes many doctors uncomfortable.

All of this is a long way of saying that medical trainees begin sorting themselves early in their careers depending on interests, drives, and personality types. Surgeons tend to be technicians. They're good with their hands and want easily identified problems with clear cut solutions. Medical subspecialists like endocrinologists or gastroenterologists are problem solvers. They like the puzzle of diagnosis. Primary care docs are nurturers. They want to know their patients as people. They recognize that 90% of the issues that bring patients into a primary care office are things that doctors don't have answers for, but the good ones develop strategies that help people anyway.

The closer docs are to the daily lives lived by their patients, especially if those patients belong to marginalized communities, the more likely they are to understand the downside of what actually goes on in our society, and the more likely they are to be advocates for policies and programs that help the people who entrust their lives to them. In American politics, this means they move left. The technicians, far removed from the daily lives of their patients, encountering them only in the artificial world of the hospital, tend to look at the world through the lens of business and personal pocketbook issues, often moving right as a result.

There's one new and very significant trend changing this dynamic: the rapidly growing influence of women in medicine. Women in this country did not begin attending medical school in any number until the 1970s. There were a few who went earlier (my grandmother graduated from medical school in 1926, the only woman in her class). One thing I noticed about these pioneering women when I started to meet them in the 1980s, 15 or 20 years into their careers, was that they had to de-gender themselves in order to succeed. The feminine had to give way to the asexual.

By the time my generation came along, there were enough women in medicine that this was no longer true, but there were other interesting trends. Women were self-segregating, for the most part in primary care disciplines. Perhaps this speaks to nurturing instincts; perhaps to something else. But the result has been more women choosing to fill much-needed roles in primary care. In my experience, women also tend to be more flexible in regards to such issues as job sharing and time off which is important when dealing with childbirth and family life.

To this day, the surgical specialties still remain heavily masculine, but even this is changing. A few years ago, the scales tipped and there are now more women than men in medical education in this country, and more and more are entering the technical specialties. I can easily see the entire profession becoming female-dominated over the next 50 years and that just might be a good thing.

Enough for tonight. Be well. Be safe. And wash your hands. Holmes and Semmelweis... Well, you know.

TUESDAY | APRIL 21, 2020

THE LOCAL NUMBERS FOR METRO BIRMINGHAM are flattening. UAB and the Birmingham VA have weathered the storm without a major disaster.

The conversation has now shifted to how to start thinking about opening things up again while keeping both patients and staff safe. The people at the top calling the shots in both institutions seem to be making cautious and wise decisions with the ability to backtrack if necessary. We'll see how it goes.

I have to give kudos to our governor as well. She has not jumped on the bandwagon of Trumpist conservative Republican southern governors who are running around trying to force things open prematurely for political reasons. She came out today and stated that lifting her closure orders is going to be done based on recommendations from scientists, epidemiologists, and the department of public health. From what I can tell, the rather odd laundry list of things opening soon in neighboring states has more to do with moving people off of unemployment programs for tax and political reasons than it has to do with any sort of orderly transition based on societal need. Nail salons? Massage studios?

I have a feeling when patient care opens up on an outpatient basis for a return to face-to-face visits, there are going to be some major changes in patterns of who comes in and when and why. I think video calls are here to stay. There are still a lot of technical glitches but those are going to get worked out over the next few months. Video calls will work fine for some kinds of routine follow-up but not for everything. I still have no idea how to do a decent physical via tele-medicine, for example. Nothing looks right to me on screen. The VA has long been using tele-medicine to get specialty care to rural areas and is way ahead of the curve, so I may be doing some of my rural house calls via nurse-carried iPad or some such in the not-too-distant future.

Something else I've noticed is that my hypochondriacs have gone dormant. Every doctor has a collection of people who are always "sick", or who have new symptoms that must be addressed, or are worried about this or that. When I've called to ask them how they're doing, they've all been fine and stable and without complaints, some for the first time in a decade or more.

I haven't quite decided why this is. They may have finally realized what sick truly means and have started to understand that they are relatively well. Or they may be so scared of visiting a health facility, for fear of coming into contact with an infected person, that they're going to be well unless something is actually seriously wrong. I have a feeling that doctor-patient dynamics are going to come out on the other side of the COVID-19 crisis somewhat changed and maybe, with people less interested in accessing health services they don't really need, those changes may be for the better.

I attended a virtual cocktail party this evening via Zoom. A bunch of folk from the opera chorus got together, each with his or her glass of wine or cocktail. (I enjoyed a peach hard cider I bought on a whim on my last grocery run). No one has quite figured out the etiquette of virtual gatherings yet, but it was good to see everyone, even in a Brady Bunch gathering of squares on my laptop.

There's something not right with my laptops and Zoom. On one, I can get video and no audio, on the other I can get audio and no video. I settled for the video and dialed in on my phone for the audio portion. A little clunky but it ended up working. Fortunately, I've had some practice with online social life, even before video was possible. When Steve was sick, I had a couple of years when I couldn't leave the house much other than for work. At that time, most of my connections were through email and chat boards. Some of the friends I made that way have remained friends for lo these 20 years. Just another one of my life experiences that seems to have readied me for this particular moment in history.

There's a new Facebook group that's sprung up in the last month or so for gay male doctors. I don't know why there wasn't one before but apparently, given the current social conditions, the time was right. It's now up to nearly 5,000 members. The majority are American, but there are a few European, Australian, Middle Eastern, and South African doctors as well. Despite a tendency of the well-built and good looking to throw in pictures more appropriate for Tinder, it's interesting to see how much has changed in the last couple of generations.

When I was in medical training in the mid 1980s, no one was out in medicine. I take that back, there were a few openly gay men in HIV medicine which at the time was in its infancy. Everyone else was strictly closeted whether student, resident, or faculty.

I understood the lesson: If I wanted to be successful in medicine, I had to be closeted and play the part society expected. Therefore, no real dating or bonding or getting to know my tribe. I also had no role models for how to live an authentic life in my chosen profession. It wasn't until I met Steve in 1989, and he let me know in no uncertain terms that if we were going to be together the closet was not an option, that I came out. Steve came out in the early 60s while still in high school, pre-Stonewall, and had fought for respect and recognition his whole adult life. He wasn't going to retreat one step.

The cultural changes associated with the late 80s and 90s, spurred in part by the AIDS crisis, led to a weakening of some of the barriers and traditions in the medical field. As a result, more people started coming out and demanding to be recognized. By the time I finished my training in the early 90s, there were one or two out residents in every class and a few faculty who began to acknowledge publicly what everyone had suspected for years.

UAB, being in Alabama, was somewhat lagging in this regard when I came here in the late 90s. To my knowledge, I was the first member of the medical faculty recruited as an out individual (everyone else having been closeted until after they got the job). I don't think they quite knew what to do with me and Steve, but they wanted me and my skill set, so I was hired. Someone, it seems, made the right decision, for here I sit, 22 years, two husbands, and thousands of patients later.

As I look at all the eager young faces in the gay physician Facebook group—internists, pediatricians, radiologists, surgeons, pathologists, and so many more—I've come to the conclusion that enduring some of what I endured was OK. My generation broke through the doors and walls and ceilings that are enabling their generation to flourish. They may not recognize the work that was done or the sacrifices made, but the results make it all worthwhile. A new generation gets to live up to their full potential instead of being ghettoized into stereotypical roles.

And so, as Samuel Pepys would say, to bed.

Stay well, stay safe, and wash yo' damn hands.

SATURDAY | APRIL 25, 2020

MY HANDY-DANDY CORONAVIRUS COUNTER shows we're closing in on three million cases worldwide (doubtless a huge undercount for both political and logistical reasons), one million cases in the US, and just over six thousand cases here in Alabama.

The greater Birmingham area remains relatively virus free due to the local population continuing to adhere to social distancing requirements. The state hotspots are Mobile (likely due to proximity to New Orleans) and the Georgia/Alabama border area around Auburn. I have no need to travel to either of those places. I haven't been much of anywhere other than work in the last six-and-a-half weeks. I'm still working on the same tank of gas I put in the car eight weeks ago.

There are still people out there who want to believe, mainly for ideological reasons, that COVID-19 is no worse than the flu and isn't worth all the fuss. As a point of comparison, we are currently at just over 51,000 deaths in the US from the disease (again, likely an undercount due to inconsistent reporting methodologies and spotty testing). At current trends, we'll hit 60,000 by the middle of next week. This means the disease will have killed more Americans in eight weeks than were killed in eight years of misadventure in the Vietnam War. Every one of these deaths was someone's child, someone's parent, someone's colleague, someone's friend. The ripple effects are going to be enormous and long-lasting as we're still in an upward trajectory.

The number of flu deaths in the US varies from year to year, depending on the heaviness of the season. The 2018 flu season, the worst in the last decade, had about 60,000 deaths. Most years it's closer to 20-30,000. The coronavirus has accomplished in the last two months what the flu does in a year, and a really bad year at that. "No worse than the flu" is yet one more piece of deadly populist propaganda.

Some are advocating opening up fully en route to herd immunity. Herd immunity happens when enough of a susceptible population is immune to a disease process so that a communicable disease cannot become established and transmitted. It's what protects the small portion of the population that cannot be vaccinated for medical reasons from common infectious diseases as enough people are vaccinated to keep the disease from ever reaching the vulnerable.

Herd immunity is one of the more basic concepts in epidemiology. It is easy to calculate, based on a simple formula which depends on the transmissibility of the disease. In its simplest form, if an infected person is capable of transmitting the disease to two people (a transmissibility rate of 2.0), one half or 50% of the population must be immune to achieve herd immunity. If it's three people, two-thirds or 67%; four people, three fourths or 75%. The more transmissible a disease, the higher the percentage must be.

The transmissibility of COVID-19 is hotly debated. Best guesses currently run somewhere between 2.2 and 5.7 meaning that between 55% and 82% of the population must be immune to achieve herd immunity. In the US, therefore, with a population of roughly 320 million, between 172 million and 256 million people need to be infected or, with luck, eventually immunized.

How many excess deaths this would cause is unclear as there seem to be significant numbers of subclinical cases—people who have the disease but never know it. The percentage of asymptomatic cases is unknown. Spot studies have revealed numbers from 5% to 80% which is too wide a spread to be of much use. What is clearer is the mortality rate for symptomatic cases which seems to be about 3.5%. This leaves us with a low of 35 million to a high of 243 million clinical cases to achieve herd immunity with 1,170,000 to 8,270,000 deaths.

It may or may not be possible to save those individuals, but the longer we can delay their becoming ill through social distancing and flattening the curve, the greater the chance of developing a vaccine or coming up with medications which, if not a cure, can at least lessen the damage the disease causes.

Then there are the issues of the health system.

It cannot cope with tens of millions of cases at once, but it can begin to cope with lower numbers over a longer period of time. We've been relatively blessed in Alabama. Few of our healthcare workers have become ill and stocks of PPE are lasting. But this isn't true for the country as a whole. Currently, it's estimated that 10,000 US healthcare workers have caught the disease on the job to date. By contrast, in 40 years of HIV care, fewer than 50 US healthcare workers have contracted this disease on the job.

I see the crowds rallying at statehouses, riled up by politicians and economic forces that do not have their best interests at heart. I do not understand this—or them. We all want it to be like it was. I miss getting together with friends, having rehearsal, going out to dinner, so many little things that now seem larger. But I know that as a responsible citizen and member of society, not to mention a health professional caring for a vulnerable population, that I have to put these things on hold for a while.

Even if lockdown orders are lifted, we're not going to go back to 2019 behavior patterns the next day. People have learned a lot these last few weeks and are going to be much more cautious in their choices. They're going to have the freedom to not do things as well as to do things and the economy is going to remain in trouble, driven as it is by consumer spending. There is no way to get through this process without economic disruption whether that's by shutting things down or by doing nothing and letting a significant portion of the population suffer and die all at once, bringing down the healthcare system with it, and with that, 18% of GDP. If my choices are to not do some things I miss or contribute to the destruction of our country, I'll happily choose the former.

If no vaccine is found, ultimately we're all going to be tested by fire and get COVID just as our ancestors all got smallpox. The majority of us will survive; life, society and civilization will go on, just differently. How differently? I don't know. There are tantalizing clues in the study of pandemics past. The Plague of Justinian effectively ended the Roman Empire in the west, leading to the development of Byzantine society. The Black Death of Medieval Europe allowed for the Renaissance, the Reformation, and the modern world. The Spanish Flu hastened the end of World War I. Unfortunately, I left my crystal ball in an old handbag at the left luggage counter of Victoria Station some years ago, so my powers of prognostication regarding the current pandemic are, shall we say, limited.

Be safe, be well, wash your hands.

TUESDAY | APRIL 28, 2020

CASES IN THE US BROKE ONE MILLION TODAY. The number of dead broke 58,000, more than the number of Vietnam War casualties. I find myself in a state of great disturbance. The milestone of mortality is deeply distressing. But something else hangs over me tonight as well.

It's not work stress (although there's plenty of that). It's not cabin fever (going to work regularly has helped keep that from settling in). It's the date.

Two years ago today, in the wee hours of the morning, I got the phone call none of us wants to get: Tommy, who had been finally beginning to recover from serious heart problems after six weeks in the hospital, unexpectedly died in the night.

I had steeled myself for the possibility of his death over the preceding weeks given the seriousness of his previously undiagnosed heart issues, but he fought back valiantly, full of plans for the future. The last time I saw him alive, he was making notes on wigs for *Beauty and the Beast* which was coming up that June. I hadn't expected his death to come that night. If he was going to die, I was thinking there would be a steady downhill course and time to prepare. It was not to be.

So, today, April 28th, is now to me, a day of unrealness, of having to tell his family, of quickly having to make funeral and burial arrangements, and of having to begin contemplating aging alone, rather than with a loving, enthusiastic, exasperating, and unconventional partner in crime.

I know the date will lose its meaning eventually from experience. I always remember Steve's birthday and our anniversary when they roll around every year, but I often don't remember his death day until several days after it has passed. It has lost its meaning with time as his illness and death recedes in my mind in favor of our years of health and adventure. I know the same thing will happen with Tommy eventually. It's just not that time yet.

This was my 7th weekend in isolation. It followed the same pattern as most of the others. Catching up on work undone from the week. Doing some writing. A couple of long walks through the neighborhood. A little more sorting of decades worth of accumulated possessions in preparation for the move.

I did add a couple of constructive moments to the usual. I got together with my moving coordinator. I can take no time off from work prior to June for various reasons, so someone else has to deal with all the niggling details. I also had an interior designer friend take a look at the new space together with her artistic daughter and give me some ideas on colors.

I think I've made final selections. Bolder than the pastels in this house, but not quite as wild as the range of colors Tommy chose for the old one. I have to come up with a name for the new place. I've named all my houses. The first thing that came to mind was COVID Corners but I'm not sure that's the best idea.

I watched the online Sondheim 90th birthday concert last evening. I had tried to watch it on Sunday, but the technical glitches that led to the delay in broadcast meant that I fell asleep about the time it started, so I had to wait until Monday after work.

Such electronic gatherings may be the future of theater in the short term. I hope not. So much of theater depends on the connection between performer and audience. You just don't get that in an electronic medium. (This is why I really don't like watching theatrical performances on film; I always feel like there's something missing—because there is.) Sondheim, however, was worth the delay, and I'm glad I was able to see it.

Sondheim's music has been so much the soundtrack of my entire adult life that any celebration, or new interpretation of the canon, always brings me joy. This time, however, joy mixed with sorrow, especially during Brandon Uranowitz's performance of *With So Little To Be Sure Of*. It's a song that's always been dear to my heart, one that always comes to mind when I think of my losses. To hear it performed so well when I was preparing myself emotionally for the anniversary of Tommy's passing hit me hard, and I cried for a couple of minutes. But the song also applies to this entire moment we're going through: "Crazy business this, this life we live in. Can't complain about the time we're given. With so little to be sure of in this world..."

I, of course, am not the only person to lose a loved one. There's a lot of that going around at the moment. Each unique individual loss, whether its COVID-19 or something more mundane, leaves a hole in the tapestry of life and the edges unraveling. Only a combination of time and other people knit it back up. We all have time on our hands at the moment, but few other people to have it with.

It took a small army of friends, family, and colleagues to get me through my losses with dinners, coffee dates, phone calls, post-rehearsal chats, and all the rest. I feel so much for those who lose someone at this moment in history who can't draw on those resources in the same way: no gathering at a wake or a funeral to share memories and tell outrageous stories, no relief of being lost in a crowd reminding oneself that life goes on, no getting down and playing with groups of children as a reminder of the cycles and continuity of the process of life. If you have lost someone recently or know someone who has, my heart goes out to you.

In the meantime, be well, be safe, wash your hands.

MAY 2020

Something Just Broke

SATURDAY | MAY 2, 2020

'VE BEEN FOLLOWING THE PHOTOS of protests of lockdown orders happening around the country, from waves of people looking like they're about to storm the beaches of Orange County, to angry overly armed yahoos marching on the Michigan capitol building.

It's clear that big money from the usual "conservative" sources is ginning them up and providing logistical support and communications infrastructure. Most of these demonstrations aren't large when you consider the population as a whole and are being amplified by a media eager for content, sensationalism, and ratings.

I stopped watching televised news and information programming years ago. Between the rise of Fox and the sale of CNN to Time Warner, with it's transformation from a legitimate journalistic enterprise to infotainment, there's no cogent analysis or impartial drilling down to facts anymore. True news and insightful analysis have been reduced to hyperpartisan sports-broadcast scorekeeping. It doesn't help anyone understand what's going on, and the sensationalistic punditry is designed only to engage a viewer's emotions.

My first prescription for older people with high blood pressure is to limit themselves to one half-hour newscast of choice daily. That's enough to keep you up to date. Everything else is filler that's going to raise your catecholamine levels. Those of my patients who listen to this advice, a minority to be sure, often don't need further pharmaceutical intervention.

The militia folk parading around with their assault weapons aren't scary to me, just sad. I see young men—raised on a media image that a major societal transformation would resemble a combination of *Mad Max*, *The Walking Dead*, and *Fallout* video games—fantasizing that they were proving their manliness and worth to society as warriors. What did they get instead? People staying home, bonding with their families, working on their gardens, and learning home baking techniques.

These are all positive social things, but they conflict with the patriarchal "a man takes care of himself and his family as a rugged individualist" ideal which permeates American cultural thought. The ways in which urban and multicultural society have been evolving over the last decades don't depend on that cowboy mythos, and those who buy into it are feeling that violent action may be their only recourse. I think they're having a major cognitive disconnect. If it ever comes down to shooting, it's going to go about as well for them as the second act of *Les Misérables*.

More frightening to me than untrained hobbyists with assault weapons is the quiet agenda playing out at the highest levels of the government and business sectors, where certain people have decided that certain classes of other people are expendable for some greater good. It's the sort of thinking we've seen before in other societies and even our own. (Remember HIV in the 80s and 90s?)

Efforts are being made to hide what's going on in senior living communities in Florida, in Midwest agricultural plants staffed mainly by immigrants, in communities of color in large cities, and in the homeless population. It's a slippery slope, and it's easy to cast the net wider and wider, especially when there's positive reinforcement.

What do I mean by this? Fewer nursing home residents means that fewer Medicaid long-term care dollars will be needed, relieving strained state budgets. A need to keep essential businesses open is an opportunity to reduce "bureaucracy" in terms of worker safety protections and environmental regulations. A shrinking of "problem" communities reduces a demand for social services.

There's a word for the merging of the needs of the state with the needs of the business elite, one that harnesses the symbols of patriotism, and holds up an idyllic and virtuous people as clean, while those that are "other" are classified as diseased. That word is fascism.

No matter the gestalt of the moment, the virus won't be beaten this way. COVID-19 isn't going away, and it's continuing to spread. Lockdowns have slowed things, but until there's widespread testing, an effective medical regimen, or a vaccine, there are no other weapons against it. We can give up on mitigating measures, and attempt to return to some semblance of normalcy, but doing so will kill people.

What I think will happen is that we will open up some, more people will die, but that we're just not going to hear much about it. The majority of those who do die will not be reported on by the media who, on a corporate level, have the same vested interest in opening things back up as all other big businesses. We are all, like the gay community of the 80s, going to have to amplify our own voices and let the moral clarity of choosing life speak for itself.

Me? I'll keep going to work. It's my ethical and moral responsibility, and I will follow the directives of my employers in the service of patient safety. The people I work for have made prudent decisions so far. I trust them to continue doing this. And even though I'm as ready to bust out of here as everyone else, I'll continue to stay at home. I have books to read, Netflix to binge, jigsaw puzzles to do, walks to take, food to eat, and I'm still trying to move one household into another over the course of the next month while using appropriate sanitation and social distancing.

Be safe, be well, wash y'all's hands.

WEDNESDAY | MAY 6, 2020

THE HOUR GROWS LATE.

I'm finally getting around to the sideshow of human comedy that is *Tiger King* on Netflix (very definitely one of those "only in America" subjects). I have to admit that this car crash of humanity is hard to turn away from, but I can only stomach one episode at a time.

A flamboyantly gay protagonist exhibiting big cats in the rural Midwest along with his meth-addled husbands. A flower child antagonist channeling Stevie Nicks and exhibiting big cats in Florida, despite possibly having offed an earlier husband. There's nothing so unreal as reality television. At least after seeing it, I'll be able to interpret water cooler conversation among my nursing staff.

I spelled myself by bingeing the new series, *Hollywood*, this weekend, Ryan Murphy's fantasy take on post-war Hollywood and the career of pimp Scottie Bowers. It began promisingly enough as a sort of dramatized *Hollywood Babylon* but was undone by weak casting of pretty faces with minimal talent, and a final episode that angered me as it discounted the years of pain endured by minorities in the Hollywood Dream Factory for a pat, happy ending that wasn't earned by the story.

It can't be all COVID-19 all the time even though it seems so all-consuming, not just to me, but to all of us. There is still art and music and sunshine and small children at play and pets and good food. We can't necessarily enjoy these things in the way our culture has socialized us to believe is proper, but human society is infinitely malleable. People have thrived and lived and laughed and loved everywhere from the depths of the Sahara to the frozen tundra of Lapland. We've developed ways of being shaped by local environments—geographic, climatic, and microbial. We've made it through other plagues. We'll make it through this one.

People misunderstand the Theory of Evolution, in particular, the idea of "survival of the fittest." The fittest aren't the strongest, the biggest, the richest, or the smartest. The fittest are the most adaptable to the inevitable changes of every living system. We like to think of our lives and world as static because it's comforting to do so, but the lives we live and the world we live in are in constant flux. As the quote from Heraclitus goes, "The only thing constant in life is change."

I was born the year of the Cuban Missile Crisis. When I see dramatizations of that era, it looks as foreign to me as an 18th century British costume drama. But clearly, the world was changing then and perhaps all that has happened since is that the pace of change has quickened, which makes fitness all the more a matter of adaptability.

To each of us, personally, even the relatively rapid changes of our age usually happen slowly enough for us to take them in stride. The change that is upon us now is so much quicker and more wrenching than anything we are used to. We're all still in a state of shock, trying to process what has happened and where we are. But with time, we will adapt, even to this.

The number of cases of COVID-19 continues to climb steadily which, of course, means that the powers that be are working steadily to end the one true weapon we have to combat a pandemic of this type: isolation. It's clear to me that those who run our society, nearly all of whom are unelected and not accountable to the public in any way, have come to the conclusion that the groups of people who will be hardest hit are expendable and easily rationalized as collateral damage—the butcher's bill that must be paid by end of day.

The complete rolling over of government institutions to this philosophy is, to me, a betrayal of the most basic of reasons for the existence of government: the protection of the citizenry. I fear that as time goes on, and the death toll continues to mount, and every single one of us loses someone we love, the strain between the will of the people and the will of the power brokers will lead to unexpected outcomes via unknowable effects. Add to this, a society full of Veruca Salts who have no concept of delayed gratification, and there is much that we cannot predict.

The Birmingham music theater types like me, knowing that performing live is out for a while, are all in communication with each other and working out alternate ways of being and sharing. We are adapting as are so many artists these days. We're working on a group choral number, each of us singing our own part at home, and then combining the videos. There's talk of remote readings, remote cabaret entertainments, remote drag tutorials.

There was an extremely sobering webinar yesterday hosted by the National Association of Teachers of Singing, the American Choral Directors Association, and other musical groups looking at what is known about viral spread and singing. This song is a somber one. There is no safe way to sing with other people without risking significant spread between performers and even to the audience as the very act of singing creates the aerosolized droplets the virus hitches it's ride on. Wind and brass instruments do the same thing.

A world without group singing—no opera, no musicals, no national anthem at the ball game, no marching band at half time, no hymns at church is a bleak one. I tend to be an Eyore by nature, but in this particular case I'm going to trust to human ingenuity that someone, somewhere is going to solve these issues medically or artistically or stylistically in some way. In the meantime, I am so sorry for all of my friends who perform, especially the professionals whose life's work and livelihoods have been shuttered completely. An opera singer is the equivalent of an Olympic athlete, stretching the abilities of the body to the nth degree in service of art, humanity, and culture. What do we do to support them if they cannot practice the craft they have dedicated their lives to perfecting? How can we, as a society, protect them—especially as we live in a society that tends to denigrate the artist in general as effete at best and parasitical and destructive at worst?

I miss performing. It is a huge piece of who I am these days, giving me a way to process my life experiences, in community with people I care about and who care about me, all striving in service of a goal greater than ourselves. Rehearsals are my social life. Without them, I feel like I'm an aging queen home alone with equally aging cats and my own aging thoughts.

If I never perform again, at least I went out on top. The four roles I played in the 2019-20 season—Mr. Pendleton in *Choir Boy*, the Ansager in *Politically Incorrect Cabaret*, Will Dearth in *Dear Brutus*, and Herr Schultz in *Cabaret*—were among the best opportunities I have ever enjoyed. I will forever be grateful for this period in my life. I proved to myself that I've still got it, and I think I surprised a few people who are only used to me in small character roles.

Meanwhile, the move creeps on, each step delayed and complicated by issues courtesy of COVID-19. Progress is being made. Tommy's wig studio was packed up by Red Mountain Theater Company and taken to storage where it will be kept until their new performance venue is ready for furnishing, after which it will be the basis of their wig department. This gives me an empty space so I can start getting the discards of practical life out of the house.

I've decided which furniture is coming with me and which is not. Now I'm going through closets. I have two major projects left in the sort: the kitchen and the basement. I am saving the basement for last as I'm looking forward to that process the least. In my more maudlin moments alone at night, I envision myself ensconced in the new place and, as the sun sets, closing all the windows and shutting myself in like Lavinia at the end of *Mourning Becomes Electra*, alone with my dead, waiting for the end. And then I think, no, life goes on. I'll get the new place set up and, assuming I'm not terribly unlucky genetically, I'll pass the test of COVID-19 along with the rest of society, and there will be music and laughter and parties and friends once more. I've got to hang on to something. We all do.

Stay safe, stay well, wash your hands, and remember social isolation isn't about you, it's about others and being a good citizen.

SUNDAY | MAY 9, 2020

T'S MOTHER'S DAY WEEKEND.

I'm two months into my socially isolated life, and still the number of cases of COVID-19 continues to grow. I use the Johns Hopkins coronavirus counter to track the numbers and trends worldwide.

We're at about 1.3 million cases in the US. Alabama will crack the 10,000 mark tomorrow. The national curves show little signs of flattening outside of states like New York, California, and Washington that responded aggressively early on. In most of the rest of the country, exponential growth continues on its merry way.

Our brilliant governor has jumped on the conservative Southern band wagon. She plans to open everything up again this weekend. Friends of mine are describing "Hooray! We're out of lockdown!" parties in suburban cul de sacs, traffic has picked up, there were lines outside of the mall with hungry consumers waiting to get in right at the stroke of 9 AM. I am in need of a washer and dryer for the new condo, but when I went past Lowes and saw the crowd, I decided to wait for a midweek afternoon. I did my every-three-week grocery shopping today. The local Piggly Wiggly is enforcing masks and is nowhere near as crowded as the Publix, so it was a relatively quick and painless (and safer) experience.

With the media full of White House propaganda reverberating through the conservative pundit echo chamber about "It's not so bad" and "Everyone needs to get back to work", I'm anxious about what will happen in two to three weeks. We've been lucky locally to avoid overwhelming the health system, and we're just now developing some breathing room. Life could all come crashing down again shortly. The amount of societal arrogance on display over the course of the last few weeks would be tossed out of a Hollywood writers' room as too far-fetched. Perhaps we deserve every single thing we're going to get.

I had an imaginary conversation with Tommy and Steve over these issues at dinner tonight. In my head, Tommy was arguing that what we're seeing are simple extensions of the nastiness that has always existed in American culture. Steve was busy planning a counter-demonstration to the next right wing "open up" rally complete with a parade float, Earth Wind and Fire on the PA system, and a socially distanced kick line of aging Act Up members.

Out of curiosity, I downloaded all entries to date in these *Accidental Plague Diaries* and found they amount to roughly 30,000 words so far. That's half to a third of a book. It isn't the one I started to write last year about the healthcare system and the coming crush of late-in-life Baby Boomers, but sometimes life takes funny turns. Much of the material I had been digesting for my book on Baby Boomer aging has made its way into these entries, albeit with a somewhat different emphasis. I suspect I'll be commenting more in the future on topics related to aging, health policy, the interaction of the pandemic with the health system, and the D's of growing old: debility, depression, dementia, dissipation.

I'm thinking I need to do a discussion of iatrogenic disease in the not too distant future (diseases caused by doctors and the healthcare system) as we're likely to see many more of these if COVID cases spike again and people start grasping at straws. Hydroxychloroquine anyone? Multiple studies now suggest it is not helpful at best, dangerous at worst. Then there's the presidential suggestion of bleach ingestion, an idea so stupid that I won't further comment upon it here. I also haven't tackled dementia even though it's my specialty. (I am well known at UAB as being one of the few doctors who knows how to communicate effectively with the demented. What this says about me, I don't know.)

On the home front, I have been modestly productive. Still working on moving things. Slowly but surely removing the discards from the house, though not entirely off the property. With the studio empty, at least I have somewhere to put them temporarily. My out-of-work-actor packers are coming on Monday for the books and the art and the DVD collection. I spent my Thursday evening on a video project involving most of the music-theater types in town, repetitively singing the Bass 2 part of an eight-part arrangement to a pre-recorded track and filming myself so I can be mixed in with 40 others by a genius sound engineer. Take after take ended with me cursing my latest mistake, but eventually I got a couple takes that I thought would do and sent them in. It was a healthy reminder that I am strictly a character singer, and that I should never be allowed to sing *a cappella* in public.

Tomorrow is Mother's Day, the first without my mother. She ceased to understand or care about such things a number of years ago as her dementia advanced, but she is still here with me, and I thought about her as the weekend rolled in. My birthday usually coincides with Mother's Day weekend (it's the day after this year), so there were often dual family celebrations in mid-May when I was growing up.

In a different life, the clan would have gathered in Seattle a couple of weeks ago for her memorial service. We could have all been together and swapped stories of the remarkable woman that was Alison Beatrix Saunders Duxbury. Her keen intelligence, her love of language, her use of the cutting word that could put Dorothy Parker to shame, her affinity for the natural world. But it was not to be.

We may be able to do something as a family later in the year, but we're getting too distant from her passing for a public memorial to have the same meaning. As international travel is out for the foreseeable future, and as I am in need of some time off, having not had a vacation since last Thanksgiving, I may work out a way to go to Seattle sometime this fall. I figure they'll have gotten air travel figured out by then. Or I could drive. I'll just have to allow an extra nine days for that round trip. But this is a challenge for another day.

Be safe, be well, be happy, call your mother.

TUESDAY | MAY 12, 2020

ANOTHER YEAR OLDER.

I completed my 58th orbit of the sun yesterday; today I begin my 59th year. 58 is an odd age to be. There's nothing terribly interesting about the number. You're not yet on the cusp, it's late in an undistinguished decade, it's not even a prime. But that's the way the world and our mathematical system works with its arbitrary divisions determined by the cycles of the seasons and the motion of celestial bodies.

It wasn't a terribly interesting day either. Monday is my double-clinic day at UAB Geriatrics, so it was pretty much work, work, work followed by a Zoom board meeting. There was carrot cake though, not once but twice: at lunch provided by my clinic staff, and at dinner provided by the friends who are my packers and movers.

Yesterday was also the first big packing day in the slow process of relocating. Covid Corners has been rejected yet again as an appropriate name for the new condo. I'm now leaning towards Clearview as it has a view of downtown from its perch on the side of Red Mountain, and I purchased it in pre-COVID-19 2020. My other thought, and another ophthalmological pun, is Hindsight.

Most of the stuff in the house will be packed by the end of the week. Then it's a matter of getting the new space ready to receive it all. That's going slower than anyone would like due to issues with the supply chain delivering replacement items like sinks but, once it's fixed and the paint is dry, I will be ready to send my stuff over. Of course, I won't be able to find anything in the new place for the next six weeks. It's a good thing that theater is out of production and no one is looking for props or costume pieces.

I keep having what seem to be good ideas for tangential subjects well worth pondering here in *The Accidental Plague Diaries*, but by the time I get home, get settled, and begin to write, I can't remember what any of them were. I'll have to start jotting them down during the day and sticking them in my back pocket for later reference.

Some days, as I start writing, it just comes to me and flows. Other days, it's the pulling of proverbial hen's teeth, and I'm quite certain that what I've laid out is complete garbage that no one would be interested in. And then I see a comment from someone after I post about how much they liked it or that it helped clarify something that had been on their mind. This is when I feel as if maybe these musings are worthwhile after all, and I decide to go ahead and write another one. I guess I didn't learn Ginny Weasley's lesson about the dangers of diaries that write back to you.

I do ask for readers to make suggestions regarding what I might write about. Someone brought up the subject of depression in aging. How do older people, who recognize that their physical and cognitive faculties are diminishing, cope with the downhill slide? Do they get depressed by this? Does debility and dementia cause depression or does depression worsen debility and dementia? What does any of this have to do with COVID-19?

I think the first thing we have to consider is that an older person and a younger person are not the same being. I've brought up evolutionary theory before. I do it because one of my big Aha! moments when I got into geriatrics was an understanding that it applied powerfully to aging. Niche Theory is the idea that all species fill an ecological niche in a vast puzzle and that, as the environment changes, each species must change to fit into its niche, its own little microcosm within the macrocosm, or head toward extinction.

Older people are like a species, existing in equilibrium with their niche of a life they've spent decades building. This niche is multi-dimensional, consisting of family, physical environment, finances, social connections, and myriad other factors. But, for the most part, it works for them and they hum along.

Then, slowly, they start to change. Maybe it's arthritis making the stairs more difficult. Maybe it's increasing living expenses eating away at a fixed income. Maybe it's memory lapses. Maybe it's eyesight changes creating problems with night vision and driving. Some of these problems can be fixed, some can't. If they can't be fixed, the person can try to live an unaltered life but, as their physical reality no longer fits key-in-lock with their life niche, things start to go wrong and disease results.

If they can't change themselves, they can change their lives and adapt to new circumstances. Move to a home without stairs, pursue co-housing to reduce expenses, use ride-share services after dark. Those who recognize that life is change and accept and embrace it, keep themselves in balance with their individual aging process and usually do well, rarely becoming seriously depressed. Those who attempt to live in a fossilized reality created by their younger self—seeing the growing mismatch between who they are, who they want to be, and having a life that no longer supports their self-image—often do become depressed. Studies of those who have broken the century mark show that they have but one thing in common: a sense of optimism, a looking forward to the future rather than a sense of regret about the past.

Where did I learn all this? From my mother. She taught junior college sciences from the time I was in middle school until her retirement. Among her many routine courses was basic biology. I remember her grading papers at the kitchen table when I was in high school, Helene Curtis's biology textbook at her elbow, and talking to her about the ideas she was looking for in essay answers. Niche Theory was nearly always on the test. I absorbed it, and it came out again years later in a somewhat different way.

I'll talk more about dementia later; it's much too complex a subject to dispense with in a paragraph or two, but I want here to offer at least a basic definition.

Dementia is a syndrome, a collection of signs and symptoms, not a disease. It's the syndrome that presents in an adult when a previously functional brain stops working in the way it used to when that individual was younger. There are hundreds of possible causes of dementia, a panoply of diseases. The most common is Alzheimer's disease, a specific disease process that creates easily identifiable physical changes to the brain. These changes are microscopic and not easily observed in a living person, although newer scanning techniques are beginning to change this.

We tend, in society, to use Alzheimer's and dementia interchangeably, but this is not accurate. Alzheimer's is a specific subset of the dementing illnesses. It is likely not even a single disease but a number of different processes with common final pathways leading to similar pathologic brain changes. We're just not smart enough yet to separate them all or to understand them as different entities.

People with dementia do get depressed. Sometimes they have difficulty accepting or adjusting to inevitable changes and loss of function. This can be treated pharmacologically and, in early stages, with psychotherapy. It's not inevitable. I know plenty of severely demented people who have been serenely unaware of their own declines and perfectly happy through the process.

We don't know why some people get depressed and some don't. I have a feeling that personality structure plays a role, as does heredity and individual neurochemistry, with some additional input from life experience. Some people are depressed in early stages when they become aware of the changes and their losses. They may lose this later on when their world becomes only the here and now and what they can immediately sense.

Some people develop change in the frontal lobe that keeps them from self-initiating: They simply stop doing things they would have normally done in the past. They can take care of themselves and their body, but they lose all interest in formerly pleasurable activities and just sit on the couch doing plenty of nothing. Families usually interpret this as depression, but it's not. As such, it's usually not amenable to antidepressant treatment. Adjustments typically have to be made, but not by the patients as much as by their loved ones.

In general, keeping people looking forward, keeping their sense of adult self and dignity intact as much as possible, and slowly helping them change their lives to keep them in line with their abilities, does more to prevent and alleviate depression with dementia than anything in pill form. Pills are occasionally necessary. They can help prevent friction in family life as much as they help the individual, and when a demented person is at home, you have to treat the family as a unit, not the individual in isolation.

This is where COVID-19 comes in and why I am both angered and saddened by those bound and determined to open society up before we have a good handle on the virus. Opening up too soon may help the lives of younger people, but will not help the lives of the elderly and cognitively impaired. It will place continued barriers between elders and their family members for fear of infecting a vulnerable person. Baby time with grandchildren and great grandchildren (especially valuable for demented elderly women) stays restricted. Family members who would meet and eat together for Sunday dinner will drop off a bag of groceries on the front porch and go. Older people who fall ill and must be admitted to the hospital will be forbidden visitors and become delirious with no familiar faces or other comforting presence.

Those whose needs are beyond what a family can provide and who live in a facility don't necessarily understand why no one comes to see them anymore or, if they do, realize that a FaceTime chat isn't the same as a hug and a healing touch. Instead, they're locked down with underpaid and overworked staff who love their charges but who simply don't have the resources to help them maintain good mental health. As a result, those with a dementing process already in place are likely to sink deeper into a confused state more quickly.

When you think about how nice it would be for you if things suddenly opened up, think about the men and women who won World War II who are still with us. Then weigh your wish for dinner at Applebee's against what it may cost them.

I'm still staying in.

SATURDAY | MAY 16, 2020

'M JUST BACK FROM A FOUR MILE CONSTITUTIONAL and I
can tell you that indeed, *Summer is icumen in.*

It's 86 degrees and this is the first day I've really started to feel
the seasonal humidity. I'll have to change my walks to evening or
early morning (fat chance of that).

While scrolling through social media this AM, I ran across a quote
from Albert Camus's novel *The Plague,* that seminal study of human
behavior under uncontrolled pandemic illness conditions. "Stupidity
has a knack of getting its way; as we should see if we were not always
so much wrapped up in ourselves." I could not think of anything more
apropos of the historical moment in which we find ourselves.

The idiotic notion that viral epidemiology can somehow be influ-
enced by political ideology, running rampant at the moment, leaves
me perpetually befuddled. Perhaps I'm too thoroughly inured to the
sciences. I've tried to balance right and left brain over the course of
my life, but degrees in biology, chemistry, and decades of work in
medicine leave me well past any chance of altering this particular lens
through which I am so used to seeing my life and that of others.

A friend of mine wanted to know about a situation where a cousin of hers and his family had made the decision to go visit his elderly
mother and traveled out of state to spend a week with her, so she
could have some grandchild time. My response was that life is risk
and that you always have to compare risk with reward. As mom lived
alone, and not in a group setting where others could be endangered,
if she thought the reward of family time was greater than the risk of
possible contagion, it was her decision to make. Ditto the decision on
the part of the cousin and his family. Trying to impose arbitrary judg-

117

ments of risk on the unique circumstances of the individual usually fails. What should we do as responsible individuals as things begin to open up? I think we need to learn better risk stratification.

Americans are terrible at understanding risk. Culturally, we accept incredibly risky things if we think we have some control over the risks involved, and we are outraged by not-so-risky things where we have no control over the outcome.

The classic example is how we think about cars. In 2018, the last year for which there are complete numbers, 39,404 people in the US were killed as the result of motor vehicle accidents. This means the chance of being killed in any given year is roughly 1/8,300, and the cumulative lifetime risk is about 1%. Most of us don't think twice about getting in a car. We know we're good drivers. We obey traffic laws. We can control unexpected situations. We worry much more about shark attacks at the beach (32 in 2018 with one death), plane crashes (393 fatalities in 2018, only one of which was a commercial passenger), or salmonella-contaminated food (420 deaths in the US in 2018). By the way, the leading cause of accidental death is poisoning. Your lifetime risk is 1/71, so don't drink the bleach.

I have long had a rule of thumb regarding choices. Is it riskier than getting in a car? The problem at the moment is, as this virus is so new, we really don't know what's risky and what's not. The federal agencies that would usually calculate and disseminate this information are in disarray. We're going to have 50 states going 50 different directions which should start to give us some data about which strategies work and which are disastrous.

Until the data starts to make some sense, I'm continuing to stay in unless I have to go out for something. I'll wear my mask in enclosed public spaces. To me, wearing a mask says, "I see you and I care about you and all of us." Not wearing one says to me "I'm a selfish Ayn Rand devotée." As people are packing and moving for me, we're keeping as much distance as possible, wearing masks, and sanitizing frequently, mitigating risks until risks are better understood.

Be safe, be well, wash your hands.

THURSDAY | MAY 21, 2020

T WAS ANOTHER ONE OF THOSE NIGHTS when I got home from work and felt completely drained of all energy and limp as a dishrag; not much constructive was done. I know it's just my body and brain reacting to being steeped in the toxic miasma of stress hormones we're all contending with. The current era is busy taking time off of our collective life spans due to excess catecholamines bathing our systems, but there's not a whole lot I can do about that. Cat videos on the Internet only go so far toward rejuvenating the soul.

I am happy to report some good news on the moving front. Most of the house is packed and ready to go. Progress is also being made on the painting of the new condo, and what I've seen of my color selections on the walls so far makes me think I've gotten those right.

On the bad news front, the HVAC at the condo is busy giving up the ghost, and my usual service guy has suggested tossing it off the roof in favor of a new unit. (There are probably HOA rules against doing this. I'll have to check.) I may be able to temporize for a couple of years with a more inexpensive repair, and there is a home purchase warranty included with the whole deal which may cover most of it, so that's a good thing. Something else to deal with. Part of the reason for moving was to get out of having to deal with such troubles. Ah, well.

Local numbers for the virus are not looking good. We're still doing well here in Birmingham with its heavily medical population, but the virus is, as I had feared, beginning to explode in rural areas as the state continues to open up rapidly and ill-advisedly. A number of the rural hospitals in the central state are overloaded. Montgomery is nearly out of room and the cases keep coming in and will soon be diverted here. As painful as social distancing and isolation may be for all of us, we really do need to stay the course for the foreseeable future. I don't think anyone will be very happy if the healthcare system, already strained, starts to collapse around us. I figure I'm spending the summer putting my home and life back together in the new space while also perfecting my Xbox skills.

The big argument in the hinterlands continues to be over the use of masks. Masks are not about protecting you from catching the virus unless you're wearing a properly fitted N-95 medical mask. And unless you were working around ill people in a hospital setting, I would wonder why you were doing so if I saw you in one due to the shortage of such supplies. Masks are about preventing you from spreading the virus to others as a possible asymptomatic carrier. They don't do a lot of good unless worn relatively universally which is why we see all the ordinances and requests for their use in public.

For general socially distanced interactions, the cloth masks folks have been running up on their sewing machines the last few months are fine. I have a number of them. I keep one in the car, one in my pocket, and one on my face if I need to be indoors around others. Today's face-covering features classic Mickey Mouse. As I move around my area of Birmingham, adherence to masks (required by local ordinance) is pretty good. I hear it's not so good in the suburbs, but I haven't ventured out there to check.

Part of the bone weariness is a certain mind-stasis that prevents me from thinking rapidly and in an entertaining way over my misspent youth. This last week marked the 40th anniversary of the eruption of Mount St Helens in Washington, an event forever entwined with my memories of high school graduation. For children of the Pacific Northwest, May 18th, 1980 will always be one of those "Where were you?" days. I remember it far more vividly than my high school graduation ceremony a couple of weeks later. I still have a bottle of ash collected from the roadside a couple of weeks after the eruption when I was down near Portland. My out-of-work actor packers found it this week and were somewhat afraid it was someone's cremains. They have been reassured. Cremains at my house ride around in car trunks or live in old shoe boxes.

Stay safe. Stay well. Wash your hands.

MONDAY | MAY 26, 2020

IT'S MEMORIAL DAY.

This is the day we are supposed to reflect on those who have given their lives for our country over the generations. In reality, however, it's the long weekend that kicks off the summer season of lightened schedules, better weather, family outdoor activities, pool parties, outdoor concerts, and all the other things we associate with a more languorous time of year.

But not this year.

We're engaged in a different fight, one that doesn't fall into the traditional conventions of armies clashing. The enemy is unseen, of completely unified purpose, and is part of the usual design of nature with no interest in honoring the rhythms and rituals of the human race.

Like everyone else, I saw the pictures and video of the enormous pool party somewhere at Lake of the Ozarks, full of squealing inebriated 20-somethings doing their best to violate every rule of social dis-

121

tancing. I saw the vituperative comments from their elders bouncing around social media. It didn't make me angry; it made me sad. They are young people doing what young people are supposed to do. Filled with energy and swirling with hormones, they are going goofy in large groups. I did it in my day. I'm sure my parents and my grandparents had their variations (although my grandparents' shenanigans undoubtedly involved more layers of clothing).

I completely understand their wish to gather and let off steam after this horrible spring. I also understand the revulsion that their engaging in what would be otherwise completely normal and unremarkable behavior engenders as well. The public health failures that have allowed COVID-19 to become entrenched and endemic in the community are putting us all in an impossible situation. The few weapons we have that we can bring to bear as a society—social distancing, masks in public—run contrary to every communal impulse present in those under the age of 30. It's a population not yet fully able neurologically to make the connection between actions and consequences. Those frontal lobes don't finish developing until after the age of 25, which is why frat boys think it's a great idea to light fire to the couch and throw it off the roof of the house. How do we balance the needs of the mature for safety with the needs of the young for socialization? My only inspiration here is that we all decide to become Shakers.

I confine myself to work and home because, at the age of 58, I've had my youth and know it's another generation's turn. I admit that I spent all of my 20s on the educational treadmill, so I was never able to get too wild and crazy. I got married to Steve halfway through which also slowed me down some. I still had my share of group road trips, late night parties, slightly excessive alcohol intake, heart-to-hearts in corner booths of all-night diners, solo travel to distant parts with groups of young people from all over the world, bonding in hostels or sleeping on the floors of train stations. It breaks my heart that we're stuck in a world at the moment where the young have such a difficult time going through these rites of passage, if they're even possible at all for a few years.

Because of my theater work, I'm around a lot of young people in their 20s and have enjoyed settling into the wicked-wise uncle role with them, telling the stories of what the world was like back before computers ruled our every move, of how things were the same and of how they are now so radically different. That's our job, of course. We of the grandparent generation must tell the stories and provide the cultural continuity. (I've finally woken up to the fact that even though I never had children, I'm definitely a paw-paw). Friendships with young people have kept me young. Without them around, I'd feel like I'm aging at an accelerated rate.

What are we to do as a society? The death toll will break 100,000 in the US in the next day or two. It shows no signs of slowing down. Locally, we're spiking again in the rural areas as Alabama's under-funded healthcare system begins to buckle. The news on Friday was that rural cases were flooding into Montgomery which was out of ICU beds. I'm assuming they'll be heading up I-65 this week putting more strain here on UAB.

We're in a damned-if we-do, damned-if-we don't situation. We can continue opening up and contribute to the spike, or we can stay the course causing additional social strain. I don't have the answers other than continuing to do my part to keep the infection rate down: Stay home as much as I can, wear a mask in public, keep my hands clean, avoid enclosed spaces with lots of other people. It's what I have to do to fulfill my pledge to my patients. I'm not ready to write off the elderly or the chronically ill en masse unlike certain other societal forces. All of us are having to look within and ask ourselves very tough questions. I think I know my answers, but it's testing my fortitude to keep moving forward.

JUNE 2020

Perpetual Anticipation

MONDAY | JUNE 1, 2020

A DECADE AGO, I was offered a slot in the Leadership Birmingham program. It's a program that takes local residents from all
types of careers and walks of life who have proven themselves
to be leadership types and gives them a crash course in how our metropolitan area works.

With full days devoted to topics such as health issues, education,
economic development, and cultural opportunities, it was a great
chance to network, develop new friendships with people in other
industries and careers I might not otherwise meet, and a rare opportunity to peek behind the curtains into the realities of local power
structures. My class included a federal judge, the school superinten-
dent, a city councilperson, various business types, activists working
on social justice issues for the African-American and Latino communities, and clergy.

By the end of that year, we had bonded and discovered many
commonalities, despite our diverse backgrounds, and we, like all
of the other classes that have gone through the program over the
decades, have used our experiences to help make our community a
better place.

One lesson I took away from all of this was one I don't think was
intended. I quickly recognized that when it came to local politics,
the lower the level, the more creative and resourceful the individuals.
Those working on projects at the neighborhood level tended to be
bright, impassioned, committed individuals who cared deeply about
their areas of town and who created great things on minimal resources. On the city of Birmingham level, the leaders had their hearts
and their energies in the right places, but were beholden to powers

and economic interests that would at times lead to contrarian decision-making for reasons of politics and expediency. Those working at the county level experienced even more of this.

It was only a few years since the Jefferson County sewer scandal had roiled the local power structure top to bottom, and most of those we met struck me as having one eye over their shoulder expecting the Feds at any moment. Those individuals we met working on the state level were to a person, far more invested in the game of politics than they were in the results or in the needs of the citizenry, and a few of them struck me as either ignorant, unmotivated, or both.

I didn't meet anyone on the federal level but I did make a general observation. Rising up the ladder requires a constant trading away of morals-oriented service to the greater good in exchange for service to self and others above them. I now wonder if this is a possible explanation for the two separate, but inextricably intertwined issues, facing us at the moment. I can't speak to the truth of this pattern in other states or in Washington DC, not having been through leadership programs there, but I have a suspicion the pattern isn't unique to Alabama.

The first problem is that of COVID-19. The case loads locally continue to increase. It's difficult for me to find out just how much as there's not a lot of transparency in the numbers. Alabama, for instance, is one of the few states which is not reporting on what is happening in nursing homes. UAB, where I work, weathered the initial surge and is starting to return to more normal operations, but everyone is on tenterhooks wondering when that other shoe is going to drop. As other stories dominate the news cycle and as people, tired of social distancing, crowd back into newly opened places of business, we could be well on our way to a fresh spike by the Fourth of July. Friends are reporting that beaches are full, stores are filling up, and then, of course, there have been mass demonstrations.

It seems to me that state leaders have abdicated their role in protecting the citizenry in a series of calculated trade-offs of their primary responsibility (ensuring the safety of its residents) by making politically expedient concessions to a vocal minority of people who want business fully open, large gatherings unrestricted, social distancing ended, and masks removed.

I haven't seen the governor or the legislature in evidence at all during the last few weeks. Our mayor, a young and energetic African-American, has been one of the few local leaders who has maintained a media presence and given sound advice.

I've been out and about a bit more because this has been moving week. In the city, the majority are wearing masks. In the suburbs, mask-wearing is minimal outside of healthcare facilities. It's as if society has made a sudden decision that this is all over. But coronaviruses don't care how bored or frustrated or governmentally constrained any of us may feel. They don't care about the economy. They don't care about politics. They care only about propagation. Until there is an effective treatment or vaccine, the only way to prevent this is distancing and masking in order to break transmission chains.

The second problem is the civil unrest currently gripping most urban areas. I read somewhere that more than 140 cities have had demonstrations in the wake of the George Floyd killing last week. While Mr. Floyd's murder by police, and it's reigniting of the issues of horrific injustices suffered by the African-American community is the proximate cause, I've tended to think that widespread civil unrest was going to happen no matter what.

An enormous portion of the populace is out of work, the prices of basic necessities are skyrocketing, and it's becoming more and more difficult for those at the bottom of the ladder to put food on the table. Many have been relegated to subsistence jobs for years, enough to survive but not enough to build wealth, get ahead, or ensure that things will be better for their children. Add to that the lockdown and the canceling of all those things that distract us or that make our lives a little more bearable like sports, cultural events, concerts, social gatherings, etc., and tensions, already high, ratchet up seemingly with no end in sight.

When there is neither bread nor circuses, the people become increasingly unhappy with their lot and more inclined toward desperate measures. The government had the chance to make grand gestures and side with the people, but instead it let big business run off with hundreds of billions of dollars from the treasury while telling ordinary folk to survive for months on $1200. I don't know where this is going, but I remain optimistic. The best scientific minds in the world are working together on methods of controlling COVID-19. I imagine we will start to see progress on prevention and treatment in the coming months.

Wash your hands. Stay well.

SUNDAY | JUNE 7, 2020

THE NUMBER OF COVID-19 CASES CONTINUES TO RISE. We're up to nearly two million cases nationally. 20,000 of those are in Alabama, 2,000 are in Jefferson County, and the numbers have been rising sharply over the last few weeks as the virus transmitted over Memorial Day weekend begins to make itself known. What we're doing today is reflected in the numbers 10-20 days from now. This is one of the reasons it's difficult for us as a society to understand the cause and effect of social behavior on our physical well-being.

The American media, unable to keep more than one big narrative going at once, has decided to turn its attention from COVID-19 to the rallies, marches, and occasional civil disturbances that have sprung up over the last two weeks. I have two thoughts about this. First, coronaviruses don't care if they're being reported on or not. They're going to continue to do the one thing they're designed to do: propagate themselves by infecting new individuals. Hopefully, we've had enough lead time to prepare, but I can tell you from first-hand experience that the healthcare system is strained, that the practitioners are tired, and that there is no end in sight. Second, though it doesn't necessarily fit media narratives, the pandemic and the BLM protests are very much intertwined.

This country hasn't seen this number of people out on the streets protesting against the powers that be for more than 50 years. The rallies I have attended have been orderly affairs, Black America, White America, all hues of America, speaking with one voice, saying that the systems that have divided us for so long and treated us so unequally must be changed.

Locally, we've had only one serious disturbance. The city's response has been subdued (some of the white flight suburbs appear to have overreacted) but the message has been sent loud and clear. I've seen the photos from NYC, DC, Philly, and elsewhere of enormous crowds braving pandemic conditions to stand up for what is right and for the ideals this country was founded upon—ideals which so many have championed in resistance to systemic and other forces led by those who have no aspirations to reach for.

I don't think this coming together of diverse voices en masse, day after day, in city after city, would have been possible without the pandemic. BLM has been around for a few years and, of course, systemic racism for four centuries. But it took the societal stress of a pandemic, a lock down, and economic uncertainty on a grand scale to get a majority of Americans to experience the stress and conditions minority groups face on a daily basis. Worries about the rent, putting food on the table, indifference from the authorities to distress, seeing the oligarchy helping itself to the treasury, watching a militarized police traumatize peaceful protesters, realizing that a government unable to meet the most basic needs of the healthcare system over months, has laid bare the myth that government is here to serve the citizenry. It has become more obvious that government exists to protect the property of the wealthy—and prerogatives of its own sustainability in service of the wealthy.

The younger generation isn't especially at risk from COVID-19. Their education has been disrupted. They have also been saddled with appalling levels of debt for that education as part of the monetization of society to benefit the wealthy. They don't have a whole lot to lose at the moment, and the pandemic has destroyed the social controls the elite have used to control them in recent decades such as student loans, entry into upper-tier schools, internships, and other networking opportunities. There's no reason for them not to continue being out on the streets working for systemic change which will benefit us all. I can't read tea leaves, but I can read the moods and machinations of my community and say that we seem to be at an inflection point where the rules of the game have changed, and the older generations haven't figured that out yet. I think this will be born out in the results of the coming election cycle.

What's next for COVID-19 is unclear. The amount of information available has been reduced. Reportage on what's happening elsewhere in the world is slim as our nation focuses on its internal struggles. Because various states present data in inconsistent ways for what seem to be political purposes, I can't always find trustworthy domestic numbers.

As a geriatrician, I am well aware that the virus continues its march through senior facilities. Some people die, some don't. It's unclear what the difference between the two groups could be. There's likely a genetic subset of us that is doomed to become incredibly ill if we get the disease, but why that is and how to determine who is at risk remains obscure.

In the meantime, everyone stay safe, stay well, and wash your hands.

THURSDAY | JUNE 11, 2020

AND JUST LIKE THAT, the novel coronavirus marches on.

The reduction in case load achieved by aggressive measures in the spring has been reversed by an easing of those measures for socio-economic and political reasons. In Alabama, there were roughly 900 new diagnoses today, nearly twice as many as the daily rate at the peak of the original pandemic.

Had the power structure not gutted the pandemic response office, had they taken tried and true approaches to the control of epidemic infectious disease, made masking politically fashionable, and done the other things that we know would have helped bring the coronavirus under control this spring, American society would be in a position of being able to open cautiously, we would be celebrating a dodging of the bullet, and the current administration would be coasting into an easy re-election campaign. But, their short term self-interest and contrarian nature towards the laws of science, and even logic, have pushed them into a position where they cannot succeed.

They could begin to follow public health guidelines but it will, at this point, require a great deal of resources to win hearts and minds to this way of thinking now that there has been such intense commitment to "open up the economy", and the party in power has been loathe to spend on the average American since the historic Reagan tax cuts of 1981. Spending on protection of wealth for the upper crust is another story. They have no easy path forward which makes me think they'll likely continue to focus on the irresponsible minimization of the disease and its consequences for society.

There will be those quick to blame the increase in infections— aimed like a dagger at the heart of the African-American community—on the various demonstrations and rallies. But the numbers don't bear that out. The rallies have been confined predominantly to Huntsville and Birmingham, and those are not the areas in which cases are skyrocketing. Virus spread is increasing quickly in suburban and rural areas. I'm not surprised. We're between two and three weeks out from the Memorial Day weekend (the demonstrations didn't begin until a week later). The spread is the result of a bored populace emerging from its cocoon, blinking at the fine weather, and taking off for the beach, the bar, and the backyard barbecue. This isn't a second wave. It's still the first wave of the virus, simply waiting until we let down our collective guard so it can continue on its relentless path.

There is a graphic running around breaking common social activities into nine levels of risk. It's not the most scientifically accurate thing, but it's easy to understand, and it serves as a good reminder of what social distancing actually means. It's not easy.

I live at level four. I can't exactly avoid a doctor's waiting room if I'm going to go to work. I'm still curtailing most of my activities. I've had to open up my life a little because of the process of moving, but life is risk, and moving was a risk I needed to take. So far, so good. I'll know in about two weeks if I've been careful enough.

I fully expect to contract COVID-19 at some point. I'm a physician. It's my duty to be around the sick, no matter the personal cost. I'm not being stupid or taking unreasonable chances, but I've tried to order my life just in case I become one of the deathly ill. Now that the moving is done, life will return to my usual work days with patients and weekends at home with books, taking long walks, and working on my Xbox skills (which don't seem to be improving much).

The condo is pretty much together. Almost everything is stowed away in at least a temporary home. The old house is empty. The discards are being picked over by various folk. It gets its repair and facelift over the next two weeks and should be on the market by the end of the month. I'll be glad when the last phase of this process is over. I'm looking forward to not having to move again for decades.

I'm an optimist when it comes to human behavior. I've worked in a caring profession that's taken me inside so many homes of so many kinds of people for more than three decades. From this I've learned that no matter how people express it, we all want pretty much the same things: a sense of safety, a few creature comforts, a better chance for our children, opportunities to feel fulfilled, and to do meaningful work within our professions and communities. It's not hard to understand this once you start seeing people as human beings.

There have been two major social trends over the last century or so that have kept this from happening. These have been deliberately implemented by the landlord class of property owners in order to protect assets at the expense of individuals. The first, and more familiar practice, is the dividing of the working class on the basis of ethnicity, of teaching both Black and White that the other is not to be trusted, of making it difficult through a thousand little social rules for them to make common cause. The power structure has long known that if they do get together—average Americans of all kinds—and start pulling in the same direction, the power class will be in trouble. Maybe COVID-19 striking at just this moment in time, when the Millennials and Generation Z are starting to ascend to the majority, that it becomes the inflection point that allows for this to change—and for our society to change with it.

The second, more insidious reason, is the co-opting of the professional and upper middle class by the power structure through economic means. As the old saying goes, if you work for money, you're not rich. When you're rich, your money works for you. Most professionals have fairly high salaries but they're still working for a living, and their economic interests are firmly tied to those of the working class. However, when the power structure came up with the brilliant idea of replacing defined benefit pension systems with IRAs, 401Ks and 403Bs, they all of a sudden got the band of people who do a lot of the heavy societal lifting to start voting based on the casino of the stock market, not realizing that their paltry gains would never make up for what they were losing in both pension systems and the systematic privatization of the Commons that has been going on for the last half century.

Can we fix this mess? I do believe we can. No one ever said it would be easy, and I think we have a lot more pain in terms of both COVID-19, along with the social unrest that its effects will engender, before we get to the other side. Fasten your seat belts. It's going to be a bumpy ride, but we will make it if we decide we want to, and we will reach out our hands to each other unafraid to take them.

Speaking of hands, you know what I'm going to say: Wash them well and often.

TUESDAY | JUNE 16, 2020

I DON'T RECALL WHEN I'VE HAD TIMES where I've been as genuinely exhausted as I have been over the last few months. But I think it's a perfectly normal phenomenon.

Everything about life and all its certainties has been upended; bits of stress seep into everything we do. Three months of unending stress, a lack of the usual activities that relieve stress, long work hours, and then a move added on top of all that when I can't take any time off work is enough to flatten anyone I suppose.

A friend posed the question the other day asking if difficulties make us stronger. My answer to that is not really. I believe they make us more resilient, more able to roll with the punches that life throws at us, but they don't necessarily give us additional strength.

I've certainly had plenty of curve balls lobbed at me through life, and I don't think I'm any stronger today than I was as a teen. What I am is more prepared to bend and change, figure out what I need to absorb, and what I can safely let go of. I suppose it's how I've made it this far. It's the adaptable creature that survives, not the strong one, if Darwin is to be believed.

Speaking of adapting, when it comes to the coronavirus, we don't seem to be doing very well. The numbers of cases locally are accelerating like crazy. Five thousand new cases in Alabama and four hundred in Jefferson county over the last week. UAB now has more inpatient COVID-19 sufferers than ever. And yet, the populace seems to have shrugged off the disease as yesterday's news.

Now that things have reopened somewhat, I see more and more people without masks, hanging out in groups, living life as it used to be. They are mainly younger folk who aren't hugely at risk for significant complications. This makes me wonder: Are we heading into a two-tiered society of the young and healthy with minimal risk in one group, living what we might consider a relatively normal lifestyle, and a more at-risk group of older and chronically ill people, acting more circumspectly? I wonder what a few years of this might do to politics and the economy. As someone whose age, profession, and general health status place him in the more at-risk group, I can't say I approve of what's going on. I worry that our already youth-oriented culture may continue down this particular path in unhealthy ways at the expense of empathy and wisdom.

When I look at the numbers nationally, especially when compared against other advanced societies, it's obvious that our government has abdicated its responsibility for keeping our population safe. The partisan politicization of science and expertise, and the elevation of feeling and belief over fact and reason, creates the perfect environment for a virus of this type to keep breeding and replicating. I don't know that there's much any of us can do as individuals about this. I keep my hands washed and sanitized and wear a mask in public and at work when with patients (which makes my job harder as most older people rely at least partially on lip reading in order to hear properly), but there are times when I feel like I'm in a shrinking minority, and I wonder just what motivates people? Are they thinking it's over? (It's not.) Are they thinking they are not at risk? (They are.) Are they thinking if no one else cares, why should I? (My parents had many pithy things to say about peer pressure when I was growing up.)

Something that's liable to happen is that those traveling on US passports will find themselves unwelcome to travel to other countries. The world will get a handle on the virus and travel will start up again, but will we be able to partake? If I were running a health ministry somewhere in Europe, I'd look at the US numbers and behavior and say no to those people coming here. This will undoubtedly shock most Americans of upper income who are used to coming and going across the world at will. It will also put American businesses at a major disadvantage. You can only do so much over Zoom.

But I have a new nest, and I'm likely to spend many hours in it as my plans for travel are in abeyance, and it's unclear when the kinds of performance I participate in will be safe to resume. Time to put all that resilience to work. More writing? Something artistic? Getting started on my retirement reading shelf? I'll eventually figure it out. In the meantime, I'll do what I can to safely make the world a better place and try not to be too much of that crotchety old man railing at the young folks.

So kids, wash your hands, wear your masks, keep your distance—and stay off my lawn!

SUNDAY | JUNE 21, 2020

OVER THE LAST WEEK, Alabama has 4,000 new COVID-19 cases, Jefferson County has 400 new COVID cases, and there have been 60 more deaths. This isn't over by a long shot, even if the media and the zeitgeist have moved on to other things.

There are a couple of interesting trends I'm following in the data. One is the divergence in case rates between areas with Republican/conservative governments versus those with Democratic/liberal governments. By most measures, Red areas are trending up in numbers and rates of infection while Blue areas are trending down. There are many sociological possibilities behind this.

Blue areas are more heavily urban and more crowded. This led to easier transmission in the early days of the pandemic. Now Blue areas, having experienced what the virus can do, are much more cautious and vigilant in their public health orders, leading to reductions in transmissions. Meanwhile, Red areas, being more concerned with the economic impacts of shut downs, have chosen not to implement the tried-and-true ways of preventing disease spread.

As the virus makes its way to less densely populated parts of the country, it's going to be more efficiently spread by people who have absorbed the political idea that the virus is a big nothing-burger and that they should not be concerned about either themselves or their neighbors. If previous trends hold true, July is going to be a devastating month in Red states as the death toll follows the increased infection rate, and it will be very hard for the governments in those areas to walk back their laissez-faire attitudes.

The other interesting trend is the age of new cases. Data out of Florida is showing that the majority of new cases over the last few months are in younger adults, with the median age falling into the 30s. Is this due to the substantial elder population of Florida taking precautions while the younger population, believing itself immune, has not? Is the virus becoming more effective at being transmitted by certain social behaviors of young people? Is the virus, as it goes from host to host, starting to mutate somewhat leaving younger people, with less lifetime exposure to viral illness, more susceptible? Fascinating questions that I, nor anyone else, have answers to at this time.

Epidemiologists and public health experts know what we have to do to get over the pandemic. The playbook hasn't changed in decades. Social distancing/isolation, quarantine of positive cases, and contact tracing. It's not that hard. It just takes political will and money. We're definitely missing the former in today's society. We're not missing the latter, we just make odd decisions about where it goes. I'm not a trained epidemiologist, but I've had my share of classes as part of my medical training, and I've rooted about in the public health world for decades due to my work trying to identify and fix the disparities of health care that exist for physically frail and cognitively impaired elders.

I remember my first epidemiology class well. It was in my first semester of medical school, towards the end of the term. On the first day of class, the professor gave us an extra credit problem to work on. It was a breakdown of a society where a condition had struck a segment, and we had to figure out what the disease was. We had breakdowns by gender, ethnicity, socio-economic status, marital status, age, etc. We were given the information on Monday and told to give our answers on Friday in class.

Friday came and I took my usual seat in the back corner, knowing that would make me one of the last called on to answer. I hadn't a clue what it was. Some disease that hit men far more than women, the poor far more than the rich, single people more than married. My colleagues kept giving their answers and being told they were wrong. I was thinking Athlete's foot and was going to go with that when something caught my eye. Only four females in the highest socioeconomic group had the condition. That rang a bell deep in the recesses of my brain. Something about only four women. Then I saw that only one child in the highest socioeconomic group had it. I scanned all the numbers again, and I knew what it was. I started squiggling in my seat waiting for the professor to get to me. When he did, I blurted out "I know it, I know it! It's the Titanic and which passengers lived and which died." The professor's jaw dropped. I was right: the first student who had solved that puzzle in the twenty years he had been teaching the course.

That's how my mind works. It absorbs factoids like only four first-class women died on the Titanic and then reorders them subconsciously, so all of a sudden I just know an answer to a complex problem. I suppose this ability of mine to subconsciously store away little bits of information from here and there, and then rearrange them until they make a blindingly clear observation regarding some other facet of life, is what's behind my writing these entries. I'm seeing trends in public health, politics, and economic response to the pandemic as whole formed patterns, bursting forth, usually in the late night hours. I write them out to make more sense of them.

I've finished one week in the new condo with pretty much everything in place. I feel like it's been the absolute right decision to move even if the process has been exhausting. I'm planning on staying put with things where they are for a few more weeks, and then spending some time fine tuning. It has, of course, shown me its little quirks, the most interesting one being two of the drawers in the kitchen island refusing to stay closed. They were fine all through the move-in process and the loading-up. Then, all of a sudden, last week, they started to open on their own. I've decided it's Tommy trying to communicate something to me about kitchen organization. Of course, this brings up unpleasant thoughts of the early scenes of *Poltergeist*. If the chairs start stacking themselves up, I may have to think twice about this place.

Stay well, stay safe, wash your hands.

THURSDAY | JUNE 25, 2020

SOMEONE POSED THE QUESTION TODAY as to what I would entitle my memoir, should I ever write one, and I've decided, given all the weird, wonderful, and serendipitous things that have occurred in my life, combined with my writing best in short essay form, that it would have to be called *Accidental Notes*. (And now all my musician friends are groaning in unison. Sorry about that but I do like a good pun.) And now, pushed on by a pandemic and a completely new way of living, it's emerging but as *The Accidental Plague Diaries*. At least I got one part of the title right far in advance.

The news on COVID-19 over the last few days has been devastating. It's skyrocketing across the sunbelt—Arizona, Texas, Florida, South Carolina. Not quite as much here, but we're not far behind. It's as if all the pain and misery we endured throughout the spring—via isolation and quarantine and flattening of the curve simply had no effect. But that's not true. It had the desired effect. The curve did flatten, the exponential rates of spread did come down. It was obvious that we couldn't all remain behind closed doors forever, and some of us including yours truly, due to the nature of our jobs, really couldn't do it at all. I've done my best to be careful, being mindful of my activities, and giving up many of the things I enjoy in life to help my patients, my colleagues, and my fellow citizens survive, and I don't regret it.

Flattening the curve was never about defeating or ending the virus. It was about buying time to allow tried-and-true public health measures to swing into place which could eventually tamp the pandemic down. What are those measures? Public education on what measures are necessary and why, social distancing, quarantine of the ill until they become non-infectious, and contact tracing of those exposed in order to separate them from the uninfected. What did the federal government do with the time our sacrifices bought them? I'll let you answer that question for yourself as my answer would likely contain a few too many expletives.

When the public reached their limit for total societal quarantine (around Memorial Day), and power-hungry forces decided to politicize public health measures for momentary gain, states began to take divergent courses. Well-governed states, following sound scientific public health measures, have been slowly reopening based on scientific data and good epidemiology. Poorly governed states have thrown wide the gates and encouraged everything to return to the way it had been. You can probably guess where the virus is spreading like wildfire. As I've said before, the virus doesn't care about your politics, your vacation plans, your comfort, or anything else. It has one purpose only: propagation. It will seek any change in your behavior patterns it can exploit.

So, while the rest of the advanced world, by using everything learned about infectious disease epidemiology over the last two hundred years, brings their numbers down and the pandemic under control, the United States is merrily zooming the wrong way. I have a feeling the rest of the world is fairly close to placing a *cordon sanitaire* around the country to protect itself. For those unfamiliar with the concept, this is a complete and total blockade around an infected locale. No one in or out. No foreign travel, no international business trips, trade severely hampered. Don't think it can't happen or that America, with its näive belief in its own Exceptionalism, is immune from the social forces of the rest of the world.

From what I can tell, there's really only one way to bring the pandemic under control, and this is for the American citizenry to change the current government into one that protects its citizens through basic public health measures. There's an opportunity to do this in a few months. We'll see if we are able. In the meantime, from what I can tell, older people will continue to protect themselves; younger people, believing themselves in no specific danger, will not. The problem is that a certain percentage of younger people are also now falling deathly ill. It may be a smaller percentage than of older people, but it's still significant. There's also the issue of long-term effects on those who don't actually die. Some studies are suggesting that even the young and healthy are experiencing serious compromises of lung function which will likely wreak havoc upon them as they age into middle and then older age.

With a failed societal response, we all have to do what little we can do. Wear our masks. It does help reduce transmission significantly when we all do that—and, please, let's stop with the ridiculousness about HIPAA and the ADA and the nonsense about how you can't breathe, or that you're going to get carbon dioxide poisoning, or any of the other pieces of garbage I've seen floating around.

Wash your hands, and stay home when you can. It isn't fun, but this is what will buy us the time to work on better societal solutions.

SUNDAY | JUNE 28, 2020

'M FEELING LOW as I'm sure many of you are as well.

Caseloads of COVID-19 are surging in my region of the country, and the mostly conservative state governments seem either oblivious or hostile to the most basic public health measures that could curb this.

People seem to have forgotten two simple facts. The first is that this virus takes time to fully manifest itself. The numbers we see now stem from what we were doing or not doing in May, and it takes some weeks after the virus establishes itself in a population for enough people to get critically ill. The death toll follows some weeks after that. We won't really know the extent of the mortality from this current surge until late July.

Second, exponential numbers don't work the way our linearly oriented brains think they do. We can get a better sense of this by thinking in terms of powers of two and the metaphor of lily pads on the pond that double daily. If the pond is covered today, then yesterday the pond was only half covered, the day before only ¼ covered, and last week you would have barely noticed there were any lily pads at all. In the same way the virus is barely there but growing slowly, stealthily, and then all of a sudden it's everywhere.

I'm not sure if I should feel angry or sad over all the examples of American entitlement that have been running around these last few weeks. From the people delivering word salad against the use of masks at various council meetings, to the people on social media complaining about poor restaurant and retail service, to the people crowding into bars and onto beaches as if opening back up means that life has somehow returned to pre-COVID-19 normalcy.

The results of this willful ignorance of how infectious disease works, has led to the USA, with 5% of the world's population, having 25% of the world's COVID-19 cases. This strikes me in a deeply personal way as the two things I have always done to renew my spirit are travel and theater, neither of which are possible, and I really am beginning to feel as though I want to reach through my computer screen at times and slap some folks silly for robbing me of my personal joys.

Where do we go from here? I wish I knew. There are a few scenarios that could happen. First, the virus continues to spread, we all get sick, most of us recover, and we develop something akin to herd immunity. We seem to be choosing this option by default thanks to inaction on the part of our elected leaders. Of course, this option is likely to pull down the healthcare system as we know it and is going to lead to a lot of other collateral societal damage. And as all this is going on, the federal government is again trying to invalidate Obamacare. This, of course, will invalidate its ban on discrimination for pre-existing conditions which will, ironically enough, include COVID-19, so anyone who does get sick would essentially become uninsurable in a hypothetical future. We have no idea what the long-term consequences for non-fatal cases might be, and I can assure you that the health insurance industry has no interest in footing the bill for finding out.

Second, the virus ravages for a while and then dies back into the background, similar to influenza, and we all learn to live with it. This will likely cause some major changes in how society operates, but what these will be is anybody's guess.

Third, we elect a new administration which takes its public health mission seriously, and we put appropriate resources and measures in place. There will be reactionary complaints against this, it will continue to drive a wedge between Red and Blue America, and it won't happen without additional civil unrest.

Fourth, someone stumbles upon a vaccine or medical treatment which allows us to go back to usual patterns. We won't go back to where we were in February, we're too changed, but at least we can cling to familiarities.

I was looking at the local statistics at Birmingham area neighborhoods. If you look at the rates of infection per population, the highest rates are not in poorer or minority neighborhoods. The highest rates are in the moneyed white neighborhoods known collectively around here as "Over the Mountain". I surmise this is due to higher collective rates of entitlement and feelings that rules and masks are for the little people.

I had toyed with the idea of going somewhere for fresh air and water, but I think I'll be much safer in my central city neighborhood among medical types who understand how serious this all is.

As always, wear your mask, stay home when you can, and wash your hands.

JULY 2020

Here We Are Again

SATURDAY | JULY 4, 2020

DREAM A LOT.

Generally, my dreams are gone within an hour or so of getting up unless I take a moment to jot them down. I've dream-journaled off and on over the years, mainly off, but I'm wondering if I should take it up again to try and make sense of all the insanity in the world today.

If dreams are the way our subconscious processes information, maybe it's time to pay a bit more attention to them. I have a dream journal on my nightstand that Tommy gave me years ago. He inscribed it "Andy, For your dreams... Good or bad. Always remember you are in my heart. Take solace there!—Tommy." Little things like this from the past are what allow me to keep going on days when it all seems to be too much.

My dreams this last week have been about travel. They've also been variations on the actors' nightmare, that dream all performers have where they find themselves about to go onstage and don't know their lines or blocking or even what show it is.

One dream was about my trying to pack for an important trip and not being able to find the things I needed which led to my being late to the airport and missing the flight. One was about being in a foreign country where I didn't speak the language and being lost in a crumbling palace. Then came the realization that I owned it and would never be able to afford the repairs. A third dream involved being trapped on a train with many unpleasant people, call it *Murder on the Orient Express* without the murder. I'm hardly a trained dream analyst, but the common thread seems to be one of anxiety and a feeling of being unprepared or unable to handle the tasks I have been given.

I'm assuming I'm having travel dreams because I'm moving on—not just in the literal sense of having completed a relocation, but also in the metaphorical sense of launching myself into an unknown future in which the rule book has been rewritten by the pandemic and has not yet been made available for us ordinary mortals to read and digest. The immediate stresses of the move are over. I'm settling into the new condo, and now I have to figure out who the new me is going forward.

The new me was going to be defined by my two great interests outside of my professional career: music/theater and travel. Neither of those things is currently possible, so there's a huge void to be filled, and I don't know yet how to make those adjustments. I have projects to work on, and my job gives me direction and purpose and uses up an enormous amount of energy given all the strain on the healthcare system. I know it will all work itself out eventually, and that patience and delayed gratification are called for (again). Still, I believe I'm allowed to think back to last Fourth of July, when I was floating down the Rhine, and wondering when such experiences would be possible again. I have a life list of travel destinations and, being a geriatrician, an all too keen awareness of the limitations of an active life span.

The local virus numbers are increasing as they are all across the Southeast. Alabama is adding a thousand new cases a day which is high for our state but only a tenth of what's happening in Florida and Texas. I put this down to our lack of large cities. Birmingham is our largest, but it's quite small compared to the megalopolises of Atlanta or Houston or Jacksonville and, with smaller and less dense populations, we can keep numbers down, at least within those communities that will take things seriously.

Looking back at the last few months, that's the major problem. We don't want to take this seriously on a political, economic, social, or personal level. It interrupts our entitled sense of comfort in the way things are, or ought to be, a sort of Panglossian "Best of All Possible Worlds". It also reveals our stubborn refusal to roll with the punches nature has landed upon us, a prideful unwillingness to adapt to a new fitness landscape many of us may not be as fit for as we thought.

Alabama is not immune to the anti-mask idiocy sweeping the land. It appears to be limited to communities of privilege, to people who feel that they should be allowed to live their lives on their own terms, and that society is to cater to them rather than they are to cater to it. Communities of color and social outsider status who understand the importance of taking care of each other are much more likely to think of others as well as themselves.

Americans seem to have forgotten that the unit of survival in human social evolution is not the individual or the nuclear family, but the tribe. We have split ourselves in two, each eyeing the other with mutual suspicion and with an unwillingness to reach out to help. This is leading to our country falling far behind the rest of the world in confronting a global threat. Those on one side of the divide may get their dream of a wall, but it's going to be built by the rest of the world to keep us in.

Like much of the theater world, I subscribed to Disney+ in order to watch the filmed version of the original production of *Hamilton* which is now streaming. I was fortunate enough to see the original production on Broadway a couple years ago. Generally, I don't care for filmed versions of stage works. Film and stage are such different mediums and what works in one often does not in the other.

This version, filmed by original director Thomas Kail, does as good a job as can be done to capture the energy, talent, and sheer genius of the work. The addition of judicious close ups, heightening of the theatrical lighting, and the clarity of the sound allowing every word to be heard make this one a winner. *Hamilton* became a phenomenon in 2015-16 at the end of the Obama era. Only five years later, watching it makes it so clear how much our civic life has changed in such a very short time.

I also picked up much more clearly on a couple of themes. First, while the show is called *Hamilton* and Alexander is the central character, the narrator, and our way into the show, our perspective comes entirely through Aaron Burr, the ultimate outsider among our critical Founding Fathers, the one unremembered on the coinage and the postage stamps.

Second, the ultimate theme of the show, which became crystal clear in the filming, and in Phillipa Soo's performance as Eliza Schuyler Hamilton, is that the most important thing in history is who gets to tell the story and thereby control the narrative.

For centuries, we have been taught a specific American narrative of progress and superiority. *Hamilton* gently reminds us that this isn't necessarily the truth, the whole truth, and nothing but the truth.

This has been my great revelation of the last few years. Telling the story is perhaps our most important function as humans. As I've realized this, I see now that it permeates all the various areas of my life. I succeed as a physician when I allow patients and families to tell their stories. If I am willing to listen, there's usually a nugget of information that allows me to crack the case and figure out how I can help.

I started writing these posts a few years ago when I came to the realization that I had a lot of stories to tell and, without Tommy, no one to tell them to. I figured it was time to send them out into the world to see if they could touch others. The evolution of these writings into this plague diary was completely accidental, simply my attempt to make sense of a crazy time in modern history.

Where do I go from here? I don't know but the story goes on.

TUESDAY | JULY 7, 2020

I CAME HOME FROM WORK THIS EVENING AT 5:30, sat down on the couch, and found myself incapable of moving for about two hours. This has become a fairly common pattern.

About twice a week I get in from the day, feeling pretty normal, and then, like someone stuck a pin in my balloon, I feel drained of all energy and can't do much besides stare out the window (thunderstorms and rain today) and wait for my faculties to return.

I assume it's my personal physiologic reaction to the never-ending COVID-19 stress we're all living in. At least the world those of us who work in health care and are paying attention are living in. A significant portion of the population seems to be running around as if nothing has changed and that we aren't living in a very different world than we were living in last year.

Local counts continue to rise. My hospital has over 90 inpatients with COVID-19 (we were running 60-70 at the height of the early pandemic in March/April), and we've increased by over 50% in a week and a half. Numbers in surrounding Southern states are appalling: more than 10,000 cases a day becoming the norm in Florida and Texas with their large populations and relatively dense cities.

The stories are spreading among medical professionals of overfull ICUs, patients being sent to other cities or even out of state for treatment, absolute exhaustion on the part of medical personnel, shortages of protective equipment, and all the other logistical nightmares that we all heard about from elsewhere early in the pandemic. There hasn't been much reportage on this. The powers that be have decided that a narrative of economic recovery is more important than one of personal safety. People have lost out to profits.

There's much speculation as to why the death toll has not spiked in the same way as case numbers. This may be due in part to changes in testing, part to a shift in infections away from older people who are taking greater precautions than younger people, and that younger people are less likely to become seriously ill. They have healthier bodies with less chronic disease burden and are less likely to be seriously affected. But this malevolent disease, that we do not yet fully understand, makes a certain percentage of young people with no appreciable health problems deathly ill. It appears to leave those who survive with chronic issues that may take months or years to resolve, if ever. No matter what, every single infection is conceivably preventable with proper public health measures that we as a society are apparently unwilling to take.

We've got huge societal dilemmas coming up over the next year or so which are independent of current partisan politics or who occupies the White House. The first is the question of getting kids back into school. The majority of American families depend economically on two incomes which requires both parents to work. This means schools must be open and *in loco parentis* during usual business hours. Children gathered together in groups are highly unlikely to keep social distancing, proper hygiene, or masks in place, and the majority of veteran teachers are of an age to be in a higher risk group.

If we send kids to school, how do we keep them safe? How do we keep teachers and staff safe? If COVID-19 starts to spread in a school, do we shut it down? What do we do with everyone for quarantine periods? When veteran teachers decide to put their health ahead of their careers and take early retirement, how do we replace that lost experience? How do we deal with the extracurriculars which are sometimes the only things that keep at-risk kids in school? In higher education, where online education is more feasible in certain subjects, what do we do with practicums like chemistry labs? What do we do about federal policies about students on visas not allowing them to remain in the country if their classes are online? This issue alone could decimate graduate and research programs nationwide.

I've certainly considered early retirement myself as it's become clear that neither my state or federal government cares much about the safety of me and my colleagues or the stress that we're being put through at the moment. If they did, they'd be paying more attention to the public health system, less to the chamber of commerce. If I were a few years older, I likely would retire, but in looking at all my options, I plan to keep soldiering on for a few years more. I'll continue to hold up my little corner of the healthcare system and hope that things get better. Maybe the cavalry will eventually show up and give me and mine a little respite.

Not every experienced healthcare provider is going to want to continue to work under these conditions. How do we replace them? We've been importing doctors to the US for years as US medical schools haven't been able to produce enough to meet demand. If we become more cut off from the rest of the world, and unfriendly to immigrants, where are we going to get people to replace them?

The right wing has been sending us down a path of isolationism for the last few years with their chants of "Build a wall!" etc. The business community understands that, in this day of global economies and multinational corporations, this has been relatively silly rhetoric that keeps the masses distracted while their pockets are picked. However, our complete failure to respond appropriately to the pandemic may lead the rest of the world to wall us off anyway, at least until we're no longer seen as dangerous.

Be careful for what you wish—for you may get it.

I see advertisements for inexpensive international travel cropping up for late fall or winter, and I can't help but think that this will never happen. We think life is bad now. What happens when the usual flu season coincides with the pandemic with no adequate responses in place? I wouldn't plan that trip to Paris quite yet.

Usually, I'm optimistic in these entries. But I'm feeling pessimistic this evening. Maybe it was that two hours of staring out the window at the rain. Maybe it's the life circumstance to have to go through this alone. Maybe the Smoothie King lunch I drank isn't agreeing.

Wash your hands. Wear your mask. Use common sense.

SATURDAY | JULY 11, 2020

W E'RE UP TO OVER 70,000 NEW DIAGNOSES DAILY in this country, more than 130,000 are dead, hospitals in multiple states are running out of ICU beds, and Walt Disney World has decided it's a great time to reopen.

I'm in a better mood than I was when I wrote my last missive. That was a low point. I'm not sure what refreshed my soul. Maybe my once-a-month trip to Target for supplies (100% masks on patrons and employees!), maybe having appointments with a couple of my favorite patients over the last few days, maybe memories of Tommy and Steve.

Today would have been mine and Tommy's sixth legal anniversary. We didn't use the date as we'd been together for nearly twelve years when we got married. That was simply a formality for taxes and insurance.

Prior to the Obergefell decision of 2015, marriage laws were something of a patchwork in this country, but the Windsor decision of 2013 decreed that, at least for federal purposes, a legal marriage in any state would be recognized by the federal government. Tommy and I looked at our taxes and other things and decided that marriage would be advantageous. We didn't want a wedding. We were a decade or more too late for that, and there was the issue of Alabama dragging its feet for state purposes, so we decided, that on our next trip to Seattle to visit the family, we would do the deed. I contacted an old high school friend, an attorney in Seattle, and she put us in touch with a judge who was willing to marry us.

On a July afternoon, we trekked down to the King County Criminal Court in Redmond along with my father, brother, and cousin for witnesses and said our "I do's" in front of the power vested by the state of Washington, right after she was done with the Grand Theft Auto case that dragged on a bit longer than anyone expected. This was followed by a dinner for family and friends in my sister's back yard.

Tommy felt that even this was too much hoopla, but I suspect he secretly enjoyed it. On the flight back to Alabama, our marriage dissolved and reformed several times depending on which state we were over and was not recognized when we returned home, but we were able to file a joint tax return that year, and a year later, thanks to Obergefell, we remained married no matter what the flight path.

Our marriage was, of course, cut short by Tommy's untimely death four years later, but it was valid and this made a huge difference in our lives in regard to dealing with various institutions. It allowed me to put him on my benefits without question, it helped at tax time, it announced to the world we weren't giving up on each other (although everybody had already figured that one out), and it changed how we related to each other in subtle but real ways.

We both knew that leaving each other would now require a lot more than packing a suitcase and walking out the door, and there was more strength to the bond when we had our fights (and believe me, we had some doozies). Most importantly, we understood that we were riding a wave of societal change forward. We had no idea where it was going to lead us, but we knew there would be no turning back.

One of the fundamental flaws of American culture—and I wonder if it's descended from the Boomer ideal of the media depiction of America prevalent in their childhood (the *Leave it to Beaver* and *Sally, Dick ,and Jane* world of perfection and safety) is that there is some sort of quintessence that must be recaptured at all costs, with its rose-colored nostalgia that causes people to look backward rather than forward. When applied to the current time of COVID-19, we all run around talking about things getting back to normal. Honestly, we have no way of knowing if that is going to be possible and, even if the virus were to fall silent tomorrow, we wouldn't be able to go back to where we were last fall. There's been too much radical change to allow that.

I'm hoping that some of our brighter thinkers (and I do not count myself among that group) will give us ways to start thinking about moving forward to what can be, rather than pining for what is no longer, and can help us redirect our energies in that direction.

Our education system, for instance, was borrowed from Prussia in the mid-19th century and was designed to create an obeisant proletariat of workers and soldiers. Highly regimented, it was grounded in an unwritten curriculum of obedience to authority, subject to the tyranny of the clock.

We no longer live in that world. Perhaps this can be a time where we take the underpinnings of the system and reinvent something for who we are today. We are the wealthiest society the planet has ever produced and where does an enormous amount of our treasure go? Defense systems above and beyond what are needed. Can some of that be redirected? Our health system is tied to employment due to mid-20th century historical accident. What are the possibilities there?

Living in the past with backward thinking is toxic and corrosive and will set you up for failure. Being the show queen that I am, and having been primed with several viewings of *Hamilton,* I went to my CD collection and to the Sondheim rack where I tend to find a lot of life's answers. I put on the Original Cast Album of *Follies*, a show about the dangers of living in the past, trying to stop time, and refusing to recognize that either you or the world has changed.

That title is a double-edged sword. It may be about the ghosts of between-the-wars young adults and their mature 1970s selves, but the same phenomenon is happening today, especially with the Baby Boomers. How many Boomer icons in their 70s and 80s are trying to project the same image they've had for the last fifty years?

In my job, I see so many people in their 70s to whom I have to break it that their disease processes are chronic and not curable due to the ravages of time. And they simply refuse to accept this. Our two candidates for president are 74 and 77. Could this be the moment when we can move forward with a cultural reset and where younger artists with a new way of looking at the world get their chance to lead us in new directions?

I'm thinking that our sclerotic, if not fossilized, social institutions are cracking under the strain of COVID-19. This may not be a bad thing, as long as the energy is channeled in positive directions. If it goes negative, let's hope we avoid 1793 France or 1918 Russia.

Time to change the CD. Switching from *Follies* to *Merrily We Roll Along*, a caustic look at where the Silent Generation and older Boomers went wrong in middle age. Seems somewhat fitting, doesn't it? I'm allowed to criticize Boomers because I am one, although at the tail end of the generation. More recent demographers define me and my cohort as "Generation Jones"—the group that always tried to "Keep up with the Joneses"—and were "always jonesin' for more." We were prevented from doing so because as we arrived at each stage of life, the sheer numbers of the older Boomers moving through before us had pretty much chewed up all of the resources leaving us a few scant crumbs.

In the meantime, wash your hands, wear your mask, and stay home when you can.

WEDNESDAY | JULY 15, 2020

I GOT A TEXT FROM AN OLD FRIEND a couple of days ago.

She's a nurse anesthetist in Houston. She said that her 290-bed hospital is completely full, 160 of those beds filled with COVID-19 patients. Every single ICU bed has a COVID-19 patient in it. It was 10 AM. She had already been called to six Code Blue situations. She was frazzled and exhausted. And that's just the beginning of the surge in Houston area hospitals.

There's a very predictable pattern happening in hot spots. Cases begin to rise with higher percentages of positive tests. About three weeks later, hospitals begin to fill up. Three weeks after that, deaths begin to skyrocket. The end of July and beginning of August are going to be brutal for Texas, Arizona, Florida, and the other states following their general curves.

Numbers are arcing up in Alabama as well. As we don't have the large dense urban centers, our absolute numbers are far fewer, but the trends are the same. UAB hospital now has over 100 COVID-19 inpatients (we were at 60 a month ago). The other hospitals in town are also seeing a rise. It's seeping into the long-term care facilities and senior communities and starting to spread among those vulnerable populations.

Our governor, never one to rock the boat, or even to be visible much of the time, emerged today for a press conference and announced a mandatory statewide mask order. Better late than never, I suppose, but it would have been helpful before the numbers started to spike. This has led to the inevitable backlash among those who have been conditioned by certain media outlets to regard anything that impinges on their sense of entitlement as a threat. I wonder what future generations will make of the Great Mask Wars of the summer of 2020? Perhaps we need to enlist the help of the Kardashians and have them run a PR campaign to make masks the must-have fashion accessory of the season.

I'm taking my first journey this weekend since COVID-19 hit when I head to Seattle to see my family. It's my first time off from work, and the first time I will have been able to see them since last November. I'll be staying at my brother's house in Wedgwood. I have no real agenda other than family time and probably a number of very long naps as the grind of work in this era has been getting to me. I'm not looking forward to flying in the age of COVID-19, but it was either that or nine days of driving round trip.

Keep those hands washed and sanitized. Wear your mask when out and about. Stay home as much as you can.

SUNDAY | JULY 19, 2020

'M SITTING ON THE LIVING ROOM COUCH at my brother's house, a couple of tuckered out dogs napping at my feet, listening to him practice some sort of stadium rock riffs on his electric guitar. It's nice to be around family after months and months of social distancing and more evenings and weekends alone than I care to contemplate.

I do all my air travel on Delta these days due to my location in the Southeast. My research into the responses of airlines to the needs of the coronavirus era suggested to me that there was no real need to change this as their protocols were about as good as you could get given the configurations of airplanes and airports. I was more concerned about time in airports than the plane itself, so I decided to drive over to Atlanta on Friday and spend the night in an airport area hotel, ensuring myself minimal airport time and no need to make a plane change at one of the hubs. I have all my points through Hilton properties, and Hampton Inn has been my go-to for years. I took advantage of the online check in and check out through my phone app together with downloading a digital key so I didn't have to linger in a lobby. The room was clean, but I wiped off surfaces before I touched them and hoped for the best.

The next morning, I drove through Starbucks, parked at the Atlanta airport in the economy lot and, mask in place, entered the terminal. I'm pleased to say that no matter what the Governor of Georgia may be up to, masking at the airport was universal with the exception of people eating in the food court. (I did not stop there).

The airport was nowhere near as busy as usual, so maintaining distance was not difficult, and I was able to get my bottle of Purell through security without a fuss, so sanitizing after every new activity wasn't an issue. The plane was about 60% full. Middle seats weren't sold except to family groups traveling together. People stayed masked and there was minimal traffic in the aisles.

I wedged myself in my seat per usual, put on a movie, promptly fell asleep, and woke up somewhere over Nebraska in time for a bottle of water, some Cheez-Its, and some cookies in a baggie. Then, more movies, which did not put me to sleep this time, and a lovely view of Mount Rainier as we flew past and descended into Sea-Tac airport. Again, universal masking, a quick trip through baggage claim, and off to meet my brother who was picking me up.

My biggest takeaway from the whole experience is how we have to do a whole new set of risk/benefit calculations with everyday activity that we just aren't used to and for which we are operating off of imperfect data. We've all been used to this since we were children.

Busy street? Wait for the light at the corner or, if there's no one coming, jaywalk to cut a couple minutes off of your time. Dark underpass at a late hour? Not a problem; I'm with three friends. We don't even think much about those calculations, especially if we're white males. We've been acculturated to them over decades of life experience.

Now we have a whole new set of risks to think about in a pandemic world and little conventional wisdom upon which to fall back. Am I far enough away from that person in this elevator? Is the need for my being able to interact with my family worth the risk of this plane flight? Can I hold it long enough not to need to use this public restroom? Perhaps, with time and additional data points, we'll get better at making these calculations.

The same thing is going on at a macro level with society. Is the need to educate and socialize our children worth the risk of opening up public schools in the usual model? Can we accomplish the same sorts of business or academic productivity without commuting into offices daily? Is it safe to stand in line with strangers? Is it safe to go indoors with them in large groups? If not now, when? What needs to happen to restore public confidence in these sorts of activities?

The criminal neglect of these basic questions evidenced by the lack of interest by current federal and state administrations is why we remain mired in a sort of stasis. We're holding at a crossroads: Either we allow the virus to spread unchecked and accept the consequences in excess mortality and morbidity, or we get serious about bringing it under control in the way most of the rest of the world has done. I'm afraid we're going to be stuck in stasis until we make up our societal minds about which way we really want to go. No choice is pleasant. The virus doesn't care.

In the meantime, wash your hands, wear your mask, maintain social distancing (which I am doing as much as I can, even with members of my family).

TUESDAY | JULY 21, 2020

TODAY WAS MELANCHOLY.

The American branch of the Saunders clan gathered at my uncle's house at Magnolia bluff to bid formal goodbye to my mother who died unexpectedly in late January. She'd had a serious genetic dementia and was non-communicative and unable to function the last few years of her life. One morning she just didn't wake up.

We wonder if possibly she may have been an early COVID-19 victim as she'd had a bit of a cough the week before her death and the disease was spreading silently in the Seattle area at the time. No one thought to look for it then, so there is no way of knowing.

Who was my mother? Alison Beatrix Saunders Duxbury was the elder daughter of a British South African colonial from an upper middle class social climbing family who emigrated to this country in the 1930s to join the faculty at what would become UCSF School of Medicine.

Here in the new world, her father set about climbing the academic ladder eventually becoming dean and chancellor. Her mother was an earthy practical Scot from Edinburgh with a steely resolve that got her through medical school in the 1920s, practically unheard of for women, and then became the quiet power behind her husband's rise in California. My mother rarely discussed her San Francisco girlhood and adolescence. Her father wanted his daughters to marry into the existing power structure. My mother had other ideas, throwing over the young doctor that was picked for her for the oceanography student of no particular pedigree who became my father.

My mother was one of the last generation to come of age before the onset of feminism and women's liberation, taught from infancy to subsume herself to the needs of husband and family. She was brilliant, could easily have had a scientific career the equal of my father's but decided her children were more important than a PhD. She was a devoted stay at home mom during our early childhood and then, when she got the last of us into school, went back to work and had an impressive community college teaching career for several decades.

She wordsmithed the textbook she wrote with my father that went through eight editions and funded their comfortable retirement. She quietly and competently ran every organization that came her way from the community club, to the Girl Scouts, the Cub Scouts, the PTA, and ended up helping to found the high school from which my sister graduated. She taught me far more than any teacher I ever had in school. More than anyone else, she was the one who taught me how to write clearly and cogently, but with a bit of a flair for the esoteric.

I am very much my mother's child, my brother is very much my father's child, and my sister always marched to her own drummer and laughed at all of us and our foibles. As I sit here and reflect on my mother, hundreds of moments and images collide from all phases of her life. Her grabbing me and running down the road at a campground in Banff when I was four because a bear was invading the tent next door. A major fight she had with Steve when we were all stressed out about the collapse of the clinical geriatrics program at UC Davis. Her coming to Birmingham to see the first musical I had directed in decades, *Kiss Me Kate,* and getting to meet my theater family. Her beaming at my graduation from medical school. Walking with her along a mountain trail on one of our many day hikes in the Cascades discussing the books I was reading in high school. Even long after I had left Seattle, we would get together over cups of tea on my rare visits back and discuss all sorts of things, always picking up where we had left off. I always knew that my parents would have my back no matter what.

We had planned a memorial for her in early April here in Seattle, but that was canceled by the spreading pandemic, so we decided to have a private family gathering to scatter her ashes at the same place as her sister.

When my uncle's parents died in the 1960s, he took the money he inherited from the sale of their house in New York and bought an undeveloped lot at the base of Magnolia bluff on Puget Sound. Just offshore from the lot was a boulder sitting on the sea bed, a glacial erratic placed there at the end of the last Ice Age by the retreating glaciers that carved the Sound and its landscape. It may have an official name, but my generation, children at the time, dubbed it Turtle Rock due to its resemblance to the shell of a turtle breaking the surface of the water at high tide.

Not much happened at the Turtle Rock property for 25 years or so other than people scrambling down the bluff for beach walks or blackberrying in the summer. But around1990, my aunt and uncle built a house there. It took some doing as the city had forgotten there was an undeveloped lot still on that road and the permitting process was a bit of a chore. He is an expert on Japanese culture and policy. She was an artist with an interest in Asian art forms. The house they built took both Japanese and Northwest design elements and has become the gathering place for our clan over time.

My aunt died of breast cancer in 2012 and, after her cremation, we scattered her ashes at Turtle Rock at the July low tide that summer. Eight years to the day later, we took my mother there to join her.

Myself, my uncle, my brother and his family, my sister and her SO, and my two cousins and families who were in town made our way down the bluff to the tide flats, went wading past the herons, the geoducks, the moon snails, and a mildly curious bald eagle, armed with the ashes, flowers, and a few words of remembrance. It was quite nice. I think she would have approved. My father was not up to the climb, so he watched from the balcony. I haven't made any specific requests regarding my remains when I die other than cremation. I won't be around to approve or disapprove, but I won't be upset if I end up at Turtle Rock as well.

WEDNESDAY | JULY 22, 2020

HERE IN SEATTLE, THE FIRST US EPICENTER back in those distant days of this past February, the population saw how quickly and silently COVID-19 can spread, and they take the potential dangers seriously.

In my wanderings around town, I've seen excellent adherence to masking and social distancing by the general population and, from what I can tell from the data available to me, transmission in Seattle proper is way down. The rest of Washington state is not quite so good. I assume that's a combination of rural population politics combined with substandard living conditions for agricultural workers on the other side of the Cascades.

The question I keep getting asked by family and friends is some variant on "What's coming next?" or "What is the new normal going to look like?" I have no degree in futurology or futurism or future studies or whatever it may be called in the future, so bear with me as I attempt to answer this. I may be right, I may be hopelessly wrong, but it's what I see from where I stand in mid-July of this benighted year.

HEALTH CARE

The healthcare system was going to enter an era of intense strain in about a decade, even without the presence of pandemic illness due to the demographics of American society. The aging of the Baby Boom generation, its wish to remain forever young, and its demands that the health system provide quick fixes to the complex issues of aging were going to tax the system. This process has just been sped up considerably. We now know where the cracks are about a decade ahead of schedule.

Some things, I think, are here to stay: More primary care will be moved away from office visits to virtual visits, especially for the management of chronic illness. People will get one or two appointments a year in the office. Additional appointments will be online, checking through a list of potential issues, looking for problems. More of these routine visits will also be devolved from physicians to Nurse Practitioners and Physician Assistants.

Access to specialty care is likely to move back towards a gatekeeper mechanism requiring referrals and more workup through primary care before a specialty appointment can be kept as the system continues to limit face-to-face contacts for the protection of both patients and healthcare providers. There will also likely be more rapid development of house call programs, home health will expand its service lines, and the home hospital model is likely to gain additional interest in an attempt to keep ill people who can be handled in a situation other than the hospital setting out of a place where the sick congregate and are more likely to become infected. Hospitals will continue to work to separate out COVID-19 services physically from other parts of hospital care, leading to something akin to the old TB pavilions and sanitariums of a century ago.

AGING

There's going to be more and more of a push for housing appropriate for multi-generational families as older people will be more and more loath to enter senior communities where they may be cut off from interacting with their grandchildren and great grandchildren. As more people work from home, there will be other adults in the home to assist an elder. I think we'll continue to see the collapse of the nuclear family as an ideal, and a reemergence of the extended family.

Elders are also going to want to be more connected to community and looking for senior housing integrated into urban areas rather than separated in suburban areas where they are trapped if they cannot drive. Older people, understanding their vulnerabilities, are going to be among the last to return to full social interactions which is going to have a huge impact on such things as audiences for performing arts events and dining patterns. There's going to be a huge demand for services that can clean and disinfect in various ways so that older folk feel more secure in their environments.

FASHION

I am not Miranda Priestly and I have no training in this, but I know enough about the history of costume to know that historical events are reflected in clothing trends. As more and more work is decentralized, and more and more jobs are done at home, there is going to be a decline in formal business apparel for clothes that will look smart and professional, but will also be comfortable and appropriate for other household tasks. I think the necktie will likely disappear. It's a vector for disease transmission (they aren't washed enough). As more clothes are bought online, they will be designed and cut to fit relatively well for various body types to minimize returns.

REAL ESTATE

As there will be fewer opportunities to socialize, people are going to want to know their neighbors more and socialize on the street. Older neighborhoods which were designed for that with sidewalks and front porches will become more desirable. Newer neighborhoods, designed strictly around the automobile, less so. There is also likely to be a renewed interest in living in central cities versus far flung suburbs. Commercial real estate is going to be in trouble as more and more businesses realize they can work perfectly efficiently without so much office space. There will be far fewer commuters. Businesses that rely on heavy commuter traffic will suffer.

PERFORMING ARTS

I think there will be a decentralization of musical theater away from NYC and other cultural capitals, and an increased recognition that good art doesn't depend on the imprimatur of particular critics or branding. Smaller, more facile companies that are willing to take radical steps to envision new ways of bringing content to a public starved for entertainment will do better than large, overhead-heavy, traditional companies that really only know one way of doing things.

Ultimately, I think we're going to get some exceptional artistic works from this period from creatives who use all of this societal uncertainty to springboard to something new. It's always worked that way. The financial structures underpinning the arts in this country are in trouble (and have been for years), so we're going to have to decide as a society what we want to do about that.

It's going to change. Be prepared. Change is neither right nor wrong, it just is. It's what allows us to move forward as a society to something better. It's scary and painful and no one likes to give up the familiar—inertia is a powerful force—but ultimately the choice is to either grab hold of it and go along for the ride or resist it and let it grind you into the past. I'm doing my best to do the former, although I find it as difficult as everyone else does. In the meantime, I'll continue to do the three basic things that we can all do to curb the pandemic.

Wear a mask. Keep my distance. Wash my hands.

MONDAY | JULY 27, 2020

HAVE RETURNED FROM THE PACIFIC NORTHWEST back to my own domicile where the weather is hot and sticky, the condo is deliciously cool due to the recent replacement of the HVAC, and I am once again being pretty much ignored by both of my cats.

A friend house-sat while I was gone, at least in part to get some peace and quiet away from her busy family life. Perhaps the cats are disappointed that I am not her. Both Oliver and Anastasia did not even bother to appear for several hours after I came back, and even then it was only to yowl about supper.

In the nine days I've been away, the number of COVID-19 cases in the county is up 2,000. The number in the state is up 13,000. The number nationally is up half a million. It took several months to generate those numbers at the start of the pandemic, now it's taking just over a week. With continued uncontrolled spread, it will start speeding up more and more as that's what exponential numbers do.

Now that it has become so firmly entrenched in more conservative states, the administration appears to finally be waking up to very real public health concerns, but their track record to date at putting politics and ideology before good public health practices doesn't give me a lot of confidence that we'll be making headway soon.

What's most irksome about all of this is how absolutely unnecessary it all is. Even at this late date, the pandemic could be controlled and well on its way to eradication in four to six weeks. It would be painful and politically difficult but could be done. We are the richest society this planet has ever produced. We can do or have pretty much anything as long as we align our political and economic systems to make it so. What would we need to do?

First, a real lockdown of at least a month. We haven't had one other than some jurisdictions in the Northeast and the SF Bay area. It would have to be nationwide, no exceptions, everybody home, no travel other than trade goods, no one on the street or gathering anywhere for any reasons. And it would have to be enforced.

Second, use that time to make and distribute accurate point-of-service testing, so that people coming out of lockdown can be tested, and we can gather an understanding of where the virus is being transmitted in real time.

Third, contact tracing of carriers with enforced quarantines until the transmission chains are broken.

Of course, to do this, the government would have to take on the economic calamities that will result from more lockdowns, and we haven't been the best at that so far, especially when compared with the rest of the developed world. But that's why the rest of the developed world is beginning to open up and we're in a continued upward pandemic trajectory.

I can't help but wonder if my little jaunt to Seattle, which I felt was absolutely necessary for both my mental health and my family, didn't in its own way contribute to the problem. I'm pretty good at my masks and social distancing (although the staff at my father's senior living facility was miffed when we removed our masks on the patio of his building to drink our coffee, even though we were outdoors and a good ten feet apart). But that's me, always over-thinking and taking on more *weltschmerz* than I need to. I have a week before I go back to work, so I'm spending it in self-imposed quarantine in my condo to make sure I didn't pick anything up on the trip. So here I am, puttering around with a list of little projects to keep me busy this week.

If I do go out, you all know the litany: Wear your mask, take your sanitizer with you, keep your hands washed.

FRIDAY | JULY 31, 2020

THE STRAIGHT LINE WINDS ARE BLOWING, the rains are descending, and I remain in the same quasi-torpor I've been in for the last few days.

I've kept myself quarantined in the condo just in case I came into contact with the novel coronavirus on the trip to Seattle and back. So far, so good. I feel fine other than a general sense of lassitude and a need for daytime napping during my staycation week. I have accomplished a few constructive things. I sorted my whole CD collection and got it stowed, got the laundry done, and made some progress on some writing projects. It's the little things.

I read somewhere that the US economy contracted by something over 30% last quarter. This compares to 6% with the recession of 2008 and 16% with the Great Depression. There's a world of hurt still to come.

I was trying to decide what to write about today but everything that came to mind seemed horribly depressing, and I am trying to keep my own personal spirits up after a particularly downbeat couple of days dominated by the death of two old friends (neither related to COVID-19) and a local scandal involving another old friend, also a geriatrician, who was arrested on salacious charges. This wouldn't have been much of an issue but when you Googled his name, my UAB promotional picture came up, so people were sharing the story around social media with my picture attached which was not a particularly good feeling. I've been home, so no one has been staring in the street, and I have sicced the UAB IT department on the issue.

The big contretemps locally is over the issue of getting kids back to school. There is a very vocal minority pushing for the schools to open normally in August with full in-person instruction. There is a less vocal majority who are concerned about all of the issues that opening up will bring to the fore.

Running schools is not an easy business. There are federal, state, and local mandates regarding instruction and subjects and credit hours. There are negotiations with teachers' and employees' unions. There are the fixed costs of maintaining the physical plants. There are the special needs children and educational programs. There are the extracurricular activities such as sports and music and theater that are often the only way to maintain older children's interest in school.

I can't even begin to imagine how you balance all of that in normal times without the stresses of a pandemic, especially in a state like ours which works on a starvation budget at best. One local school district sent out a memo noting that the budget allowed for only one bottle of hand sanitizer and one box of sanitary wipes per classroom—to last the entire school year.

There are times when I wish my life had allowed for children of my own, but this is not one of them. I can't imagine the kinds of decisions that parents and families who rely on public schools are trying to navigate at the moment. The lack of central leadership means that every school district is trying to work it all out for itself. I'm not particularly worried about the children of America. They appear to be resilient and relatively unaffected by COVID-19, but what happens when they start coming home to parents and grandparents and great grandparents?

The at-risk populations in this country are much more likely to live in multi-generational households, not isolated nuclear family units, and I can see another surge in October and November as those people become exposed through school children and sicken. What are we planning to do if children end up orphaned? What happens if the teachers and their unions go on strike due to unsafe working conditions? Is the federal government going to send in their newly constituted riot police to force them into working at gunpoint? (I'm being ridiculous there, but many of what I would have considered ridiculous things a few years ago have come to pass recently.)

Large segments of our society still seem to be living in denial that COVID-19 is a serious problem. Yes, the percentage death rate is relatively low when compared to a viral illness like Ebola, but it's still a good deal higher than the flu—about ten times higher. We still don't know what the long-term sequelae of those who recover from serious cases are likely to be.

The numbers will keep going up until there is a coordinated federal response of some sort. And yet, the Senate appears incapable of acting due to partisan bickering, and the executive branch appears to be continuing to try and re-enact Poe's *The Masque of the Red Death* (without remembering how the story ends). I need to see if the Roger Corman/Vincent Price film adaptation is on one of the streaming services. It's been years since I've seen it, and it strikes me as being perhaps the best metaphor for our times.

I go back to work on Monday. I'm not looking forward to climbing back into the pressure cooker, but I must, especially with two mortgages to pay until someone buys my house. My fashion masks are all washed, I have plenty of hand sanitizer, and, if the rain stops, I'll spend as much time as I can out of doors.

AUGUST 2020

Water Under The Bridge

TUESDAY | AUGUST 4, 2020

ALABAMA CONTINUES TO EXPERIENCE A SURGE. The number of COVID inpatients at UAB is roughly double what it was late March-May as the infections that ticked up with the opening of the state in June turned into serious infections leading to hospitalizations in July which will turn into a spike in deaths in August, just in time for us to open up the schools.

I come from a land where schools don't start back until Labor Day, but here in the Deep South, they tend to begin mid-August. From what I can tell, the departments of education in the southern states, like most other governmental entities, rather than grappling with the problems posed by the coronavirus, are simply passing the buck further and further down the chain of command and leaving things up to individual school districts.

There are a number of school districts in my metropolitan area, and they all seem to be completely at sea as to what they should be doing in regard to in-person learning, distance learning, after school activities, and the safety of teachers and staff. Each one seems to be taking a different tack and sailing off a different edge of the earth. New emails come out daily, causing parents to be more and more con-fused and completely unsure about what is actually going to happen as schools gear up over the next few weeks.

The largest entity, Jefferson County schools, decided today that it will have no-in person classes for the first nine weeks of the semes-ter. Teachers will report to school and conduct classes remotely. How that's supposed to work for students without laptops, or how a teacher is supposed to effectively teach 25 kids via Zoom, was not explained. Some of the rural Georgia districts started back this week, and the first-day-of-school pictures beginning to circulate on social media do not look promising. They show teenagers being teenagers in the halls with no social distancing and only a rare mask. COVID-19 spread in 3... 2... 1...

I see the country as a whole beginning to have a major surge this fall, far worse than we are seeing now as all those young people mix and mingle and carry each other's microbes home. Add to that the fact that high school football programs (a near religion in this part of the world) are going great guns, and Friday Night Lights will soon be here, and we're going to have even more issues.

I'm not overly worried about the kids. The data suggests that the vast majority will not get seriously ill (although vast majority doesn't mean all, and some previously healthy children and teens will die). I'm much more worried about the teachers and staff who have dedicated their lives to nurturing our young and who are already horribly undervalued.

When teachers have to decide between their calling and their mortality, which will they choose? What happens if a significant portion of the teachers in this country quit because it's just too dangerous for them to be around crowds of young people? Do we redesign schools to be smaller and less centralized? Do we make more education home-dependent? What happens in those families that can only make it economically if all the adults work, sometimes at multiple jobs? Families are likely to start doubling up and becoming more multi-generational in order to have an adult in the home for child-rearing and supervision. When that adult is a grandparent or great grandparent, what does that mean in terms of their risk for coronavirus infection? I don't have answers for any of this, but it's the sort of thing that keeps me up at night.

It fascinates (and infuriates) me that the attitude of our governmental institutions towards the pandemic is one of "If we pretend it isn't there, somehow it will go away." Nature doesn't work like that. Viral illness can't be swayed by op-ed columns, mean tweets, or 30-second campaign commercials. It obeys only the laws of biology, chemistry, and physics, but we seem somehow determined to shunt aside the findings of science for feelings or wishful thinking.

We can keep doing this, but as long as we do, things are not going to be "normal". No one is immune to the virus, and we don't know what protects some of us and keeps us from getting ill, or what causes some of us to end up for weeks in the ICU despite no previous health history. There are tantalizing clues and the scientists are working overtime, but I'm not sure the politicians are listening.

My handy-dandy coronavirus counter says we're at 4.77 million cases in the US as of this afternoon. That's 1.45% of the population. It's likely an undercount as so many young people are asymptomatic. Let's say we've missed half of them, so 2.9% of the population has been infected to date. At this point, we are somewhere north of 155,000 deaths. That's roughly three Vietnam Wars. If we continue to do a whole lot of nothing to stop the disease, and it continues until we reach herd immunity (roughly 80% infection rate), we're looking at about four-and-a-half million deaths and who knows how many chronically ill or disabled. That's 50% higher than the number of US military casualties in all of the wars and actions we have ever fought over the last 250 years. Or the population of the entire San Francisco Bay area if you want something a little less military.

We can't have normal unless we put the good of society ahead of our own personal convenience. Until that happens, we're going to continue to have disasters, both major and minor, and whole sectors of the economy, those that depend on groups of people being able to get together, won't be able to function normally, if at all. Most people I know are doing the things we can do as individuals—masking, distancing, staying home, washing hands—but this only goes so far.

We need other things as well, and I'm pretty sure we won't get them before January at the earliest.

Maybe I'll watch *Hamilton* again. Must wash hands first.

SUNDAY | AUGUST 9, 2020

T'S BEEN AN EVENTFUL WEEKEND, even though I've spent a good deal of it in a T-shirt and sleep pants lounging around the condo. It's the perfect attire for snuggling with the cats and writing a lecture on COVID-19 and its implications for older adults that I'm giving via Zoom as an adult education class. It's been a while since I've written a lecture on a brand new topic for a lay audience. I think I've got all my ducks in a row and my facts checked. I should be ready, but everything changes so quickly on this topic that I've had to double- and triple-check dates on sources. If it was published before June, it's likely out of date at this point.

My so-called coronavirus life continues in its usual patterns. Go to work during the week, sit at home in the evenings and weekends with plenty of reading, binge-watching television, some Xbox time, and Zoom meetings with various boards trying to help arts and other nonprofits weather the storm and plan for the future. I am no seer, but I can help people understand the real science and medicine behind the pandemic, so they aren't relying on media reports tainted by politics or other agendas. I miss a life of rehearsals and performances and social gatherings, but I'll make the best I can of what I've got. I am so fortunate to have a career that's rather impervious to pandemics, a nice place to live, people who care about me, and to live at a time in history where creature comforts are not that hard to obtain.

The house is finally ready for market and the listing went live yesterday. No firm offers yet, but a few swirling around in the ether. It looks gorgeous in the photos. I've decided they must have taken the picture of the facade by drone as there's no way to get that vantage point unless you climb the tree in the parking strip and then shinny out onto a branch overhanging the front lawn. I'm not worrying about it selling quickly for a good price. Location, location, location. It will be nice to completely close that chapter and no longer have to pay two mortgages and sets of utilities.

This morning's surprise was the general reaction to my having PopTarts for brunch. They're one of my weaknesses. I typically only eat them on Sunday with my online church service. The Unitarian Universalists are meeting regularly, even if it has to be on YouTube. In all innocence I put up a picture of my brunch on social media only to discover that PopTarts are a bit of a flash point for my friends, engendering strong emotional response. I'd rather walk up over the hill for fresh pastries from The Continental Bakery but the proprietress has temporarily shut her doors as she cares enough about her employees not to expose them to the population around here who refuse to take COVID-19 and masking seriously.

Our local numbers continue to increase by leaps and bounds. Nearly 100,000 diagnosed cases in our state of 5 million, and 13,000 in Jefferson county. Our positivity rate (the percentage of tests done that are positive) is running about 15-16%. Public health experts recommend that this be below 5% before societal lockdowns end, and we aren't having much of one at all around here these days which is why our numbers continue to rise. I'll continue to do my part of socially isolating and wearing my mask in public because I want to get back to theater and traveling.

The one thing that is likely to get local attention, and maybe change the equation around here, is the spread of the virus among returning college students who are back on campus early for football practice. The country is about a week away from canceling college football completely. When Alabamians can't worship in the temples of Bryant-Denny and Jordan-Hare this fall, there may finally be some willingness to take the pandemic seriously and change behavior.

War Tide. Roll Eagle. Hands wash.

FRIDAY | AUGUST 14, 2020

ALABAMA HAS EASILY CRESTED 100,000 CASES of COVID-19, the US death toll has climbed to nearly 170,000, and the world watches aghast as we prepare to send students back to school at all levels with community transmission still at unacceptably high rates.

There is some good news on this front. The percentage positive rate of tests in Alabama over the last week has come down from double digits, and locally the number of people in the hospital with COVID-19 has started to drop from a peak a few weeks ago. If these trends continue, the healthcare system is going to get a little breathing room. Any bump in numbers from back-to-school won't occur for about three to four weeks.

I didn't lose too many of my long-term patients to COVID-19 early in the pandemic, but I'm starting to lose more now. Three or four in the last two weeks. Some had been ill for some time, some were relatively newly diagnosed. I suspect that in pretty much all of the cases, a family member or friend brought it into the home after being out and about and a bit more cavalier with their masking and social distancing due to summer weather and a wish for good times. When the grandkids and great grandkids head back to school, I expect I'll see another uptick. I've also had friends lose spouses, parents, grandparents, and siblings recently. It's not over until it's over.

I've accepted an offer on the house and the real estate wheels are churning along. Everything should be over and done with by the first of October. Just one more month of double mortgage payments. If the contract stands, it's going to a family with young children where both parents work from home. Tommy would like that. He adored kids and working with them. I think the happiest I ever saw him was when he was teaching and leading his beloved children's choir.

Steve adored being the wicked uncle to children, leading them into mischief and then vanishing before there could be any consequences. There are days when I think I've missed out not having children, but then I realize that the unit of survival is the tribe, not the individual, and my role is to ease the burdens of the older generation and their nurturers so that they have time and energy to give to *their* children and grandchildren—and then I feel a bit better about my choices.

COVID-19 and its roiling of healthcare finances has hit how my job works. The hospice I have medical-directed for many years and UAB are parting ways. Fortunately, it is happening at the same time that the VA part of my job is working diligently to expand the rural house call program to a new population centered in Huntsville, so it's all going to come out in the wash.

Most of the house call work is still being handled through video conferencing, but plans are afoot to get back into the field later in the fall. I will probably ultimately be doing a mix of field work and call work. I hadn't planned on working in a call center late in my career, but nothing ever stays the same in life, no matter what. As long as I can cobble together enough funding to keep my bills paid, I'm happy. I'm only about twenty months away from instituting the first part of my retirement plan. I am vested in the University of California pension system from my years there, and it stops accruing when I turn 60, so I'll officially become retired faculty from there when I hit that birthday. Funny—when I was young, I was sure I would flame out and be dead by 35 and never have to worry about things like retirement accounts.

I was industrious this evening after I made my dinner. I washed all of my face masks, got the iron out, blew the dust off, and gave them all a good steam ironing for disinfecting and de-wrinkling purposes. In case you're wondering, Rodgers and Hammerstein is good music to iron to.

The weekend has a few chores lined up. I have to get my office supplies organized (currently they're thrown in a closet). I bought some shelving to help with that which I need to assemble. Tommy and I bought a lot of do-it-yourself assembly furnishings and shelves over the years. We would sit in the living room trying to insert tab A into slot B with screwdrivers and rubber mallets, kvetching at each other that one of us wasn't doing his part right. I guess I'll have to complain bitterly to the cats when something doesn't want to fit this time around. I also have a couple of lectures to write for community education programs, and there's a dozen-and-a-half progress notes from this week calling my name.

Now that the initial shock of the COVID-19 world has worn off, I'm puzzling out how to keep myself motivated. Over the last couple of years, since Tommy's untimely death, I've done it by having about one thing a month to look forward to: a trip somewhere, a show to rehearse and perform, a special concert.

All those self-rewards are now on indefinite hold and I haven't figured out how to replace them yet. The effects of COVID-19 on my job plus the craziness of moving have kept me sufficiently distracted in recent months, for the most part, but it's unclear to me, now that things are settling down into a new routine, what should come next.

I have a few more projects to accomplish around the house, several of which will take some time, but those feel like obligations, not rewards. Maybe I'll do a little weekend road-tripping this fall, depending on what happens to the COVID numbers once the school impact becomes clear—and all the Sturgis motorcyclists make their way home and spread whatever they've picked up.

I've always been one to cope, pick myself up after reverses, and keep chugging along. This resilience has been present since I was very small. My parents tell a story about a camping trip we took when I was three or four. My parents were very outdoorsy types in Washington State, so we did a lot of backpacking and car camping when I was a child.

My parents and I had gone up into the mountains where we had put up the tent and were enjoying the sights and smells of the Pacific Northwest woods. Next to our campsite was a large tree with some invitingly low branches, and I wanted to climb it. My parents said no, it wasn't going to be a good climb for someone of my size. (I was a tiny child). I wheedled and cajoled and put forth all my best-reasoned post-toddler arguments.

Eventually, I was told "Fine, but if you fall, don't come crying to us." So I climbed up, and sure enough I fell. It wasn't a big enough fall to really hurt me, but it knocked the wind out of me. My parents watched to see what I would do. I picked myself up, bit my lip, and uttered not a sound. I had been told the consequences and I accepted them. I'm still that way.

So go ahead and climb your trees everyone but, if you fall out, deal with the pain and shock you were warned about. Just do it in a mask, and wash your hands while you're at it.

TUESDAY | AUGUST 18, 2020

AFTER A TEN-HOUR WORK DAY followed by an hour-plus Zoom lecture for my church's adult education program, I really should be curled up in a tight little ball watching some bad movie, but my mind is racing a dozen different ways.

The local COVID-19 numbers are falling. This is good news. It remains to be seen what back-to-school is going to do to them. The news from elsewhere is not good. Both UNC and Notre Dame, which went back this past week with in-person instruction, have shut again after flare-ups.

UAB is in the midst of move-in. There is a brand new private student apartment/dorm development across the street from my academic office. I walked past it this morning on my way to the VA and watched move-in day for a moment. Lots of excited young people with boxes doing what young people have always done. I doubt there's going to be a lot of social distancing or mask wearing. I doubt I would have masked and distanced at 18 or 20.

I'm both sad and mad that it's quite likely their chance to explore the joys of youth, and higher education might just be jerked to a halt in a couple of weeks; it didn't have to be that way. If this country had listened to those who know how to handle pandemic viral illness instead of to politicians with personal agendas, there's no reason why we couldn't be in the same position as most of the rest of the civilized world, cautiously opening up, returning to normal life patterns, and prepared to stomp out pockets of disease which are quickly and easily detected.

If your life hasn't been touched by this disease yet, just wait, it will be. It's too widespread and the numbers are too high for it to pass you by. The average American has a circle of acquaintances of roughly 5,000 people. At current rates, 30 people you know are likely to die before it's all over, and hundreds more will have serious health problems, likely permanently.

My lecture tonight was on death, dying, and advance directives. Not the most light-hearted of subjects, but I have figured out ways to make even the most lugubrious of geriatric-related topics interesting over the years.

I first began public speaking in the early 1990s, and it didn't take me long to realize that having a certain patter, along with a willingness to tell jokes and drop one-liners when discussing relatively heavy subject matter, kept people engaged, helped them remember what you wanted them to remember, and made them not want to slit their wrists after a talk on the upcoming infirmities and indignities we all age into eventually.

I picked a bit of it up by watching good lecturers in medical school, a bit from *Monty Python* and *Saturday Night Live,* and a bit from my own idiosyncratic background and early theater experiences. I've had a few people suggest I need to come up with some sort of one-man show/comedic monologue about all the craziness of geriatric medicine and how it intertwines with the rest of my life. I could probably write it, but I'd need a lot of help making it into a theatrical piece.

I did tell one story tonight about death.

There's an odd quirk in Alabama law. You are not allowed to authorize your own cremation. Cremation is only allowed if your surviving next of kin allows it. I've been told it was crafted by the funeral industry to allow for more burials—and it works. I believe Alabama is the state with the lowest rate of cremation. I don't know if that's true or not, but it sounds good.

Twenty years ago when Steve died, we'd had plenty of time to prepare. He was sick for two years. He had gone down to a local funeral home and made pre-need arrangements. He told me he had handled it, so I didn't think anything of it. He was in hospice when he died, so hospice handled the transfer to the funeral home, and I went down the next day to see them and to make arrangements for the cremation he wanted.

When I got there, the very nice young man told me he was sorry, but they could not possibly cremate Steve. There must be a release from legal next of kin. Despite our 13 years together, I didn't count. (It was 2001, legal marriage was still a pipe dream). I held it together and calmly said that was nice, but that Steve's parents were dead, he had no children, he was estranged from his siblings, and I had no means of contacting them. What did the nice young man want to do about that?

We sparred for a few moments, then he got a twinkle in his eye and said "I have an idea." He went off and made some calls, coming back to me in a few minutes. He suggested we transfer Steve to the low-cost mortuary across town where they didn't ask too many questions. I consented, Steve was moved, and off I went to mortuary number two. There, the mortician, who reminded me a bit of a pawn shop counter person, basically said "We'll keep him for three days, if no one comes to complain, we'll cremate him." Wink wink, nudge nudge, say no more.

So, if you want to be cremated in Alabama, make sure your family knows it. Your word, even in a will or final instructions isn't good enough. Personally, I'm going to take Tommy's approach. When I asked him about his preferences, he said "I won't be here, you'll have to figure it out," and refused to return to the subject. I trust my family to figure it out. Conservation of mass and energy will return my physical being to the cosmos no matter what they do.

SUNDAY | AUGUST 23, 2020

HAVEN'T FELT WELL THIS WEEKEND, so I've spent most of it in bed, bingeing on Netflix, and babying my stomach with ginger ale and ramen.

No fever, no respiratory symptoms, so I doubt it's COVID-19, just the usual crud we all tend to pick up now and again. I figure one more good night's sleep and I should be ready to face the coming week.

I put off most of my to-do list this weekend other than the few things I had to get done. The only one that remains is writing the talk I'm giving to the church adult education program next week on the impact of Alzheimer's on caregivers and family systems. I have most of it in my head, but I will need to get an outline down on paper in order to not sound like a complete idiot Tuesday evening when I fire up my Zoom camera.

With a quiet weekend, I've done some catching up on my coronavirus reading, leafing through articles on treatments, promising and not-so-promising, vaccine development, and current epidemiological trends. After doing that for a few hours, I usually emerge with a combination of anger that the adults in our society who were in a position to do something about all of this thoroughly abdicated their responsibilities because it's hard stuff, and sadness at the difficulties we will all continue to bear until the adults in the room where it happens decide that the lives of the many are of equal importance to the wealth of the few.

The latest round of news stories over the opening of colleges and universities cements this. It's become pretty clear that the money flowing through academia is more important than the lives and safety of faculty, staff, and students in a number of cases. My university, UAB, appears to be trying to do things correctly with constant surveillance testing, but I can't say this of all institutions of higher learning.

There seems to be a societal tendency to blame the students for misbehaving when they simply act like students. Young adults in their late teens and early 20s do not have fully developed frontal lobes and are not yet capable of completely understanding the consequences of their actions. Humans have known this for millennia.

We don't get all our neural connections until age 25 or so. College students aren't capable of making the choices we're trying to force on them. The adults who should be making those choices are pushing them off on young people and then blaming them when they aren't made in the wisest fashion. It's just one of the hundred-and-one ways in which mature generations are shafting the future out of selfish motives.

I believe this is an unintended consequence of social attitudes put in place in the 30s and 40s. From October of 1929, with the Wall Street crash, until August of 1945, with the end of World War II, America went through a whole lot of bad—more than fifteen years worth. New parents of the late 40s and early 50s, determined that their children would not know bad in that way, created a society that coddled and protected their offspring. This privileged generation, growing up in a Disney-fied world, were imbued with a sense of entitlement to the good life that has followed them through their life cycles. These kids, now in their late 60s and early 70s, run the majority of our social institutions and don't seem to be able to act when bad comes round again.

The magical thinking emanating from various high government offices has reached epidemic proportions, and while abdicating responsibility is a choice, it does little to help us cope or move forward.

Those in the upper reaches of society also seem to have little care for younger generations who are now adults and need to be brought into decision-making capacities. Rising young leaders are dismissed out of hand.

COVID-19 trends locally and nationally have been positive over the last few weeks. The reopening of schools may change that, but there is no way to know right now. I'll keep my fingers crossed that numbers will continue to inch down, but I don't have a good feeling about what's to come. I'm going to continue to do my part with my quasi-hermit existence. It's all I can do.

At least I have some creative outlets coming up: a cameo in a Zoom theater production of *Henry IV, Part II*, and a major role in *Tartuffe* in a similar format.

As performing artists start exploring the capabilities of online and other mediums, I have one piece of advice both for artists and audiences: Don't go into projects trying to recreate what was. That's just going to provoke nostalgia and feelings of sadness. Go into them determined to forge something new, something we haven't seen before. In the words of Sondhiem, *Move On*...

Speaking of Sondheim, I was cleaning out a drawer and found the letters I have received from him over the years, including my favorite one. Back in the early days of the Internet and listservs, I devised a number of puzzles around his songs and shows, some of which I sent to him. He solved most of them easily other than one. And when I sent him the solution to that one, his note back was "I could shoot myself, but I won't."

Be like Sondheim. Wash your hands.

SATURDAY | AUGUST 29, 2020

LIFE IS SETTLING DOWN INTO A NEW NORMAL. I can't say I like it, but it is what it is and must be dealt with. The coronavirus has profoundly altered so many things that even the mundane day-to-day existence of my life feels very different from what it felt like only six months ago.

I look at the numbers and trends here locally and nationally and there is guarded cause for optimism. The trends are down, likely due to better adherence to mask wearing and social distancing in public, leading to broken transmission chains and a decline in the infection rate. Will they remain down with the spikes beginning to arise in schools and on college campuses? Time alone will tell.

What are the changes? On the University side of my job, which revolves mainly around outpatient ambulatory clinics, the amount of time I need to spend outside of actual clinical hours dealing with patient needs has roughly doubled. A four-hour clinic session used to create about one to two hours of out-of-clinic work (paperwork, charting, phone calls, emails, patient messages, etc.). Now it generates three to four. I think COVID-19 is directly responsible.

People no longer save up their questions for their next visit to the doctor. They're uncertain about life. They want some certitude at least about their current health and are much more likely to make multiple calls or send multiple emails, each of which must be dealt with individually by me or my staff. In order to ensure safety and isolation, our bar for enlisting home health services for patients is a good deal lower. We'd rather have a professional go in who understands infection control than have patients go out and rub shoulders with multiple individuals who may not. Each of those referrals generates a mountain of paperwork, required by Medicare for documentation, so that the Center for Medicare and Medicaid services knows for what it is paying.

On the VA side of the job, I'm managing all my house call teams from my bunker in a VA out-building. This saves many hours of car trips to such exciting destinations as Holly Pond and Nauvoo, but sitting there staring at a computer screen for hours on end, whether it's with patients and families or with federal systems stressed by COVID-19, makes me cross-eyed after a few hours. We're also using this period for program building, and over the next six months my patient panel will increase by 50-100% as we create new teams based out of Huntsville.

I just know that when I come home in the evening after my usual ten-hour work day, I sit on the couch and just zone out for an hour or so. That's not something I've done in the past. My usual pattern was to grab dinner, head for rehearsal, and not get home until sometime between 9-10 PM. And I would still feel perfectly energetic for a few more hours and be able to get the necessary chores done. I can't imagine doing that right now. The fatigue is probably a stress response. My limbic system and primitive brain reflexes are making me store up energy to fight the omnipresent danger later. I'd rather go to rehearsal. I even miss technicals.

So far so good on the personal COVID-19 front. My surveillance testing has been negative. I haven't had a repeat of the feeling rotten of last weekend which I am fairly certain could be traced to something I ate. As I wander through my life at UAB, I've noticed that about a third of the population wears their masks below their noses, completely defeating the purpose, so I figure it's only a matter of time, especially as I have to keep closeting myself up in my too-small exam rooms with demented people who have child-like or toddler brains, and who won't keep masks on for love nor money. I'll continue to trust in providence and the fact that the majority of the demented tend not to hang out in sports bars.

I'm not completely sure what to make of the social battles over the opening of schools and universities. Not a day goes by currently when I don't hear about a younger friend from theater circles or the college-aged child of a peer being diagnosed at school. They've all been fine and should recover without major incident (although the long-term effects remain obscure and potentially dangerous). The smaller schools seem to be doing better than the larger ones, although they have smaller problems to solve.

UAB itself seems to be doing well and has policies in place that are well thought out, and there haven't been any major clusters or super-spreader events that I've been aware of. Down the road in Tuscaloosa, it's been a different matter, but the culture of the institution is not the same. UAB is an urban, mainly commuter campus while Tuscaloosa is an isolated traditional campus in a small college town. The biggest question is going to be the effect of the football season. The SEC has not canceled (big money, I expect), although the stadia are supposed to be socially distanced in seating. I just don't see how that's supposed to work and will not be in the least surprised if one of the early match-ups turns into a super-spreading event.

The debate over whether schools should be in-person or online continues. I don't know all the answers here. I just think that the administrators of educational institutions have been put in an impossible position due to the political failures of six months ago that allowed the virus to become so firmly entrenched. They have so many constituencies they must try to satisfy. The needs of students, the needs of parents, the needs of faculty and staff, mandates on education from the local, state, and federal level, the rules of accrediting bodies, the needs of donors in the case of private institutions. It's a nigh impossible task to please all of these disparate viewpoints, and I like to think that the majority of educational administrators are trying to do their best with inadequate resources in a highly stressful time. Of course, I also feel that some I have read about are complete boneheads, but that's just me.

I did get my creative juices going this week by writing some parody Christmas carol lyrics for a friend's choral group. I'm hoping that *Walkin' in a COVID Wonderland* and *Have Yourself a COVID Little Christmas* will be heard in heavy rotation on the radio this yuletide. If anyone else needs some quick satire, you know where to find me. In the meantime, I'm going to finish my hard pineapple cider and put on a movie.

Wear your mask, wash your hands, keep your distance. It's really that simple.

SEPTEMBER 2020

I Know Things Now

TUESDAY | SEPTEMBER 1, 2020

I T WAS THE BEST OF TIMES, IT WAS THE WORST OF TIMES.
I don't know about anyone else, but I keep being whipsawed between extreme highs and lows with what's going on in the world today. Something happens to make me think I still live in a country full of generous and compassionate people, and then something else comes along an hour later which makes me feel like Thomas Hobbes was not only right, but that he's also busy directing events from the next world. The truth is, as always, somewhere in the middle of extremes. It's not easy to remember this when your brain is being asked to absorb far more than it has the capacity to parse on a daily basis.

On the good news front is a story out of Tuscaloosa where there was a Black Lives Matter march. BLM marches aren't uncommon these days. I've been in a few myself as I strongly support racial equity and the reassessment of social structures that prevent it from happening. What made this one special was the figure leading the march: Alabama football coach Nick Saban. Those not of Alabama may not understand the import of this image. College football is a religion in these parts, and Saban is a major deity in the pantheon, ranking only slightly below the legendary Bear Bryant.

I spend a lot of time in small town and rural Alabama due to the part of my job where I am the medical director for the local VA's rural house call program. University of Alabama football fandom is one of the few things that's common to pretty much every household I enter, no matter where that household may fall on the socio-economic scale or what political beliefs they champion.

The sight of Saban, this divine being, not just supporting, but leading a group disdained by rural Alabama culture (thanks to a steady diet of Fox News) has set up an enormous cognitive dissonance. It will be interesting to see how it plays out. I can't think of a better way to get the people of this region to actually start considering what BLM actually stands for and means.

Moving on from a high to a low, I have a number of friends on the opposite side of the political spectrum from myself, and I make it a point to read things written by people of widely divergent views. I swore off televised news years ago, but I try to read a good deal of political news and commentary, searching for nuggets of truth within the spin.

On Monday, I was greeted by a few of my more conservative friends passing around the ridiculous idea that only 6% of COVID-19 deaths were actually due to COVID-19. In tracking down where that insane idea had come from, I found that it was a gross misinterpretation of some data published by the CDC where they stated that only 6% of the death certificates filed had COVID-19 as the sole cause of death. All the others mentioned things like respiratory failure, heart disease, etc.

The people advancing the idea that 94% of non-COVID death certificates are part of some grand conspiracy theory don't know how death certificates work. If the certifying physician is doing them correctly, there should almost always be several contributing causes of death and often a cascade of events documented that lead to death. Very few natural cause deaths are completely cut and dried.

Rejecting death certificates with other causes would be akin to saying that someone who was involved in a serious car crash, and died later at the hospital of cardiac arrest, died solely of cardiac disease, and that the accident had nothing to do with the death. Most of us realize that this is ridiculous and that it would prevent us from getting good public health data on motor vehicle accidents that can be used to keep us all safer.

The need of a certain segment of the population to continue to deny the pandemic for political and economic reasons of their own drives me mad. In the end, you can believe what you want, but the virus will remain the virus, do what the virus does, and all your philosophical arguments will come to naught, for the virus doesn't care.

I'm not sure what to make of the reportage on vaccine development. The FDA and the CDC have been so heavily politicized in recent months that I don't completely trust the information coming out of them. The FDA seems ready to approve anything that will help more than it hurts whether there is sound science behind it or not. That strikes me as a recipe for either grand failure (after all, we could construe an injection of normal saline as helping more than it hurts) or utter disaster as something improperly tested is widely distributed and only later found to have a major negative effect.

Given my reading of political tea leaves, the FDA is likely to release or at least announce a vaccine in the last week of October, just as we head to the voting booths. Even if something is available, I have a feeling there will be major distribution issues, and I won't be the least bit surprised to start reading news stories of corruption and profiteering in the supply chain.

In the meantime, you know the drill. Wash your hands, wear your mask, stay out of crowds.

SATURDAY | SEPTEMBER 5, 2020

I T'S ANOTHER EXCITING SATURDAY EVENING CHEZ ANDY. I sat out on my terrace after dinner and watched the sun go down in a flurry of lavender and tangerine while sipping a warm-weather concoction I just invented with a tumbler full of ice, limeade, ginger ale, and a generous dollop of gin.

Not quite like watching the sun set over the Great Rift Valley in Eastern Africa, especially as the only nearby wildlife were my two obnoxious cats complaining that they hadn't yet had their evening kitty treats. The yowls of *felis domesticus* can't be interchanged with the roaring of the big cats of the Savannah in any way, shape, or form.

It's going to be a quiet long weekend. I don't feel like going anywhere and rubbing elbows with crowds; I am still taking COVID-19 seriously and don't want to be the one who brings it into the UAB and Birmingham VA clinical geriatrics programs. I do get out some, but I try to do it at non-peak times, and I'm still not really comfortable going into indoor spaces I don't have to be in when they are filled with people I don't know. I'm fine with small group and outdoor socializing, but nothing much has presented itself recently. I do have a dinner with Tommy's family coming up on Monday. It will be good to catch up with them.

I remain perplexed at the number of highly educated and supposedly rational people out there who seem determined to throw out centuries of careful study of epidemic disease, microbiology, and virology in favor of politically expedient puffery. The tried and true mechanisms for dealing with pandemics weren't invented out of whole cloth. They come from a series of brilliant minds. Giants standing on the shoulders of giants have brought us to the point where the deadliest of diseases can be corralled through time-honored principles. As recently as a decade ago, Ebola, a much more deadly disease than COVID, was contained with US CDC leadership and beaten back. Number of US fatalities? Two.

We are now approaching 200,000 US fatalities and, at current trends, that's expected to double before the end of the year. It may easily top 500,000 by inauguration day when there may finally be a change in the political class in this country to one that relies on evidence and rationality rather than emotion and expediency.

The journey of knowledge of microbiology is a long one, beginning in the 1640s with the invention of the microscope by Kircher, later perfected and popularized in the 1670s by Anton van Leeuwenhoek. Their discovery of a plethora of living things, previously invisible to the human eye, led to a revolution in the understanding of the mechanisms of disease. By 1700, physicians were beginning to postulate that some of these newly discovered micro-organisms were responsible for infections, but it wasn't proven until experiments done by Agostino Bassi around 1810. Once the Germ Theory of disease took hold, Holmes and Semmelweis demonstrated how unwashed hands caused puerperal fever on OB wards in 1843, and John Snow traced a cholera outbreak in London to the handle of the Broad Street pump in 1854.

By the late Victorian period, the need for hygiene in medicine and society was well recognized, and various social campaigns began to modernize sewer systems, provide for indoor plumbing, and create aseptic nursing and surgery in healthcare settings. The result? Life expectancy skyrocketed as more and more of us were able to avoid what were previously common infectious diseases. In 1900, life expectancy in the USA was 42 years. Today, it's 79 years (and we're low on the international totem pole; in most of Western Europe it's well over 80 years). The biggest contributor to this? Your ability to access a sink for hand washing pretty much anywhere you go—and, of course, a flush toilet.

The brains of the late 19th and early 20th centuries recognized the importance of public health measures, the importance of understanding the epidemiology of disease, and the importance of educating the populace in good health habits like regular bathing. They gifted us with our much longer life spans and, in the process, took away our general fear of epidemic disease. As we live now in a culture where there hasn't been much of a serious epidemic striking the general population in several generations, we've collectively forgotten the lessons of the past and haven't adequately funded the institutions needed to protect us en masse. Mother Nature doesn't care. Let down your guard, cease your vigilance, and she's always there with her rules which have nothing to do with political, economic, or sociological structures.

More of us are going to die.

As we drift towards some sort of mythic herd immunity, we'll do it at the expense of hundreds of thousands, if not millions, of individuals who didn't have to die at this time. We have no way of knowing what the long-term morbidity will be. A recent study showed that something over a third of college athletes who developed COVID-19 and recovered have residual myocarditis (inflammation of the heart muscle). If this continues, will it lead to a weakening of heart tissue and early onset congestive heart failure 20 or 30 years from now when they should be in the prime of life? Will it interfere with their cardiac conduction system, greatly raising their chance of sudden cardiac death in the future? No one knows. We'll be studying and learning from this virus and its effects for decades—likely the rest of my personal life span.

The one thing we can all do is follow the playbook that's been around for the last couple of hundred years for dealing with epidemic disease. Maintain good hygiene, isolate, and break transmission chains—in this case, wearing a mask to contain aerosol and droplet transmission. There's an old saying that when you save one life, you save the world entire. Doing the basics, like washing your hands, will do that many times over.

WEDNESDAY | SEPTEMBER 9, 2020

'M FEELING UNMOORED TONIGHT, adrift among the uncertainties of modern life. Hopefully, some egotistical rich person with no cares for the little people will not come roaring by and swamp my small craft in their wake. If the events of the weekend with the Lake Travis flotilla were not the perfect metaphor for our current socio-political "greed is good" vulture capitalism, I don't know what else is.

I should be careful about such idle wishes; these days, anything outlandish is usually topped within the week. It's one of the reasons why I am finding it so much more difficult to write political satire than I have in the past. How can I possibly top reality?

We're about to hit another milestone: 200,000 US deaths. The toll around here is lighter. About 2,500 deaths in Alabama, 17,000 cases in the county, and 125,000 cases in the state, but we're a mostly small town, rural state. Pretty much everyday I hear about a case affecting someone of my acquaintance. They are sick, a family member is sick, a good friend is deathly ill. I've lost a few friends, others are recovering. My experience is probably typical.

I was as naive as most of the rest of us back in February and early March, trusting that the structures of the federal government and world-renowned institutions like the CDC would swing into action. I assumed that we would get regular informed updates backed up by data synthesized by brilliant minds, and that government agencies at all levels would start working together to make sure the pandemic would be contained before it could become a serious problem.

As the spring advanced, and it became abundantly clear that our significantly dysfunctional government either would not or could not do anything of the kind, I retreated into a shell made up partly of disbelief, partly of morbid humor, and partly of focus on the real problems that had to be solved quickly to make the health systems, to which I owe responsibility, responsive to the needs of patients in an unusual time.

The news that's been breaking over the last day or so of the absolute proof of incompetence and malignancy at the highest levels of governance in response to the emerging pandemic—which has more or less been sat upon and kept under wraps for the purposes of journalistic profit through book contracts and media appearances—is making me by turns furiously angry and incredibly sad: angry at the fact that people with the means to get information out that could potentially sway public opinion and action chose their personal profit over public good; sad that the system we live under has become so corrupt that hundreds of thousands of people will end up giving their lives so that a very few can continue to pretend that the world isn't changing around them.

I've always been more of an incrementalist by nature when it comes to change. When I started reading philosophy and sociology in high school, I was most attracted to the Fabian socialists of the late 19th and early 20th century who believed in a slow, natural evolution to a more just society. I'm starting to think I've been wrong for most of the last few decades, and that maybe it's time to pull a whole lot of rotted structures down completely and begin again.

It's become a lot easier for me to see how the Jacobins and Trotskyites of the world were able to move forward as quickly and decisively as they did at their particular historical moments. I think we're racing toward a similar inflection point, and it's going to be here faster than any of us can believe.

Steve, who was very much a child of the 60s and described himself as a communist when he was asked what his political philosophy was, would have been very much in his element were he here today. I think Tommy was seeing where we were headed fairly clearly before his death and was planning on coping with it by ignoring it and throwing himself into his work.

This is what I am likely to be doing as well. There are patients to care for, systems of healthcare that remain imperfect to which I can contribute a few innovative ideas, people to mentor, theater groups to support through a very tough time, and friends to counsel.

I'm not able to fix the problems of the country, much less the world. I can only, as Voltaire wrote, cultivate my garden without regret for yesterday or hope for tomorrow. I don't like that sentiment. I'm a big believer in hope. The idea that things will get better is what motivates me to get up in the morning and throw myself back into the fray.

But now it's time for a nightcap, a hand wash, Netflix, and bed before entering once more into the breach, dear friends.

SUNDAY | SEPTEMBER 13, 2020

S UNDAY, SWEET SUNDAY, WITH TOO MUCH TO DO.

I don't think that's quite what Oscar Hammerstein II wrote, but it does make a certain amount of sense. I haven't quite figured out how my "To Do" list gets longer and longer when I'm spending most of my time away from work by myself, but that seems to be the way of the world these days.

It probably has something to do with the fact that there are many days when I don't feel like accomplishing much, so things of low priority get carried over week to week to be joined by an ever-growing list of somewhat higher priority items. As we've all gotten more facile with Zoom meetings and the like, things that were more or less in abeyance for some months are steadily creeping back into my life. Like 7 AM QA committee meetings.

We're just about to hit 200,000 deaths in the USA (that's 50,000 Benghazis or 67 9/11's for those keeping track), and there's not a lot of evidence that we're going to be turning a corner anytime soon. Locally, the college spike in Tuscaloosa seems to have been stemmed by the city having closed the local bars. The numbers here at UAB have remained relatively low due to a great deal of vigilance on behalf of the administration.

Out of curiosity, I looked up the current demographics for my patient population. The mortality rate for those in nursing homes is 25%. Long-term morbidity is unknown. The mortality rate for those of an age and illness burden which could place them in nursing homes, but who live in the community is somewhat lower. However, there is disagreement among authorities as to what it actually is. Those living in the community are far less susceptible than those in group living, probably due to the success of isolation measures leading to far less exposure.

My takeaway from all of this is that the simple tried-and-true measures for pandemic control are working when they are being allowed to work. The fact that a significant part of the population is being talked into ignoring these basic public health measures for political reasons means that our lives of discomfort are going to continue far longer than we want. A building is only as strong as its weakest stone.

One thing bringing me hope is the stirring of life in the local performing arts community. There have been some safely produced out of doors entertainments, some work towards small-scale indoor socially distanced pieces, and a lot of work at figuring out how to adapt Zoom and other video conferencing platforms to the requirements of theatrical and musical performance. Large-scale musical endeavors don't work due to the lags in sound inherent in the software, but that doesn't mean there aren't other things that can be done and, as brighter minds than mine enter the fray, I think there will be more and more technical improvements with time. I'm currently working on *The Importance of Being Earnest* with a group based mainly in South Carolina, and that's something positive the pandemic has wrought. When working online, you can pull your cast and your audience from anywhere. And I think I've figured out how to pass hand props across state lines without violating the Mann Act.

The hardest part of getting live performances back on track is not going to be able to figure out how to keep cast, crew, and musicians safe, it's going to be how to keep the audience safe from each other, and how to make them feel comfortable attending live events in enclosed space. Our theaters, concert halls, recital rooms, and all the rest, are not designed for social distancing—actually the opposite. This is the Gordian knot of a problem that must be solved before live entertainment returns in full. Do we retrofit existing venues? How? Do we build new ones that will allow for appropriate social distancing? Do we take a page from the Santa Fe Opera and make performance spaces indoor/outdoor?

I think we're going to see a democratization of theater in this country over the next decade. Theatrical success will not be limited to a few dozen early 20th century theaters within walking distance of Times Square. As bright minds solve more and more technical problems, allowing anyone to access theater performance from anywhere, and allowing a theater company anywhere in the country access to a potential international audience, things are going to change. Research has shown that release of a filmed or taped theatrical performance does not diminish audience demand for the live product, it increases it. As more people have a chance to see what it is, more and more people want the chance to experience it live. Innovative companies, authors, and performers who use this pandemic-enforced hiatus to create content suitable to the needs and interests of today, cultivate audiences, and move towards something new and different, are likely to be well-positioned with a huge demand when things open up again. And successful theatre will be able to be accessed by those whose household budgets do not allow for the average $150/seat price tag on Broadway.

As usual, everything comes down to Sondheim. You keep moving on. Too bad he didn't write a handwashing lyric.

WEDNESDAY | SEPTEMBER 16, 2020

I T'S HURRICANE SEASON AGAIN.

Sally (not to be confused with my sister-in-law) has been busy battering the Alabama coast line and is slowly making its way northeast into Georgia and points beyond.

Here in Birmingham, about 200 miles from the coast, we only got a few of the outer bands which brought lovely cool temperatures, some wind, and a smattering of rain. Nothing to cause any difficulties for us.

Friends on the gulf coast have been checking in and everyone seems OK, but there's been a lot of flooding and wind damage in the beach towns. There are four more storms lined up out in the Atlantic, so we may get something worse in the days to come. Fires in the west, flooding in the south, pestilence everywhere. Just another week in the life of 2020.

Jefferson County, the most populous county in Alabama and home to Birmingham, has generally posted somewhere between 70-130 new cases of COVID-19 daily over the last month or so. Yesterday, they posted over 1,000 new cases.

The number is so out of line with where things have been that I assume it's an anomaly due to a data dump or an adjustment in the statistics. Either that or we're seeing the result of people getting a little too friendly with each other at their Labor Day picnics and barbeques a few weeks ago. Time will tell. The numbers at UAB hospital have remained relatively steady. Far more than we would like, but low enough for the system to handle without buckling.

The medical residents are back on their usual rotations and I have had a flock of new interns rotating through my UAB Geriatrics Clinic over the course of the last month or so. Residency is hard enough. I can't begin to imagine what it must be like with the added stresses of duty on COVID-19 wards and the shut down of the many ways young people like and need to blow off steam after grueling weeks.

Our rotation is pretty easy for them compared to others they endure. We give them a chance to explore some of the more interesting things geriatrics has to offer in the hope that it might rub off a little and one of them might be willing to make it a career choice. We occasionally succeed, but we need a lot more of them to look our way.

I continue to tire of video evidence of "anti-maskers" or "mask deniers" or whatever they're calling themselves these days. It's a piece of cloth on your face, you wear coverings on most of the rest of your body without incident. It's not chain mail or barbed wire, but the amount of carrying on from people for political reasons strikes me as being completely out of proportion with what is being asked. Perhaps if people would stop posting video of ordinary folks behaving badly in Target or Wal-Mart, there would be less self-aggrandizement and less monkey-see, monkey-do.

I was reading Andy Slavitt's notes the other day. He was the head of the Center for Medicare and Medicaid Services under Obama, and he's a fierce defender of science in public health. Not surprisingly, he's become a significant critic of the Trump administration's response to COVID-19 and does a routine deep dive into the science which he puts out on Twitter and on his podcast. He did some modeling based on what is known about the $R0$ ("R-naught", a measure of the infectiousness of the virus in a naive population) and the Re ("a measure of the infectiousness of the virus in a population taking steps to control the pandemic) and came up with a rather startling figure.

Every 1% of the US population that refuses to mask will result in an extra 10,000 deaths from COVID-19 over the next year. So, if 30% are anti-maskers, there will be an additional 300,000 deaths in this country that doing something as simple as universal masking would prevent.

Masking is not just a personal choice as it has effects on people far beyond you. Your decision not to mask, based on whatever idea is politically advantageous to you, raises the chance that you will pass the disease along if you are an asymptomatic carrier to others who will then pass it on to still others. Masking has implications for the family, especially if you have elders or others with chronic illness in the household. It has implications for us as a nation in regard to the amount of disease burden we will bear.

Refusing to mask is a rejection of scientific fact. If we condition ourselves to reject facts in this area, what other facts will we end up rejecting and what impact will that have on our social institutions?

When I see someone unmasked in public, my takeaway is that this is a person who is unwilling to accept a minor inconvenience for a healthier and stronger community. I can almost see the thought balloons reading "It's All About Me!" hovering over their heads.

I highly recommend following Mr. Slavitt and reading his notes. They are literate, easily understood by the lay public, and point out the real issues. He is also incredibly experienced in how public health and governance work together.

A couple of days ago, I brought up the old saying that the one who saves one life, saves the world entire. Encouraging an additional 1% to mask up saves 10,000 lives. Morally and metaphorically, that has to be more than the world, perhaps the galaxy, or at least our quadrant.

I don't understand the lack of empathy our culture seems to have bred into a considerable percentage that leads people not to want to do something so simple to help others. It doesn't compute. Or maybe it computes all too well with human nature, or as George Orwell put it: "All animals are equal, but some are more equal than others."

The ultimate message of almost every religious tradition is one of caring for the stranger as you would care for your own, so I don't see how people who profess to follow any sort of spiritual life would have any qualms about not only masking up, but assisting their neighbor in doing the same.

Perhaps it shows how poisoned some religious traditions have become in a lust for secular power. But until we all take this seriously, I and my co-religionists in our church choir will continue to meet via Zoom and discuss how we can have a safe community sing/rehearsal in the church parking lot where we can be masked, socially distanced, and out of doors.

SATURDAY | SEPTEMBER 19, 2020

THE NOTORIOUS RBG IS GONE.

It's not often that older women become pop culture icons, but once in a while, one breaks through and is embraced by all ages as a symbol of the strength and wisdom of the elder. Or maybe it's a testament to the very human need to believe in endurance, no matter what life throws at each of us, and those few who work and live their best lives into their 80s and beyond come to embody that hope for continued relevance as time marches forward. It's been marching across my face recently. I looked in the mirror this morning when I got up and was not happy with the cross of Christopher Walken's Headless Horseman and Christopher Lloyd's Doc Brown looking back at me.

One of the curses of being a well-trained geriatrician is hearing news about the health of aging public figures and being able to draw far more conclusions about life span than most. I've got a good deal more data to work with than the average American. I wasn't in the least surprised by RBG's death. I had hoped she would hang on a while longer but frankly, I was surprised she made it as long as she did given what I was able to glean from news reports about her overall health.

As much as I admired her and her jurisprudence over many years, I was never able to cast her in my mind as this tiny, but towering figure holding dark forces at bay, and I doubt she ever conceived of herself that way either. She just showed up, did her job, and did it well. She combined a keen mind and a sharp wit with deep knowledge and an unshakeable commitment to make the law serve as many people as possible—rather than serve the few and bludgeon the many—and she was well aware that some of her opinions were going to be in the minority. She never fussed, she never went to the media trying to rally the court of public opinion. She simply dissented with vigor and well-honed argument, knowing full well that her dissents and their legal reasoning might help form the basis of a win sometime in the future.

The biggest problem with the American political system at the moment is the American preoccupation with instant gratification. We want results and we want them now. The system wasn't built that way, yet we are constantly forcing it to fit that mold via an unrelenting two-party slugfest with one side constantly trying to score a TKO and proclaim victory. Many things have gone into this devolution. The rise of the 24-hour news cycle, consolidation of media outlets, politicians playing to the camera rather than to the public, the expense of campaigning requiring constant fundraising, etc., etc.

RBG knew this all too well and avoided it. Her best friend on and off the court for years was Justice Scalia. Despite their diametrically opposed judicial philosophies, they bonded over their love of the arts, especially opera. The two of them may have lived in different ideological worlds, but they inhabited the same cultural sphere as Americans, and it strikes me that we need to start doing more of that as a people—get out of our confirmation bias echo chambers and spend more time together in common space. Of course, that's been made a tad more difficult due to our good friend COVID-19.

And here's where I cleverly segue to an event scheduled for November 10th. On that day, the Trump administration will argue California v. Texas in front of the Supreme Court. For those of you who have forgotten, this is a case brought by a number of conservative states claiming that the Affordable Care Act is fundamentally flawed from a constitutional point of view, and that the entire law must be declared unconstitutional and therefore, null and void. It is highly unlikely that RBG's seat will be filled in seven weeks no matter what happens, so only eight justices will hear the arguments with a decision likely rendered in the late spring before the court retires for the summer.

What happens if the ACA is found unconstitutional? The most important thing in regards to COVID-19 is the provision about pre-existing conditions. Since the ACA was passed in 2010, it has been illegal for health insurers to discriminate against you based on your past health history. If this goes away again, then pretty much anyone who was infected with COVID-19 will become uninsurable.

No insurance underwriter in their right mind is going to allow someone to purchase their product who has been infected by a disease that causes significant changes to nearly every organ system, and for which the possible long-term sequelae are essentially unknown. That's roughly 7 million people so far and growing rapidly. Given that the attempts to limit its spread on any sort of a national level are sorely lacking, we may get to the mythical herd immunity at some point, but only after the numbers of those infected are in the tens of millions.

How do we change things for the better? We do this by using the system the way it was designed to work. It's a slow, sometimes tedious process which requires a lot of labor, patience, and a willingness to accept defeat, learn from it, and move on. We have to let go of the idea that a single election or a single figure is going to either save or condemn us. We have to be willing to understand and play the long game.

As Tip O'Neill famously said, "All politics is local." If you want to see change, join the local chapter of your preferred political party. Volunteer to be a precinct chair. Be willing to do a lot of thankless work in terms of door knocking, get-out-the-vote campaigns, and learning to compromise while crafting platform positions. When you lose an election, take a day off to mourn, then start working on the next one. That's how the game is played.

The national parties bubble up from the grassroots. The work that has come to fruition in conservative circles over the last decade is the result of this kind of effort starting in the early 1970s. It took them nearly 50 years to get where they wanted to be. If you want something different in the future, go to work now. Of course, you can always tear the entire system down in some sort of revolutionary action, but movements like that are often either hijacked or take on a life of their own, and you end up somewhere very different from where you intended, so I can't recommend that course of action. Just mask up and wash your hands before heading off to political meetings.

TUESDAY | SEPTEMBER 22, 2020

I'T'S ONE OF THOSE EVENINGS when I'm in a French existentialist mood.

Everything's terrible and nothing I can do or say can make it any better. Time to break out a beret, a black T-shirt, an unfiltered Gauloise, and yammer on about the futility of modern living.

Thankfully, this sort of thing generally doesn't last with me. I have a deep-seated optimism by nature that no matter how bad things seem to get, human beings eventually get their act together and start responding to their better selves. The question just becomes how low we can go before that kicks in, and whether it will kick in quickly enough to save us from our worst impulses. I don't know the answer to these things.

I may have to take a sabbatical from my usual diet of political news for sanity's sake. I don't watch any of it on television. I'm not that much of a masochist. But I do read extensively on politics, especially as it intersects with health policy, so that I have some clue as to how to begin positioning the little corners of health care for which I have some responsibility to weather the storms of administrative and financial craziness that have become all too frequent recently.

I'm not sure what's put me in such a dreary mood. Nothing too horrible has happened at work. In fact, most things are ticking along. There have been some hiccups with expanding the VA house call program into the Huntsville area, but nothing that can't be overcome with some training and attention to staff. UAB is functioning relatively normally in the outpatient arena. Perhaps it's a side effect of my annual flu shot which I received earlier today. They generally don't bother me, but one never really knows how the central nervous system is affected by the state of one's physical health. You are living inside of it and are usually the last one to notice anything different.

One of the problems with being alone after so many years of coupledom is that there's no one who can look at me at home, tell me when I'm a bit off, and that my personal barometer may not be the most accurate. I'm hoping a cocktail, some leftover chicken massaman, and some reading of Sondheim studies before a decent night's sleep will take care of the issue.

We officially passed 200,000 COVID-19 deaths in the USA today. That could easily double again in the next few months. If only those who led our country would approach matters of public health with the speed and gusto they are approaching the prospect of filling a vacant Supreme Court seat. SCOTUS will still be there after the first of the year. Another 200,000 Americans may not be.

It's become painfully clear that the powers that be consider all those not of their class expendable. Couple this with economic imbalance of the type that led to the French Revolution, and I fear sometimes we may be dancing on the edge of the abyss. And then I decide, no, its not that bad, and start trying to figure out when I can next go to Seattle to see my family.

I think the thing I'm the most scared of at the moment is the opacity of information regarding COVID-19. The combination of lack of interest from the federal government with the strict control of information that flows from federal sources such as the CDC and the FDA (which is the prerogative of the executive branch as they are all executive agencies) makes it difficult to know where to turn for well-sourced science regarding spread, responses, impact of morbidity over time, and the like.

When the CDC recommendations flop back and forth in a rather ham-fisted way, one can only surmise that non-scientists are calling the shots for political expediency. If the political system tries to hide the true extent of the virus and what it's doing to the population, we're going to have a world of hurt.

I am not a conspiracy theorist. Anyone who has ever been a project manager knows that you can't keep a dozen people on task and not talking about what they're working on. You can't have nefarious complicated cabals of tens of thousands without somebody somewhere accidentally spilling the beans. For this reason alone, truth will always eventually out, and if the public ever decides that their loved ones died because the government decided they were expendable or acceptable collateral damage, there's going to be hell to pay.

Usually, by the time I finish one of these entries and I've been in a funky mood, I've straightened my head out a bit. Not so much this evening. Anastasia kitty has decided to snuggle, so I'll finish this up and go back to my reading for a bit followed by my *Schitt's Creek* binge-watch marathon.

You know the litany: Stay in when you can; wear your mask; wash your hands. It's that simple.

SATURDAY | SEPTEMBER 26, 2020

T ODAY, I WAS EITHER A SLUG OR A SLOTH or some sort of hybrid. It took me something over three hours after waking up to actually get out of bed. I've had two additional cat naps so far, and I may be heading for a third. I think my lizard brain has permanently switched from hyper-vigilance in the face of danger to a state of chronic play-dead-and-conserve-energy for further perils to come.

I sometimes really do feel like I'm slowly being ground to fine powder between the Scylla of COVID-19 and the Charybdis of Social

Isolation. I have to remind myself that no matter how horrible things seem to be, I have a roof over my head, food in the pantry, a job that continues to pay me, and a large supportive circle of friends who remain part of my life, even if we can't be together in the usual ways.

I started these meditations two-and-a-half years ago to help myself puzzle out thoughts and feelings and reinvent myself for a new phase of life. I assumed they wouldn't be of much interest to anyone, but I quickly got a response and a loyal readership, especially to my anecdotes about some of the odd things that have happened throughout the course of my life.

I started to write those as it was dawning on me that I had aged into being an elder in the traditional sense. The elders are those with the life experience to understand the human condition and to translate it into forms palatable for consumption, originally around the campfire, and then later on in poetry, prose, and song that could transfer collective wisdom from generation to generation. They are the storytellers. My stories, without Tommy in my life, no longer had a home and were going to die with me if I didn't start telling them in some form. This seemed as good a way as any to send them out into the world.

I assumed that these posts would revolve around the areas of my life in which new stories might arise: theatrical endeavors, travel, encounters with new and interesting people. But six months ago, all that changed as the whole world shifted, and I started to write more and more about COVID-19 and its effects on the healthcare system, my personal life, and the world at large. And thus, *The Accidental Plague Diaries* were born. It just happened. I didn't set out to do it.

When I first started these COVID-19 essays, I assumed that the institutions that have saved us from serious trouble with infectious disease in the past would swing into action, and that the whole thing would likely be over in six months or so, at least in terms of writing.

Now, I can clearly see my own naïveté. There is no end in sight at this point, and my words on the subject are now at book length.

Everywhere I go, when I see people whom I haven't seen for a while, they bring up my writing—how it has helped them make sense of a nonsensical world, and how they are grateful for the combination of trying to stick to fact and trying to navigate a centrist position through the hysterical hyperbole that informs reporting on the subject on both sides of the political spectrum.

I'm immensely gratified that people like these entries, but I hope they realize that I am as lost and confused in modern life as they are, and that sitting down a couple of times a week to let my fingers dance over the keyboard is more about educating myself than others. If I can find the words for difficult concepts that others can understand, then I know I've gotten things straight in my mind. And if I can get it together in my head, then I can pull it together to make it through the next day, the next week, the next month.

We're now at seven million cases of COVID-19 in the US. We were at six million only three-and-a-half weeks ago, so we are in no way getting the pandemic under control. It's now the third highest cause of death in the country (superseded only by cancer and heart disease). The long-term effects on those who recover remain unknown. There are tantalizing glimpses of why it is so serious in some people and essentially asymptomatic in others. If those could be figured out, we might be able to figure out protections for the more susceptible and let the less susceptible get on with life, but we're a long way from clear understanding. Life is beginning to return to pre-COVID-19 norms in other parts of the world (reporting in US media is spotty as it becomes more concerned with election politics), but rebounding countries are those with robust public health programs, not undermined by politics, and committed to the judicious application of their authority to implement tried-and-true public health measures.

There's a piece of me that wonders if part of the predicament we find ourselves in comes from the Baby Boom generation's refusal to accept elderhood. I've written before about how Boomers refuse to consider themselves as old, even though the leading edge is now in their 70s.

I use what I call the "Cher Scale" at work. Cher was born in 1946, the first year of the Boom. I have my med students rate patient age based on Cher: Cher plus 3 years equals a 78-year old; Cher minus 2 years equals a 73-year old. This helps them understand just what a demographic watershed that year has proved to be.

Part of the reason that the Boom has always felt young is that the generation above them, the Silent Generation, has smashed all actuarial tables in terms of living long healthy lives. Many of this cohort, now in their 80s and early 90s, remain with us and in quite good shape. The Boom, having always had stable elders to look up to, thinks of themselves as young in part because of that generation who have always been old to them. (Old is always 15 years older than you are.)

There are many theories as to why the Silent Generation have lived such a long, healthy life. The one I like is known as the semi-starved rat hypothesis. This is a phenomenon first noted in rats, but replicated over time in many other species including primates.

If you take the young of a species and calorie-restrict them, it extends their life span. The Silent Generation was young during the Depression-to-World War II years. They didn't starve, but weren't able to glut either. The long-lived Silent Generation have helped keep the Boom from embracing their own aging and mortality and, as the Boom have been the political and economic power generation of the last 30 years, they haven't developed a generational empathy for aging.

What does this have to do with COVID-19? If the Boom can't be old, then they can't be in danger from things that happen to old people, and therefore those things need not be worried about, and policies that might help older people aren't as important. This is being played out in very real threats to the ACA and Medicare which a shift in the makeup of the Supreme Court is not likely to help.

WEDNESDAY | SEPTEMBER 30, 2020

T'S ANOTHER EVENING OF FEELING A BIT LIKE NEVILLE, my favorite Gashlycrumb Tiny with whom I have always identified.

I should be celebrating as the sale of the old house closed yesterday, but there's not a lot of joy in life and society, and I really don't have anyone to rejoice with once I leave work these days.

I did get to meet the new owners at the closing yesterday morning. I knew who they were through some mutual friends, but had not yet had the pleasure of meeting them.

They seem sympatico with the ideas that Tommy and I had for the house had life turned out differently and we had stayed there for a few decades as originally planned. Their plan for the much-needed kitchen remodel was pretty much exactly what we intended, so I feel the house is in good hands. I wish them much joy in the years to come.

There's not much exciting going on in my new abode other than a few lessons learned in regards to the production of Zoom theater. The Festive Green plastic tablecloths from Party City ($1.49 apiece or a roll of 100 feet for $10) make an acceptable green screen for inserting virtual backgrounds, but if you cut them too long and they hang too low, your cats will love batting at them and trying to pull them down at inopportune moments.

These projects are taking up a little time and creative energy, but I still have more hours to fill, so I bought myself the unlimited access

Rosetta Stone language plan and am going back through all the basic languages I've studied over the years for some additional ear training and grammar. I've started with French, which I learned as a child and is still fairly intact when I need it, but I have to use it routinely to have it come with any fluency.

I haven't come up with a new or interesting angle on COVID-19 to write about this evening. How can I keep this subject fresh and impart new insights without getting tiresomely repetitive?

I think I generally do a good job but there are times, like this evening, when the pandemic has dropped to a dull roar out there in the world, and I can't think of much of anything to say about it without going down a path I've trod before. New things are published routinely and there are constantly shifting battles and skirmishes between the population and the microbe, so tonight's stalemate is unlikely to last.

The thing I'm thinking about is this: What's going to happen later this fall in response to the outbreaks traceable to college and university reopenings? For the most part, the students won't be overly affected, but what's going to happen to the populations of college towns and institutions in close proximity to colleges such as hospitals and elder care centers?

We now know the well-recognized pattern: population behavior changes; case numbers reflect that change three or four weeks later; mortality statistics reflect that change another month or so after that. We're about a month into fall quarter. Cases are rising in places like Utah driven by university exposures. What happens a month from now? What happens when the flu starts circulating?

I'm keeping fingers crossed on flu season. A good percentage of the population are being careful about viral exposure. This will interrupt seasonal flu transmission as well as COVID-19. Washing your hands will help as well.

OCTOBER 2020

I'm Calm

FRIDAY | OCTOBER 2, 2020

'M TRYING TO PROCESS THE EVENTS of the last 24 hours or so.

In my ongoing saga of chronicling my peculiar take on the effect of COVID-19 on my life and American society, we may have reached a turning point.

I can't say I'm the least bit surprised that the President has caught the virus. His public behaviors over the last six months more or less made that inevitable, but I am surprised at the rapidity of change and the escalation from "He's fine," to "He has significant symptoms," to "He's being airlifted to Walter Reed." None of us has reliable data on his health, and speculation, while intriguing, is not especially useful.

I've compared the White House's response to the novel coronavirus to Poe's *The Masque of the Red Death* a number of times. I have a feeling that midnight has struck and that Prince Prospero and his guests are going to pay the price of believing that wealth and privilege somehow insulate one from science and fact. You can believe in virology and epidemiology or you can pooh-pooh them for political reasons, but that doesn't make the science any less true. Viruses have no political allegiance.

There are those who are descending down the black holes of various conspiracy theories regarding COVID-19 now that it has reached the highest offices in the land. It's a little silly.

The current group of politicians in power hasn't been able to run the government with all of the tools at their disposal. The thought of them running some sort of shadowy network of interconnected outrageous plots out of Ian Fleming or Robert Ludlam defies belief.

Anyone who has ever been assigned a group project can tell you that human beings in groups just aren't capable of such Byzantine and opaque maneuverings without the whole thing crashing down because someone wanted to binge-watch the latest season of *Schitt's Creek* rather than do their portion of the assignment.

The Ancient Greeks would have loved the current situation. President Trump very much fits their mold of the leader who rises too high, too fast, in mockery of the gods, and is undone by his own nature and character flaws. All that's missing is the public catharsis.

The rapid fire revelations about the President's tax and financial status, the economic collapse of his campaign, and now the illness, are likely linked to the stubborn refusal of him and his followers to obey even the simplest precepts of public health measures to prevent viral transmission. We don't know how the next act of this drama is going to play out. I know what I would write if I were creating a drama of hubris, but it's not up to me.

I've tried to leave politics out of these diaries for the most part. When it comes to COVID-19, politics is immaterial as the virus is completely apolitical, and I feel very strongly that what I've been able to learn about the disease and how it affects our lives is a subject that should be of interest to the entire spectrum of opinions.

Politics sneaks in occasionally because the US response to the virus has been allowed to become politicized at nearly every step of the process. We are the weaker for it, hundreds of thousands are dead and, within a month or so, the pandemic will move from the fourth worst mass casualty event in American history to the third, surpassing World War II. (If it kills more than 600,000, it will surpass the Civil War, leaving it only behind the Flu Pandemic of 1918.)

Would the impact of COVID-19 have been lessened with a less political response? It's tough to say, but we probably wouldn't be having a mask war in society, adherence to things like social distancing would be much greater, and our casualty rates would likely be more in line with those in Western Europe.

I hope I live long enough to be able to read the definitive history of the Trump presidency that a Barbara Tuchman of the future will write sometime after 2030, when enough time will have passed for us all to be able to get some perspective on what we are living through. I also have the feeling that this particular moment in history is going to inspire some great artistic works. Trump, himself, is too big a character for traditional film or stage. He is an operatic figure, and I think only a grand opera in the Verdi tradition can totally explore his psychology and motivations. The Black Death gave us the Italian Renaissance. What is COVID-19 going to give us? I, too, will be checking my news feeds in the morning for the next chapter.

In the meantime, you all know the drill: Wash your hands; wear your masks; keep six feet apart.

TUESDAY | OCTOBER 6, 2020

LIKE EVERYONE ELSE I KNOW with formal medical training, I've been watching the events unfolding in Washington, D.C. over the last few days with increasing puzzlement.

Absolutely nothing that's happening makes any sense from either a personal or a public health perspective. There are those who claim that the president's recent diagnosis with COVID-19 was some sort of elaborate ruse, but that seems exceedingly unlikely considering the thick and fast news of multiple collateral diagnoses within the executive orbit.

Then there was the very real evidence from yesterday. I have more than 30 years experience at sizing up aging adults and determining whether they are sick or not in the first few seconds of walking into the room and beginning to converse with them. It's dozens of little cues from behavior to body posture to the look in their eyes that allow you to either tense up and prepare to send them immediately to the emergency department or relax and let them tell their story while you leisurely ponder differential diagnoses in your head. The man I saw walk up the stairs to the South Portico of the White House yesterday evening was sick.

His walking into the White House, a crowded workplace, with full blown COVID-19, while blithely removing his mask, told me everything I needed to know about the situation. I don't think there's any sort of sinister cabal going on. I think we're in full blown the-inmates-are-running-the-asylum mode, as anyone with either the knowledge or ability to deal appropriately with highly communicable infectious disease has either been purged or silenced.

The virus will therefore continue to keep leaping around the executive branch, and I expect the vast majority of those with easy access to the White House will likely be positive by the end of the week. Will any of them die? That remains to be seen. Likely not many, but some may become incredibly ill and others may end up with permanent health complications.

There's been a lot of posting about karma and *schadenfreude* recently. As much as I detest the politics and policies coming out of this administration, it is made up of human beings, and one thing that my religious tradition of Unitarian Universalism teaches me is that every human life has dignity and worth, so I cannot wish ill on any of them. I can only say that when you go swimming in a lagoon posted "Danger: No swimming. Alligators!" don't be surprised if you come back to shore missing a limb. Actions have consequences. People who take certain actions better be prepared to live with them.

Will the president recover uneventfully? Will he get worse? Will he be well enough for his next scheduled debate appearance? I can't answer these questions. All I can say is that by all objective evidence available to me, he's sick, possibly seriously ill. The puffery coming out of his medical team makes no sense from either a diagnostic or a treatment perspective, so there's really no way for me to have any sort of informed opinion.

Things will happen as they will. Hang on! The wild rollercoaster of the last few days isn't likely to slow down for a while. In the meantime, there will be more and more blather of the uninformed, opining on the unintended consequences of the actions of the uncaring. It's all making me a bit tired, so I am going to bed early.

At this juncture in history, I'm glad I live in a smaller city with a relatively informed population and a high percentage of good folk employed in health services. In Birmingham proper, most people are pretty good at social distancing, wearing their masks, and not doing anything too crazy. This has kept our caseload relatively constant and kept local hospitals from getting overloaded.

Watching those to whom much has been given in terms of money and power blithely wander through life as if those were any sort of protections against the way the world actually works makes me a bit sick. As I have said, actions have consequences. I just hope that my positive actions in favor of protecting people I don't know lead ultimately to positive consequences in my life. I'm a past master at delayed gratification. I can wait a while longer to find out. Better wash my hands while I'm waiting.

SATURDAY | OCTOBER 10, 2020

HURRICANE DELTA IS BUSY CHURNING somewhere to the west of us as it takes its leisurely course inland. It's expected to stay well west and north of the Birmingham area, so we shouldn't have any major issues around here. The outer bands have been passing over all day causing intermittent rain showers with rainbows in between, but we haven't had much in the way of wind.

It's a good weekend to stay sequestered in the condo and work on various projects coming due: a couple of distanced theatrical things, a taped story for UAB's Arts in Medicine program, several legal cases that need reviewing, and the slow methodical clean-out of various bins and files as I keep working on life simplification.

Of course, a weekend alone and cooped up does nothing for my existential angst about the rising tide of insanity in the world outside. I speculated some on the president's medical condition with my last entry. Nothing I have seen these last few days has suggested to me that his health has improved markedly. There was some sort of rally at the White House today. I did not tune in, but someone in the campaign decided to give all the attendees periwinkle blue T-shirts to go with their red MAGA hats. With that color scheme, the few pictures I saw made the south lawn of the White House look like it had been suddenly taken over by a group of fractious garden gnomes.

One wonders who is in charge of such things and whether they think before they order, or if they're just trying to enrich a certain vendor. The president's appearance and remarks were about 15 minutes in length. He usually spends several hours extemporizing at his rallies, so I assume his stamina is way below what it normally is. As the adulation he receives at such affairs appears to be his oxygen,

I doubt he's out of the woods yet, and I don't see him being able to stand up to the rigors of campaigning during the home stretch if he remains in this condition or if his condition worsens.

There's an interesting set of moral questions regarding his treatment with the monoclonal antibodies manufactured by Regeneron, a company in which he appears to hold financial interest if various media outlets can be believed. First, the treatment is not FDA-approved, so there is no good science that it works.

Second, the antibodies are developed from lines of fetal stem cells. The pro-life movement would say they come from aborted babies, and has successfully campaigned Republican administrations, including the current one, to halt any science using such tissues. But actually, they are usually obtained from embryos made during an *in vitro* fertilization process, and which would be discarded as no longer needed after a successful pregnancy.

Third, the cost for such a drug would likely run to six figures and, as it is not approved, would not be covered by even the most generous insurance plans. The claims that anyone can and will get the drug for COVID-19 are, excuse my French, horse shit.

So what happens next with monoclonal antibodies? Does the FDA fast-track them for approval, possibly undercutting long established safeguards for a political win? Does a Republican administration embrace a drug that owes its existence to a line of scientific research that is anathema to its evangelical base? Do they open up additional public coffers to pay for the treatment when much of that money will go into private hands tied to the president? I can't answer these questions. All I can do is stay home alone with my cats and my projects as I am not stupid enough to attend mass gatherings at the White House which seem to turn themselves into super-spreader events.

COVID-19 is going to have some very peculiar effects on this election cycle. It remains to be seen who will choose to vote early, who will choose to vote in person, or who will be forced into voting through a means not of their choice due to various voter suppression tactics such as limiting all counties to a single drop-off box, be they population of 1500 or 1.5 million.

Anyone who says they know what the outcome of November 3rd is going to be is deluding themselves. The dozen weeks between the election and the inauguration will also be anybody's guess. There are so many unknowns regarding the behavior of the population under these stresses, and so many knowns such as unstable personalities and large quantities of money wanting certain outcomes, that it's likely to be a very wild ride. One thing I'm fairly certain of is that the president has lost the loyalty of the Secret Service to his person rather than his office. I think the ride in the hermetically sealed limo which endangered them did that. Various Caesars found out that alienating the Praetorian Guard during times of political instability was an unwise choice.

There is an old curse that goes "May you live in interesting times." I've had enough of interesting, thank you. I'd rather have some boring times instead. At least boring enough for me to plan an interesting trip and an interesting show or two. In the meantime: work, home, work, home. Lather, rinse, repeat.

May you all stay well and remember: Wash your hands; wear your mask; stay out of crowds.

WEDNESDAY | OCTOBER 14, 2020

FINISHED SHOOTING MY BITS for the Fine Arts Center of Kershaw County's online Zoom theater production of Oscar Wilde's *The Importance of Being Earnest* this evening.

We may be all in some form of quarantine/separation these days, and gathering together in a playhouse is going to be one of the last things to come back from coronavirus restrictions, but theater people are going to theater one way or another. Online theater does allow you to pull together a cast from all over with minimal technical requirements: a laptop with a camera, a Zoom hookup, a green screen for a virtual background, and there you are.

I am considering driving back and forth to Seattle for my November vacation. One of the reasons I'm thinking about driving, other than giving myself some very long stretches to let my brain decompress and think about plenty of nothing while making my way across Kansas or Wyoming, is to get a sense of how the country is truly reacting to COVID-19.

Most of the reporting on community issues is tainted by a certain amount of political agenda. Given a crisis where we should all be pulling together, politicians and the media do their darndest to push us into one of two camps—the red or the blue for want of a better shorthand—one group for political advantage, the other for ratings and the money those ratings translate into over time.

I wonder what would have happened if, after Pearl Harbor and FDR's call for entry into World War II, half of the population had enlisted and gone to work manufacturing armaments while the other half had paraded in the streets waving Nazi and Rising Sun flags, and calling those that were preparing for war all sorts of unpleasant epithets, and the press had covered it all with both-sidesism and egged on domestic disturbance? The ultimate outcome of the conflict might have been just a bit different.

Now that we have managed to create two very different approaches and attitudes toward a single universal problem, what do we do? The red side's denial of the seriousness of things angers me personally as I watch more and more of my patient population fall ill and hear of more and more young healthy people who have succumbed. To me, these are lives wasted, not acceptable collateral damage.

Rates per unit population are surging in less populated conservative states but, as their populations are low, absolute numbers are low, so there is a feeling in these communities that COVID-19 isn't a problem other than for certain at-risk classes of individuals. The trouble is that somewhere between 25% and 40% of the population falls into those at-risk classes, and it is not possible to isolate those individuals.

Take the elderly, for example. Only about 10% of older Americans live in some sort of congregate facility. The vast majority are in the community trying to live their lives day to day just as the rest of us are. Even those in congregate living cannot be completely isolated. Staff, caregivers, delivery people, and all the rest who keep a housing facility running cannot be isolated with them. They are going to come and go in the community, and many of them will return home to school-age children who seem to be among the primary vectors.

Urban blue populations have adapted relatively well to new ways of living. Most city dwellers mask up, gauge six or so feet appropriately, don't crowd into small spaces, and have figured out how to protect themselves and their families through a thousand-and-one little changes and risk stratifications. They look down with scorn on red populations and their unwillingness to adapt. The trouble is that scorn and shame aren't going to make anyone do things any differently. People respond negatively to it, and a huge piece of our current divide comes from nearly 50 years of urban populations in service and tech economies looking down on rural populations in resource utilization economies.

Something I learned very early on when I was involved with the mine workers' programs in Appalachia that I medical-directed for many years was that if I, a doctor at a medical school in an urban center, were to call a doctor in a rural community to suggest a different treatment plan for a patient, I would be frozen out and unheeded. No one likes an outsider butting in, telling them how to do their job. The strategy we hit on was to make sure we hired nurses of and from these small rural Appalachian communities. I would teach them modern approaches to geriatric medicine and how to think through problems. These nurses could then go to the local doctors, their friends and neighbors for decades, and present things that would be listened to as they were of that world.

We need something similar at the moment to bring red and blue Americans together in better public health planning. I don't think it can happen under the current administration which has basically withdrawn the federal public health system including the CDC and the FDA from the battlefield but, if there is a change in administration, there can be strategies adopted that then flow to the states and then to the counties.

If untrusting populations see trustworthy information coming from local sources, they may begin to change their behaviors and we may start to make some inroads on bringing things under better control. If we don't, I feel we're going to be in for a very long time of it with deaths approaching, if not over, seven figures.

In the meantime, do what you can do: Wash your hands; wear your mask; stay out of crowds. It's not that difficult.

SUNDAY | OCTOBER 18, 2020

W E MAY ALL BE PREOCCUPIED with dodging coronavirus but, against that background, life continues on with its minor domestic triumphs and tragedies.

There's part of me that wants to hide from the little curveballs life throws as I'm just tired of things happening, and there's another part that revels in them as it's proof that I'm alive and that the story goes on.

I'm reminded of the period when Steve was so sick and much of my energy went to taking care of him. The little ups and downs of daily living felt greatly magnified as the battle against his disease process took so much of normal happy life away from us. Now it's COVID-19 stripping things away and leaving that which remains to occupy time and energy. It may not be much, but when all your general connectedness is gone, it can feel like too much.

I had my annual review on Friday, and I'm happy to report that I have a job for at least another year. My 22nd anniversary at UAB comes up in a couple of weeks, and it looks like I'll be with them a total of 25-30 years by the time I get around to retiring. It seems strange to be contemplating that milestone as it doesn't feel like it was that long ago that I was in college, med school, residency, fellowship, but it was all a lifetime ago at this point. I have two things to do before I can contemplate stepping down: making sure health insurance issues are covered (Medicare or otherwise) and paying off this condo. I want the mortgage gone.

Numbers are spiking again in Europe, leading to further shut downs. Numbers remain way out of control here. On the other hand, in most of Asia, things are pretty much back to normal. COVID-19 has never gained much of a foothold in Africa. If you look at rates in First World countries after mid-May (the time when there was enough understanding of the disease, its spread, and modes of transmission, for governments to get their act together), some interesting things appear when you consider case rates normalized to population.

Most of Europe and the rest of the First World was wildly out of control in March and April but came into control as more strict lockdowns were imposed. Now, case rates, low throughout the summer, are beginning to increase just in the last few weeks.

The two major outliers with much higher case rates are Sweden, which made a societal decision to let the disease spread and herd immunity take effect, and the United States where there are two populations divided by politics, one of which is vigilant in undertaking basic societal containment measures, and one which takes great joy in flouting those measures. Rates in the US are higher than in Third World slum districts.

Why has Asia fared well and the First World not? I think there are a couple of cultural factors at play here. First, Asia is well-versed in the spread of pandemic respiratory illness, having been through SARS and various avian flu strains. Their populations, as soon as it became apparent that COVID-19 was going to be a problem, did the things they have been trained to do. They masked up, started practicing social distancing, and obeyed their public health authorities as they have done many times in the past. As a result, the virus had difficulty getting a foothold and, where it did, was easily detected, and abatement measures were targeted and put in place without public outcry.

Asian cultures are not cultures of individuality. They are cultures which put the well-being of the group or the society ahead of the well-being of the individual. People are willing to endure personal inconvenience as they innately understand a greater good is being served. We don't do this well in the US.

Modern Eurocentric culture comes into being in the post-Renaissance world with one of the linchpins being that of Cartesian dualism with its corollary that every mind and individual is unique, and that the needs of the individual and the ego are paramount. Four centuries later, we have constructed a technological society (with a heavy dose of Ayn Rand's Objectivism thrown in for good measure) in which people are not only unwilling to endure inconvenience for the sake of the collective good, but are downright hostile to the idea. This "I-have-the-right-not-to-do-anything-I don't-want-to-do" mentality is so ingrained in American thinking that it's going to be difficult to even begin to bring COVID-19 spread under control.

The populations of those who understand what needs to be done and those who bristle at what they view as governmental intrusiveness are so intermixed that things will be dragged down to the lowest common denominator as the virus doesn't care about these issues. It will spread where human behavior allows it to spread.

If there's a change in administration in a few months, will we be able to start emulating societies with better track records? Not without good leadership, and I am afraid that governmental leadership has been badly damaged. It's going to take some sort of institution that a majority of Americans still trust to deliver messages and model behavior to turn things around.

I have some hope that faith communities might start filling the gap. From what I can see, some of the leadership there has begun to figure out that they have been rendering more to Caesar than to God in recent years, and that this has seriously damaged their reputation and standing. This might be an area of the love-thy-neighbor variety that they could enter and start turning the tide.

Beyond this, I'm not sure if there's a societal institution that both red and blue America trust in the same way. The military, perhaps, but public health isn't its role. Both sides tend to trust doctors, but we aren't given much of a public platform these days. The concerns of practicing physicians, especially in primary care, are overwhelmed by the concerns of the administrators and the money side of the system, and that's the narrative that makes it into the media and public discourse.

As the Emcee sang in the last show I did before theater vanished: "Money makes the world go round."

THURSDAY | OCTOBER 22, 2020

THE THIRD AND FINAL PRESIDENTIAL "DEBATE" is on this evening. I am not tuning in.

There is nothing either candidate could say that will sway my mind in the top-of-the-ticket contest. Besides which, I have already filled out and filed my ballot in early absentee voting.

I'm a big believer in the old adage that democracy is not a spectator sport, that it is a civic duty to vote, and that those who do not vote don't get to complain about the state of the country. I'm very good about voting and have been for 40 years now. I even turn up for some of the odd city elections and primary run-offs that have very low turnout. Generally, I get up a bit earlier on election day and vote on my way to work, but this year I decided to vote absentee given all of the uncertainties regarding COVID-19.

The state of Alabama does not make voting absentee terribly easy, but I qualify under the "works more than ten hours on election day" statute, so I sent in for it around Labor Day with the correct forms and a copy of my state issued ID, filled it out a couple of weeks ago, got it witnessed by two independent adults, and returned it via the post office. The ballot tracker told me yesterday that I had dotted my i's and crossed my t's correctly, and that my ballot was in the accepted pile awaiting counting week after next.

The news from the front lines in the COVID-19 wars is not good, despite the optimistic drivel emanating from the White House. Locally, the number of patients hospitalized with the disease is slowly inching back up to the numbers we had in late spring. Nationally, in a majority of states, the percentages of positive tests, which had been declining towards the 5% benchmark, are back up over 10%. (WHO suggests that there be a number of weeks of community testing prevalence of less than 5% before societies emerge from lockdown, and the current 10% is a public health emergency.)

Deaths keep going up. Morbidity seems to be a bit on the decline, but the reason for that is uncertain. It's probably due to the fact that the majority of the spread these days is in populations with less susceptibility to severe complication, mainly young adults. It doesn't stay amongst them, though.

The majority of senior and chronically ill adults in this country dwell in multi-generational households, and even those in isolated senior communities rely on younger staff coming in and out. This is where the whole herd immunity thing falls apart. It's not possible to isolate those in danger from the rest of society while we let the virus spread.

The epidemiologists are starting to get a better hand on the big data. We're at about 220,000 official deaths. The excess mortality for 2020 to date is about 285,000 deaths according to the actuaries and demographers. (285,000 more people have died in the US in 2020 then would have been predicted given the trends from 2019). Most of these are COVID deaths. A few are probably from people who delayed health care due to fear early on in the pandemic. A bunch are probably COVID cases that were not diagnosed.

As the disease rolls on, it's becoming clearer and clearer that it's actually a disease of clotting and the circulatory system that shows up in the lungs rather than a respiratory disease, so some of the deaths were probably coded as heart attack, or stroke, or from whatever long-standing chronic illness the victim was suffering that the altered physiology of the infection allowed to run rampant and tip a previously compensated person over the edge. Considering that we're only about seven months into the pandemic, I expect these numbers to shoot up a lot higher before the end of the year.

Between an incompetent federal response, a third of the population believing that even the most basic of public health measures is some sort of cabalistic plot, and that science should and must be ignored, I don't foresee us having much success getting out of our current patterns this winter. I know we're all bored with sitting alone in our rooms; we all want to get out and hear the music play, but it's just not a very good idea. Performing arts people are going to do what they do anyway, and I am encouraged at the creativity that's starting to pop up in the arts world: *Rigoletto* performed on a baseball diamond; *La Boheme,* stripped down to its essentials, performed in a bay front stadium; opera arias from the back of a flatbed in a parking lot; any number of online videos where people are stretching the capabilities of Zoom and other video conferencing software to create new hybrid virtual forms of performance.

I tend to keep my two careers of medicine and performance somewhat separate although they have been known to bleed into each other from time to time. Obviously, those in my theater life know I'm a doctor by day and those in my medical life occasionally turn up at something I'm performing in to see what I do in the evenings but, in general, they are separate arenas of existence. The overlap has been a bit more pronounced since the pandemic began. Generally, when I go to work and put on my white coat, I put on a persona that's different from what I consider the usual me. It's a role. One I've been playing for 35 or so years, so I have it down pat. The pandemic, however, has shaken up the system so much, and created a major need to unleash my imagination to problem solve, that my more usual self is popping up at work. I think it amuses the staff somewhat who are used to me being a bit more buttoned down.

I had a mental health day today. I'm not sure it worked as I'm still neurotic. But I do remember the litany: Wash your hands; wear your mask; avoid crowds. It's that easy.

SUNDAY | OCTOBER 25, 2020

TODAY HAS BEEN AN ODD DAY.

When awake, I feel like I'm about to explode out of my skin and take off like a rocket. Then I sit down for a minute, promptly enter torpor, and fall asleep.

Neither state is conducive to getting much of anything accomplished, so I'm going to have to settle for having finished up my progress notes of the week for work, a self-taping for a Halloween project, and several loads of laundry. Not the most exciting of Sundays, but it will have to do.

I'm not good with emotions. I have a hard time differentiating between them and can't always even tell positive from negative ones, so when I have a day like today where they're swirling around, my first instinct is to try and figure out how to tamp them down and wall them off somewhere, so that I don't have to feel uncomfortable and can get along with life and make a couple of further steps forward on my endless "To Do" list.

The key to both of my relationships was that Steve and Tommy, each in their own way, were able to figure out how to block those natural impulses of mine to lock my emotional self away, so that we could connect and build something together. It takes a particular kind of personality structure for that to happen with me, which is one of the reasons why I'm not holding out a lot of hope for a third husband. The number of eligible men in my age group with whom that would be possible is shrinking.

I went to Opera Shots this afternoon. It's something that Opera Birmingham has been doing for the last few years: Gather a bunch of singers together recital-style in a bar or brewery and have them belt out their favorite songs and arias while the audience sits around, has a few beers, and catches up on old times. COVID-19, of course, has changed the game.

Opera Shots is now taking place in parking lots, and it's BYOLC ("Bring Your Own Lawn Chair"), BYOB, stay six feet apart, and wear your mask. Still, it was nice to see people. Part of today's funk comes from some of the programming.

The second half was musical theater songs, and half way through, someone sang *Someone to Watch Over Me*. That was Tommy's and my song. He serenaded me with it very publicly when we were courting, and it was the last song on his recital for his music degree—a gesture of thank you to me for having helped him to achieve that long-delayed dream of his.

Sitting there in the parking lot, I experienced waves of feeling. I held it together, but the follow-up was a friend singing *You'll Never Walk Alone*. That one-two punch was a bit much, so I had to close my eyes and try not to feel for a while, or I was going to become a complete basket case.

So, at least two of the things roiling around inside me are sadness and grief, stirred up by the great American songbook. When I got home, I put on the original Broadway cast recording of *Mack and Mabel*. Jerry Herman is always good for restoring happy thoughts. Sondheim for intellect and introspection, Herman for dancing around and singing along.

I think the other major emotion is a feeling of righteous anger over this morning's headlines about the usual subject of these *Accidental Plague Diaries*. I have desperately tried to keep politics to a minimum in these writings, and to be as even-handed as possible, but I just can't today, two things having come to my attention.

The first were remarks that the president made at one of his rallies last night which more or less accused physicians of over-diagnosing COVID-19 so that they could be paid more.

I have worked with thousands of physicians over the course of my career. Most of them set much of themselves aside in order to do the best work they can in caring for the health of others. The number of times I have seen credible evidence of gaming the system for payment is very, very small. Besides which, there is no system which would increase payments for a COVID-19 diagnosis over other diagnoses. The very suggestion that those of us who are getting up and going to work daily under very trying circumstances, and putting ourselves in harm's way for the good of our patients, our profession, and our country, are somehow only in it for the profit motive makes steam come out of my ears.

One thousand seven hundred US healthcare workers have died so far from COVID-19 caught on the job. Many thousands more have been sickened and may have permanent health effects. How dare you, Mr. President! As Joseph Nye asked of Joseph McCarthy on June 9, 1954: "At long last, have you no decency?" (McCarthy never answered the question either.)

The second was Chief of Staff Mark Meadows' remarks to CNN this morning where the administration finally made full admission of what has been apparent for months to anyone who has been paying attention. The administration more or less has no plans to bring the power and resources of the most powerful and richest society the world has ever known to bear on the worst public health crisis in a century. They're just going to let it infect the population, and good luck to us all.

This complete abandonment of the foremost responsibility of a government, protection of the citizenry, also has me internally enraged. Even though I have known that this is what they have been doing for quite some time, to hear it finally articulated in an official way makes me want to punch a wall.

What does not fighting COVID-19 with good public health measures mean? It means the virus will continue to spread, because that's what viruses do.

To date, it has infected somewhere around 7% or 8% of the US population, so it's got huge inroads still to make. Without mitigation, it's likely to infect somewhere between 70% and 90% of the population before it's done. To make the math easy, we'll say the population is 320 million, and that it will infect 75% or 240 million. Currently, it appears that about 40% of those who become infected, mainly children and young adults, never know that they are sick. Another 40% become ill enough to recognize that they are sick and get tested but do not become so sick that they require hospital care. About 20% are sick enough for the hospital. So, of our 240 million cases, about 100 million are well, 100 million get sick at home, and 40 million are sick enough to require advanced care.

Of those requiring advanced care and support, about 20% require ICU care, with about half of those needing a ventilator. That's 8 million ICU patients and 4 million ventilator patients. We only have about a million hospital beds in the country and only about 130,000 ICU beds.

We've developed a model of just-in-time medical care without excess capacity in order to maximize profit, and there's no easy way to get the system to accept millions of cases at once. That was what the whole "flattening the curve" thing was about: slowing the rate of spread so as to not overwhelm the health system's ability to handle it.

The overall mortality for the disease is about 0.6%. Six in a thousand. That doesn't seem very high until you consider that's about one-and-a-half million deaths for the population. That's nearly 500 9/11's, 25 Vietnams, or more than two Civil Wars. As the average American has a circle of acquaintances of roughly 5,000, that means every one of us will lose roughly 30 people we know before this is all over.

I've lost friends, patients, close relatives of friends—colleagues and family are likely coming, and I'm steeled for it. Smaller cities are out of ICU beds. (I read a news report earlier this weekend that the entire state of North Dakota was down to one). We're getting close to the medical system becoming overwhelmed in some areas. And there's the downstream issues: Me and my colleagues are getting burnt out.

Disruptions in the healthcare industry are leading the more experienced among us to move up our retirement plans. Our complete inability to react to a thoroughly predictable pandemic as a modern nation will continue to make us a pariah state when it comes to such things as travel. Institutions which require us to congregate indoors in social groups will continue to suffer.

I don't know how to fix any of this. All I can do is report on it, on how it impacts me, and how I see it impacting health care and society at large from my vantage point and a little bit of knowledge. I can, however, wash my hands.

FRIDAY | OCTOBER 30, 2020

HURRICANE ZETA AMBLED THROUGH TOWN in the wee hours of the morning.

We're a few hundred miles from the coast, so it did not have hurricane force winds by the time it passed through Birmingham, but it was still enough to blow limbs and trees down all over town, creating massive power outages. I lost power briefly around 2:30 AM and would normally have slept through it, but the restoration some minutes later caused things to go slightly haywire in my personal electrical grid.

The smoke detector outside my bedroom began to speak to me in an overly chipper electronic voice demanding I get up and poke its reset button. While I was up, I noted that power was on in certain circuits but not in others. I had lights in the dining room, but no outlet power and no lights in the hall, refrigerator, or Wi-Fi. Flipping the circuit breakers did nothing to rectify the situation, and by now I was thoroughly awake and disgruntled, so I went back to bed with a book to wait until morning when I could talk to building maintenance.

Today marks the day that the US surpassed 9 million cases of COVID-19. This got me interested in the mathematics of big numbers when it comes to COVID, so I went back and looked up the other seven-figure anniversaries that have happened so far this year and constructed this little table:

0 cases - 1/19/2020 (the first US case was reported on 1/20/2020)

1 million cases - 4/28/2020 (99 days later)

2 million cases - 6/11/2020 (44 days later)

3 million cases - 7/8/2020 (28 days later)

4 million cases - 7/24/2020 (16 days later)

5 million cases - 8/10/2020 (17 days later)

6 million cases - 8/31/2020 (21 days later)

7 million cases - 9/25/2020 (25 days later)

8 million cases - 10/16/2020 (21 days later)

9 million cases - 10/30/2020 (14 days later)

The next data point will take us to eight figures and a whole new order of magnitude, and will probably happen sometime a week or so after the election given current trends.

South Korea, an early hot spot, had its first case of COVID-19 on the same day as the US. To date, they have had roughly 26,000 cases and about 450 deaths. They are, of course, a smaller country with roughly 1/7 of our population. If we multiply these numbers by seven, we get 182,000 cases and 3,150 deaths. Compare this to our 9,000.000 cases and 225,000 deaths to date. Our fate wasn't inevitable. It's the product of deliberate decision-making on both governmental and individual levels.

As a society, we have all become conditioned to quick and convenient services and results. We have little patience for the slow pace and rhythms of the natural world. We want our needs met instantly with same-day service, fast food, drive-thru convenience, and all the other things we have constructed to allow us to live over-scheduled busy lives.

Given what I do for a living, I run into this all the time. When my patients become acutely ill in their 70s and 80s, we can usually get them over the hump and get their physiologic processes on track so that they can begin healing. As the Baby Boom has begun to enter this age group, they expect their recoveries to take no more than a few days at best. That's all they can allow for it in their lives. But nature doesn't work that way.

A body in that age group generally needs 4-7 days of recuperation for every day of acute illness, so four days in the hospital may equal a month before things are back to normal. Patients and their families get angry at me all the time as I gently explain that this is the way it works, and that no amount of money or social position or wanting it to be different is going to change that.

Why do we do this? Aside from our infatuation with instant results, I think it has to do with brain development. Our brains are growing and changing and maturing until our mid 20s. At that point, they're done and we have our fully developed adult brain that will guide us the rest of our lives.

When we're younger than that, and our brain is changing as our bodies change, we're used to looking in the mirror and seeing some-one different look back at us as our physical, cognitive, and emotional selves mature together. Then the cognitive self comes to a halt, but the physical self keeps on going and changing in ways that most of us would rather it not. So by the time you're my age, you're looking in the mirror and seeing an unfamiliar older person looking back, and you're wondering, "What happened?"

Those of us with a little education and access to health care can keep our bodies in pretty decent shape with minimal fuss until our late 70s or early 80s these days. All the while, that same brain that still conceives of itself as 25, maybe 30, is rattling around inside and not really understanding that our physiology has changed nearly as much as it has.

On an evolutionary scale, when most of us were dead by our mid-40s at the latest, this wasn't a big problem, but in the last few generations when aging has become equal opportunity, we're creating huge numbers of people with a cognitive dissonance between mind and body.

As this is a new phenomenon, there isn't a huge amount of accumulated common wisdom to have been passed down genera-tion to generation about what it means, and how to cope with being a healthy 80-year old, and what you should worry about, and what you shouldn't. The leading edge of the Baby Boom turns 80 in just five short years. It's going to be awfully interesting in my professional world when that happens.

This lack of understanding of natural processes is, of course, playing out in our response to COVID-19. We want everything to stay the same, the way we're used to it being. We want a quick fix. Slow methodical fixes require significant behavior change. But long periods of time just aren't in our cultural DNA. Therefore, we want to get back to our restaurants and our parties and our football games and our school events.

I'm human; I do, too. But I also know that the virus exploits our inability to maintain good habits and uses that to spread, and every time it spreads, there's a good chance that someone is going to become seriously ill or die.

It keeps hitting close to home. There hasn't been a day in the last week or so where someone looking for advice or support hasn't reached out to me with a story about an ill friend or family member. I do what I can, but there remain no magic bullet treatments. The one thing that seems to be happening is that there are fewer catastrophic cases, probably as more and more cases are happening among younger, hardier populations.

As for me, I'm getting tired. I have a lot of energy to help, but I'm not an infinite well, and my usual restoratives have fallen victim to the pandemic. I am counting the days until I get some time off. This isn't the flu. It's much deadlier, and the chronic health issues of those who are seriously ill but survive remain unknown. It takes out perfectly healthy young people.

We can all help bring it under control with a few relatively easy behavior changes: hand washing, mask wearing, social distancing, staying out of crowds

And then on the societal level: ventilating public spaces, contact tracing, and testing. None of these is perfect, but when used together, you get South Korea.

If we don't do these things, the virus is going to exploit our behaviors, and behavior leads to rising infections (going on now), leads to rising hospitalizations (happening in many states; there are no hospital beds available in many Midwest communities), leads to rising deaths with a few weeks lag between each step. Ten million will become 20 million will become 30 million. Wearing your mask today ensures that someone else will be here for Christmas.

NOVEMBER 2020

Every Day A Little Death

MONDAY | NOVEMBER 2, 2020

"Tomorrow we'll be far away
Tomorrow is the judgement day
Tomorrow we'll discover
What our God in Heaven has in store
One more dawn
One more day
One day more."

ALL THE THEATER PEOPLE who read these essays of mine are busy singing that particular quote in their heads, if not aloud. All I can say about tomorrow is that I have done what I personally can do about the current state of the country and, as of tomorrow, we will have the government we deserve as a people.

Our current government has made clear what it stands for over the last four years. If we choose to retain it, we will all be responsible for the consequences. If we choose to change it, we will all be responsible for forging a new path. I am taking a news and social media hiatus tomorrow evening and curling up with a good book. I'll know the outcome soon enough and will live with the results like everyone else.

So where are we with the *Accidental Plague Diaries?* Tired. Cases are increasing again locally and in the hospital. I've had three long-term patients test positive since Friday. They are all, so far, doing well, but with the age and general physiologic condition of my folk, they are not out of the woods by a long shot. Despite the ominous signs, Alabama is doing better than a number of other places around the country. A quick skim of the headlines on my news feeds this morning revealed a lack of ICU beds in the Midwest, the need for a fourth mobile morgue unit in El Paso, and a study tracing roughly 30,000 cases over the last month to infections spread by the President's rallies.

Someone was complaining today about how the virus keeps changing its behavior, making it difficult to know how to react. This is fallacious. Viruses do not change their behavior. They don't have central nervous systems, brains, emotions, reasoning, or anything else with which we might wish to anthropomorphize them. What changes is our behavior, and this is what determines how and where the virus spreads.

The significant uptick in cases over the last couple of weeks probably relates to back-to-school behavior and COVID fatigue, which leads to people relaxing their guard and being more likely to head off to a restaurant or a small informal party, and colder weather starting to push more people indoors.

These are all trends that started some weeks ago, and it takes a while for the change in behavior to lead to a rise in cases. The rise in hospitalizations comes next. We're already seeing it in some places, and I am worried about where we may end up over the next few months.

We've got the equipment and the hospital beds. We're running out of staff. There's 168 hours in a week which means you need four full-time shifts of workers to staff acute care beds. As nurses and other staff are getting burnt out, sick themselves, or are otherwise not able to handle the rigors of COVID-19-related hospital and ICU work, we may run out of bodies to keep the system going.

Nurse staffing companies are offering huge bonuses to travel RNs due to demand (causing some regular hospital RNs to quit their jobs for the better dollars of the travel/PRN life), but even these inducements aren't going to work forever.

In the past, we imported many nurses, but the current administration's crackdown on immigration, plus COVID-19-related travel restrictions, hamper that solution. Seventeen hundred healthcare providers have died, and the chief cause of death among active duty peace officers this year is—you guessed it—COVID-19, not guns.

My little corner of healthcare is pretty stable at the moment, but I wonder for how long. We've been trying to find some new geriatrics faculty for years but have had little luck. It's a deeply unpopular specialty among American medical school graduates because it is non-procedure-oriented and, therefore, not especially lucrative. It does not lend itself to being taught and understood in the standard four-week rotation given to trainees as the specialty is longitudinal; it requires months or years to understand how interventions actually work with patients and families. It also requires a lot of creative, right brain thinking which physicians, selected for their ability to analyze and work with scientific rigor, feel very uncomfortable with.

Doctors want answers. There aren't a lot of them in geriatric medicine, and you have to be able to look patients and families squarely in the eye sometimes and say, "There is no science on this subject" or "We have no data about this" or simply "I don't know."

I think late fall and early winter are going to be hellacious when it comes to COVID- 19 cases. I just hope it's not so bad that the healthcare system starts to fail in any appreciable way. I think it may do so in certain localities where the number of ill people simply overwhelms the ability of the system to cope. I think we've got enough resources and resilience locally that it won't be us, but one never knows, does one? Our saving grace is that the protective behaviors against COVID-19 will also be protective against other viral respiratory illnesses including flu, so hopefully it will be a light flu season.

After much discussion, my family has canceled our usual Thanksgiving gathering. Too risky with octogenarian seniors, college students coming home from school and bringing buddies with them, travel exposures, and the like.

I am still going to go to Seattle in late November to see the family, but probably after the holiday rush. My father's 88th birthday is the Tuesday after Thanksgiving, and so I will make this the centerpiece of my trip and travel on less-crowded days, making it safer for me and for him.

We are having a family Zoom on Thanksgiving night. I don't know what I'll do for dinner yet. I'm not wedded to Turkey. Steve and I, on our first Thanksgiving together, more than thirty years ago, had Lasagna at a Swiss Restaurant in Mexico City, so maybe it should be Lasagna in commemoration. I have a few weeks to think about it.

FRIDAY | NOVEMBER 6, 2020

TODAY WOULD HAVE BEEN MY MOTHER'S 88TH BIRTHDAY. It's the first one she's no longer here for.

I miss her, but I've missed her for years. As dementia stole her faculties over a long, slow, painful period, she became less and less present, less able to be the touchstone of my life that she had been.

I love my father deeply, but I am definitely my mother's child in so many ways. I inherited from her my somewhat British sensibility, my love of language, my puckish sense of humor, and my enjoyment of a good single malt scotch.

She taught me to love literature for its own sake; encouraged me to read widely and deeply, and with a sense of inquiry (although she was somewhat taken aback when she found me ensconced in Kurt Vonnegut at age ten); taught me how to choose my words carefully and how to put them together into cogent ideas; how to hold one's head high and move serenely through life no matter the obstacles.

The vagaries of life that led her, the child of British émigrés, brought up in San Francisco society in an era where women wore hats and gloves downtown and married men of good families and prospects, to venture afield and meet and marry my father, never cease to amaze me. Wherever her energy is these days, I hope she's happy and contentedly smiling down on her successful descendants and their collaterals.

COVID-19 news has been knocked off the front pages by presidential politics this week, but that doesn't mean it's over by a long shot. I've seen a few of my more conservative friends post some silly memes suggesting that the coronavirus will now just go away. I'm afraid that's not happening.

Both Wednesday and Thursday of this week, there were more than 100,000 cases reported in the US. I won't be surprised if that proves true for today as well when final numbers are tallied. The numbers locally are skyrocketing. I can tell by watching my Facebook feed as well as by looking at the various case counters constantly updated online in real time. I have had five or six friends post that they have been diagnosed this week. Two have been hospitalized. Neither is serious enough to require ICU care at this time, but it's early days.

I've had four long-term patients admitted to the hospital with COVID-19 this week. One has died. For most of this year, it's been running about one a week, so that's a four-fold increase, although the sample size is too small to make a statistical inference.

As has been proven time and again, the sequence goes like this: Behavior change leads to increased cases some weeks later, leads to increased hospitalizations some weeks after that, leads to deaths some weeks after that. I am assuming this huge wave that we seem to be rolling into is coming from the opening up of various social institutions over the last few months, schools being chief among them. If the usual patterns prevail, we're just going into the case spike now.

The hospital spike should arrive just in time for the holiday season and we'll start seeing a significant increase in the death rate for Christmas and New Years. So, unless you want to gift someone with premature death this year, keep up the usual: masks, hand hygiene, social distancing, avoiding crowds.

The presidential election, while not yet complete due to the enormous numbers of absentee and mail-in ballots yet to be tallied, looks to be pretty much a done deal. We will have a new administration as of January 20, 2021.

What will this mean for COVID-19? That's hard to predict, but I suspect a few things will happen. There will be some restoration to executive agencies such as the CDC and FDA of principles of science in decision-making rather than principles of politics and wishful thinking. Congress retains the power of the purse, and while the House is likely to appropriate money for public health measures, the politics of the Senate are far less certain, and it remains in dispute which party will even be in control.

All eyes go to Georgia between now and its run-off election slated for January 5th. With luck, Stacey Abrams will be allowed to do what she knows how to do. I will repeat my mantra: Black Women should be in charge of everything in this country. They know how to get things done. I also suspect that there will be some new federal initiatives put in place to make it easier for states to cooperate regionally for better pandemic control. There may be a vaccine in the next year or so, and it will help some, but it will be like the Flu Shot. It will reduce morbidity and mortality, but will be no cure-all.

The thing I am most afraid of in terms of thinking through what's coming over the next few years in regard to COVID-19 are the unknown long-term consequences of the disease. As it becomes more and more clear that this is not a respiratory virus, but a vascular virus with damage to multiple organ systems, there may be all sorts of ugly little surprises awaiting those who have recovered. I won't be taken aback in the least if in a decade or so, there are significant cardiac, renal, or neurological late complications that surface in those who were infected. What these complications will be and what they will mean for health, function, and life expectancy are entirely unknown. But every time I read of a young healthy theater friend who has been diagnosed and is recuperating at home, I can't help but wonder what happens next. A change in administration may lead to more of an emphasis on people and less on profit, but I'm not holding my breath.

Stay safe. Be well.

TUESDAY | NOVEMBER 10, 2020

HI, MY NAME IS ANDREW, AND I HAVE COVID-19 FATIGUE. There, I said it. I've been writing these *Accidental Plague Diaries* for eight months now and I'm tired. I'm tired of otherwise intelligent people ignoring science for political purposes. I'm tired of a government allowing ordinary citizens to suffer and die from a predictable infectious disease that can be mitigated by tried-and-true public health methods. I'm tired of working in a health system that's under incredible pressures between the needs of COVID-19 patients and the needs of everyone else. I'm tired of giving up much of what I find pleasurable in life for the greater good to see hordes of people out and about just not giving a damn about what their behavior means to others. I'm tired, tired, tired.

I knew it was all getting to me this past weekend when I kept falling asleep most of the time. I didn't have much on my docket, so any time I sat down on the couch with a book, I nodded off yet again.

It reminded me of how I felt when I would come home from college for vacations and sleep 12-14 hours a day for two weeks, recuperating from the quarter just past and resetting for the quarter to come.

So where are we now? We've passed 10 million cases in the US and for the last week, have been averaging over 100,000 cases daily. At current trends, we'll be up to 11 million before Thanksgiving week. Hospitalizations are up by about 75% over the last month with some of the smaller Midwest states completely out of hospital and ICU beds. The death rate is up 15% over last week.

All of this has been pushed off the front pages by the political news of the last week in the aftermath of the election. The way things are going, I won't be surprised if we end up with a president in the White House and a "president" in Florida trading barbs at each other for the next four years. Actually, the whole saga is unfolding exactly as those who read the political currents closely predicted it would some months ago with a Democratic victory and a lot of Republican sound and fury signifying all kinds of things but without much substance behind it.

We're now in the third wave of COVID-19 cases in the US: the first wave having happened in March and April when the disease first began to spread, and the second having happened around July. This one is bigger and more widespread than the first two. Fewer people seem to be dying as the health system has learned how to save lives, but more and more people are getting sick with unknown future sequelae.

My brothers and sisters in health care were running on nervous energy, adrenaline, and the combined fear and hope of the unknown for the first wave. They received the second wave with grace, having more or less learned what they needed to do. However, they're just as tired as I am. They've been doing this for eight months without respite, the numbers are climbing again, and I'm afraid we're going to start seeing some of them crumble. Those older than I are researching their retirement options. Those younger are looking at career paths that aren't quite so stressful. Those my age are plodding forward one day at a time. We have a healthcare provider shortage, especially of skilled RNs in this country. We've imported them in the past. The current administration has shut that down.

I'm worried that we're going to see some major fractures in the healthcare system over the next few months, just in time for the holidays. Large university systems like UAB will be fine. They have all sorts of resources they can draw on. I'm worried about community hospitals in more out-of-the-way locations, with much smaller systems behind them and smaller talent pools from which to draw. These have already been heavily stressed by the general changes in health care over the last few decades, and greatly exacerbated by the political refusal of Medicaid expansion funds tied to Obamacare.

I've spent much of my career serving patients in rural poverty, going into their homes, learning the way they think and how they relate to health care culturally. I hate to think of the richest nation in the world failing some of its citizens in so basic a manner.

Speaking of Obamacare, the Trump administration, together with a coalition of a number of Republican state Attorneys General, went before the Supreme Court today arguing in California v. Texas that it should be completely invalidated. Nothing says I care for my citizens like stripping 20 million of them of health insurance during a pandemic and stripping all 320 million of them of protection against discrimination for preexisting conditions when we're facing a disease with unknown long-standing repercussions. I wouldn't count on the conservative majority throwing the whole thing out, though. There were remarks from the bench from surprising sources that suggest it won't happen. But we will see what we will see.

Rant over. I'm still tired. I should move on to a constructive project, but I'll finish my box of Oreos and turn on Netflix instead.

SATURDAY | NOVEMBER 14, 2020

I T'S THE SECOND SATURDAY IN NOVEMBER, not quite two weeks after the election. Neo-Nazis are busy marching in DC, we have an administration that refuses a gracious concession despite a major defeat, and COVID-19 marches on at disastrous levels.

In the last week alone, 1 out of 378 Americans tested positive for COVID-19. Since the beginning of the pandemic nine months ago, roughly 1 out of 31 Americans has tested positive. We're at something over 250,000 deaths. For those of you still hoping for "herd immunity" which will require roughly 2/3 to 3/4 of Americans to test positive, basic math tells us 5-to-6 million will die.

I opened up my Facebook feed yesterday and started to scroll through. The first four posts were all related to serious COVID-19 problems: a friend mourning the death of a parent from COVID-19 earlier that afternoon; another friend celebrating release from the hospital but still requiring home oxygen; a friend bemoaning a positive test that day which will require two weeks quarantining off work with concomitant loss of income; a friend two weeks out of the hospital who still doesn't have the strength to do much besides rest up.

I can't help but wonder how much longer I can keep avoiding it. I'm not stupid. I don't take unnecessary risks. And I have clamped way down on my activities. But I still march into hospital buildings every work day that are full of the ill, and I don't believe for a minute that everyone in them is negative, no matter how much checking of temperatures they do at entry.

I have a lot to say about what's about to happen to the health system in certain parts of the country, but I think I'll save that for the next entry.

I'm tired of writing about doom and gloom. I want to write about positive things today, and there are a few positive things going on as a result of the pandemic that should be celebrated.

A few nights ago, I came home grouchy. I've learned over the years that there's no better cure for that then to put on a Jerry Herman show, so I put on the Carol Channing 90s revival of *Hello, Dolly!* (I like this one because it includes a bunch of the dance music and the tempi are quicker than usual which gives it even more energy). It got me thinking about the times I've done the show in the past. There are a number of speeches, usually monologues that break the fourth wall and which are straight out of the Thornton Wilder source material, that are important.

Wilder really understood how to dig down to the essence of humanity in American culture in *Our Town*, *The Skin of Our Teeth*, and *The Matchmaker*, and remind us of what's truly important. "Money, pardon the expression, is like manure. It's not worth a thing unless it's spread around, encouraging young things to grow." "For years I had not shed one tear nor had I been filled with the wonderful hope that something or other would turn out well. And so I decided to rejoin the human race." "Even if I have to dig ditches for the rest of my life, I'll be a ditch digger who once had a wonderful day." I think it's these moments and the deep humanity of the characters that make it one of my favorite shows despite the gooey trappings.

So what is the good? Keeping these posts up has helped me to hone my writing and has given me the discipline to write these essays a couple of times a week as a record of how at least one person has been affected and reacted to the pandemic. It has also allowed me to explore a number of topics in epidemiology, sociology, and psychology that I might not otherwise have encountered. It has given me an excuse to be in touch with old friends that I might not otherwise have communicated with. It has made me withdraw from some of my over-scheduling, a coping device I've used for years to run away from having to face emotions, and made me actually confront and process some of the things that have happened to me over the years.

I see a lot of good as I look around me at society. People are learning to cook again. I should join their ranks (I'm actually not a bad cook; I just had the luxury of a trained chef in my kitchen for fifteen years), but I've never been interested in cooking for one. When things open up, and I can have people over for dinner, I'll break out some of my favored recipes from years past.

I've seen a lot of people return to long-neglected hobbies and crafts. People are sewing, knitting, painting, building, and expressing themselves practically and creatively. Items created in 2020 with love and care will come down through the generations in the future with a story attached, much in the way that we prize great grandmother's shawl or the chest great grandfather made. Performers are becoming more and more creative in how they use new technologies or how they gather an audience. I have been to drive-in performances, bring-your-own-lawn-chair-to-a-parking-lot performances, and seen people on Zoom or other streaming platforms actively creating new entertainment hybrids between stage and film.

We've got a long way to go, and given current trends, things are going to get worse before they get better. States rejecting public health science for political reasons are going to continue to fuel the spread nationally. Can that be fixed? I hope so, but it's going to take a lot of work and a lot of education, and a removal of those media vectors that propagate disinformation. We'll see what happens. As I've said repeatedly, viruses don't care about your politics, only that your behaviors allow them to spread. I'll keep trying to do my small part to reduce the spread by (everyone all together now...) washing my hands, wearing a mask, and minimizing my time indoors with crowds of other people.

Stay well.

WEDNESDAY | NOVEMBER 18, 2020

'M SAD THIS EVENING.

It's all related to COVID-19, of course, how could it not be? The number of US deaths passed a quarter million today. That's 250,000 families that were intact in February, now irretrievably broken. Widows without spouses, children without parents, parents without children. And none of it had to be. Given the nature of the beast, we were always going to lose some, but with good leadership and public health practices, our losses should be lower by an order of magnitude.

As I read through my COVID-19-related news feeds, I'm reading about North Dakota, now the hotspot for the disease not just in the country, but in the entire world. One out of a thousand people there has died of COVID-19 since the beginning of the pandemic. South Dakota, just across the border, isn't faring much better, and their seemingly delusional governor is busy running tourist ads to try and get people to come visit. They are completely out of hospital beds in Oklahoma. New York City schools are shutting again. Lockdowns are taking shape on the West Coast.

The current surge, which is much worse than either the initial outbreak of the spring or the higher numbers of July and August, is absolutely predictable. The sages in the epidemiology and virology community stated succinctly what would happen this summer if the country did not take things seriously and mask up, social distance, and cancel significant gatherings of people.

What did America do? It turned the wearing of masks into some sort of Star-Bellied Sneetches political statement to delineate in and out groups. It sent its children back to school and its young people back to college where they engaged in the behaviors that young people are wont to do. It couldn't live without its motorcycle rallies, its football games, its nights out at the restaurant. It would not exert political leadership to make it economically possible for Americans to choose to take care of each other. With no other source of income, everyone had to go back to whatever work they could find, risks be damned. I've worked very hard to be careful but I'm human. I've slipped a few times and done things that might have put myself or others at risk. I want my old life back just as much as everyone else.

The virus, of course, cares nothing for any of this. It simply takes advantage of the opportunities afforded it by human behavior and, with a third of the population convinced that COVID-19 is likely a hoax and certainly not a threat, there's no way to contain spread in the population as a whole and you get what we have now: uncontained community spread everywhere.

The saddest story I read this week was from a nurse on the COVID-19 wards. When calling families of patients who were about to be intubated and likely to die, she would ask if they would like a chance to say goodbye to their loved one. She was told over and over again that this wouldn't be necessary as the virus was a hoax. The next call she had to make was, of course, to tell them that their loved one had died.

The cognitive dissonance that must be causing I can't even begin to imagine. I have heard that families have come in demanding that death certificates must be changed. It can't possibly be COVID-19, they insist. It must be pneumonia, flu, an undiagnosed cancer, but not COVID-19 because COVID-19 doesn't exist.

On a personal note, I'm sad that I won't be able to see my family as I had planned. After much discussion and reflection, I've come to the conclusion that it's best not to go to Seattle at the moment. Washington state is heading back to mandatory quarantining of out of state visitors, and I can't take the time for a two week quarantine before seeing anyone. There's also the heightened chance of exposure through travel and the risks this potentially poses to my soon-to-be 88- year old father.

What I'm going to do with my time off I'm not sure now. I am going to go down to storage to haul out Christmas this next week. As Mame says, "We need a little Christmas. Right this very minute." At the very least, it will give me time to figure out which of my multitudinous decorations will work in this new space and which should be rehomed. Then I have to tackle boxes of ephemera and sort out pictures and mementos.

I'm sad for my patients, who were just starting to feel safe coming out of their cocoons, but who now have to go right back into an isolated existence. I'm sad for their families, who are often stuck outside a window or glass door. I'm especially sad for the demented ones who don't understand what's happening and why routines have been so disrupted. They need touch and laughter and small children to stay anchored and present in the world, and these basic needs are denied them. I try to be a bright spot in their day when they visit me either in person or via video conference, but it takes a lot of energy to play that role I've perfected for myself over the last three decades.

I'm sad for my colleagues who were, earlier in the fall, starting to feel human again as the pressures of COVID-19 were letting up on the system, and old patterns and schedules were starting to fall back into place. They haven't recovered, and here they're being asked to gird up their loins and prepare for worse yet.

This is all taking a major toll on mental health. I can see it and feel it. People are snappier, less tolerant of minor snafus, more likely to pick fights over turf or disagreements in treatment plans. I know when I get like that, it's time for a vacation, and I schedule one post haste, but there's not enough of us to handle what is happening as some retire, some burn out, and some fall ill. I'm not worried about UAB, but nationwide, one fifth of hospitals are at or over capacity as of today, and the numbers show no signs of trending down.

I made a deal with myself after Tommy's death that the way I was going to cope with life was to schedule one thing a month that I could look forward to: a vacation, a long weekend away, a theatrical project. Something that would nurture my soul. I was doing pretty well until March when the world fell apart for me as well as for everyone else. I've had little to look forward to, and I look out at the horizon and still see a long stretch of months where my usuals still won't be possible. I have to figure out something to take their place. I just haven't been able to do so as of yet.

Sorry to be Debbie Downer this evening, but some days are like that. In the meantime you all know the drill: Wear your mask; wash your hands; social distance; avoid close crowds.

SUNDAY | NOVEMBER 22, 2020

AN OLD HIGH SCHOOL FRIEND with whom I have recently been in communication (the positive joys of social media) asked me my thoughts on the COVID-19 vaccines that have been in the news recently and what may come of them. I am not an immunologist or a virologist, just a geriatrician trying to make sense of this brave new world along with the rest of you, but I have been seeking out information where I can. So, this evening's entry in *The Accidental Plague Diaries* can be called something like "When Can I Get My Shot?"

The basic answer is "I don't know." There are something like 100 vaccine candidates out there being worked on worldwide. There are a couple of motivations. The first is the beneficence of being able to protect us from the virus. The second is the potential of enormous sums of money to be made by successful products. Given the politics and sociology of this moment, I don't think we're going to see the kind of gestures made in the past such as the discoverers of insulin refusing to patent or take recompense or, more recently, Jonas Salk's not wanting to profit off the polio vaccine.

For a vaccine or any other pharmaceutical to come to market, there's a three-step process. First, you have to show that the drug or vaccine does what you think it does in a test tube or cell culture. Second, you have to show this in an animal model and provide data that it's safe for humans. Third, you have to present data on human trials showing efficacy and safety, and then you can get approval. The incredible need for a vaccine in this particular case has allowed a certain fast-tracking over this system, and a rapid development of phase three human trials.

Two different vaccines have completed a phase three trial and showed roughly 90-95% efficacy in preventing COVID-19 with minimal side effects. The first is a vaccine from Pfizer in association with a small German biotech company BioNTech. Despite certain politicians touting it as an American solution, it was developed in Germany with German money. The vaccine works by using mRNA (synthetic messenger RNA) targeted to encode a piece of the RNA the virus uses to manufacture its proteins.

This idea is relatively new and has only been in use in the lab for about fifteen years, so these vaccines are not the same as older virus vaccines like flu or measles which actually use the viral proteins themselves to confer immunity. The mRNA is injected into your muscle tissue where it is taken up by muscle cells, and the muscle cells use this mRNA to make the viral proteins. Your immune system recognizes these as foreign and gears up antibodies to them. Therefore, if you run into the actual virus later, your immune system is primed to take it out before it can ever establish itself in your body. It's a nifty idea and, as you're not actually shooting foreign proteins into someone, you're less likely to have negative reactions.

The hitch is that mRNA is not a very stable molecule. In order for it not to degrade or transform into something that would cause your cells to start making the wrong protein, it has to be kept very, very cold (-70 degrees Celsius). This is a good deal colder than your average freezer. Therefore, in order to be able to distribute the vaccine, you have to have a cold chain in place that can ensure the vaccine stays at a super-low temperature from the time and place of manufacture to its end destination where it is defrosted just in time to be used. This can be done. The Shingrix shingles vaccine requires similarly cold temperatures and has been safely distributed for some years.

The Moderna vaccine, which is an American product, is also an mRNA vaccine which works in essentially the same way as the Pfizer/BioNTech vaccine does. Moderna's big selling point is that their formulation is more shelf-stable, does not require quite as cold a temperature, and will last longer at room temperature than the other product.

Mind you, neither product has yet obtained FDA approval. Pfizer has filed for an Emergency Use Authorization that will allow them to circumvent much of the usual red tape. Moderna is expected to follow suit within the next couple of weeks. Once the EUA is granted, it will be legal for them to manufacture, distribute, and administer the products. When will that be? I'm going to trust that there are still scientists at the FDA who will know how to interpret the data and will make decisions based on that rather than on drug company press releases (the source of the vast majority of the news coverage on these products.)

I have a healthy skepticism of drug company press releases. Go back a century or so, and you'll find lovely ads for "Heroin: the new sedative for cough." I'm sure the makers of thalidomide had great things to say about their product when it was released. You can ask me about my experiences with the Merck Corporation and Vioxx next time you see me.

The chances are good that there will be something available in the next few months, but we'll have to see what happens when it's released to a general, rather than a study, population. And then there are the issues as to who should get it and how quickly.

In the meantime, the numbers don't look good. Those of you who have been reading these essays for a while may remember I wrote up a table of how many days it took for a million cases to occur in the US. We passed 12 million yesterday. Just six days after we passed 11 million. Which was only seven days after we passed 10 million.

For those who run around saying things like "I'm not worried; it's only a 1% mortality rate," think about what that means. There are roughly 200,000 cases diagnosed daily at the moment. That means 2,000 people have been told they are going to die. The problem is we don't know which 2,000. So we're having between four and five 9/11's a week in terms of mortality alone, and that doesn't even begin to touch what the morbidity both short and long term might be.

Those of us who work in health care are tired. We know that the numbers today means the hospitalizations will be skyrocketing in four to six weeks, just in time for Christmas. What's going to make a difference in terms of life and death for many is going to be the number of functional acute care nurses and other staff available. If they're sick or burned out, we gots nuttin'.

If you're going to have Thanksgiving with the family, set up card tables on the lawn. (Or in the carport if it's raining.) And wash your hands. And wear your mask. And check on your healthcare worker friends and neighbors.

THURSDAY | NOVEMBER 26, 2020

HAPPY THANKSGIVING EVERYONE.

No turkey here. I was hardly going to cook a turkey for one for dinner. I do have a few goodies in the fridge for later along with a bottle of wine for our family Zoom hour coming up later this evening. Family stretched across four time zones combined with alcohol will either end up in hilarity or disaster. Knowing my people the way I do, it will almost certainly be the former.

There's a couple of new wrinkles on the vaccine front that I've learned about in the four days since writing the last one of these diaries (which shows just how quickly things are moving). The first is that there is another vaccine that has emerged with a successful track record. This one, from Astra-Zeneca and the Jenner Vaccine Institute at Oxford University, is very different from the two mRNA vaccines I discussed previously. It is a live virus vaccine and, because of this, it does not have to be kept at super-cold temperatures for shipment and storage. It is stable at room temperature for some time, making it easier to distribute, especially to parts of the world that have less-developed infrastructure. It is also, due to funding promises from various sources, likely to be a good deal cheaper than the mRNA vaccines.

This vaccine has its roots in the Ebola and MERS (Middle East Respiratory Syndrome) outbreaks of the last decade. Knowing that there would eventually be a worldwide pandemic of something, scientists at the Jenner Vaccine Institute decided that what was needed was a vaccine that could be easily modified for any particular disease that came down the pike. They took a cold virus (an adenovirus to be specific) from chimpanzees, modified it slightly to make it non-infectious to humans, and then started to work out ways that it could be a messenger that would drop any particular engineered payload to human cells, allowing the immune system to activate against it.

They were quite far along with their ideas when COVID-19 hit and were able to pivot to using the spike proteins of the coronavirus as the target, completing ten years worth of work in less than ten months. The original trials of dosing of this vaccine weren't especially promising—50% protection rather than the 95% of the mRNA vaccines—until there was a happy accident and, by error, one of the test cohorts got only a half dose in their initial shot of a two shot series. Those individuals in the half dose group showed 90% protection. No one's quite sure why, but the studies are being hurriedly looked at and replicated.

So there now appears to be a bit of a three-way horse race to see who can first get an FDA emergency use authorization and get their product out. I'm thinking Moderna is likely to be the winner here. It comes down to money. The Pfizer vaccine is backed primarily by Germany, the Astra-Zeneca is backed primarily by England, while the Moderna is American. It doesn't hurt that Moncef Slaoui—the vaccine guru behind Operation Warp Speed was on the board of Moderna and was reaping benefits from the company until Elizabeth Warren pointed it out and pushed for him to divest.

I have a feeling that a number of individuals well-connected to Moderna are going to make a killing over the next six months, and there will be a lot of mutual back-scratching along with the congratulations. Societal upheaval and disaster have always created new wealth—like Procter and Gamble growing from a local Cincinnati company into an international powerhouse on the strength of contracts to supply the Union Army with soap and candles. Perhaps Honoré de Balzac said it best: "Behind every great fortune is a crime."

Numbers are continuing to skyrocket everywhere and will continue to do so while we have rules and regulations governed more by politics and judicial fiat than by sound public health principles. We're just lucky that the mortality rate is as low as it is. If this were SARS (and technically COVID-19 is SARS-2) with its 15% mortality rate, we'd have nearly two million dead at this point in the pandemic, and our social and health institutions might be close to a state of collapse. I hate to think what the numbers are going to look like at Christmas given the widespread flouting of these simple rules that continues to go on. I'm tired of hearing about people I know and love falling ill or losing loved ones.

Y'all know what to do: Wash your hands, wear your mask, social distance, stay out of crowded buildings if you don't have to be there.

MONDAY | NOVEMBER 30, 2020

A ND THE LONG HOLIDAY WEEKEND IS OVER.

All of the people who traveled against CDC advice have traveled again to get themselves back home, and the numbers continue to mount.

I canceled my personal travel plans when the numbers began to skyrocket in early November. I'm fairly savvy and could have made the trip to Seattle and back safely, but the odds for such things are tipping away and don't look good to me until numbers start decreasing again. And I don't think we're going to see that until Spring given that the weather will drive us all back indoors.

We're having an unseasonable cold snap in Alabama at the moment with a light dusting of snow here in Birmingham. This is not conducive to outdoor activity. I was going to take a walk earlier but the weather was really too ugly.

When judging risk, not just from COVID-19 but from all activities of life, I apply the car test. If, as an American, you get into a car with any regularity, your chance of dying in a car accident in any year is 0.02%. That's pretty low, so the risk-benefit calculation to most of us is pretty easy, and we all get into our cars without thinking about it.

Now let's compare that to the risk of death from COVID-19 which seems to be somewhere between 0.6% and 2% for all comers and is even higher for my gender and age group. In other words, about 100 times as dangerous as driving. That starts to give me pause. When evaluating risk, if it's less risky than driving (flying, being struck by lightning, being attacked by a shark at the beach, etc.), I never worry about it. If it's orders of magnitude more risky, I shy away.

Seattle will still be there in a few months and hopefully, when spring comes, risks will start descending as human activity again starts to move outdoors, and, with luck, we have a vaccine that should provide at least partial protection and an executive administration guided by science rather than by political whims.

The Moderna mRNA vaccine was presented to the FDA for an emergency use authorization, so we should hear about approvals for it and as well for Pfizer's similar vaccine in the next few weeks. There are still many questions about distribution to be answered. The last thing I saw was that the federal government was going to distribute it to the states based on population, and then let the states decide for themselves how to allocate it from there. While this fits in with the administration's passing the buck and every state for itself strategies, I don't think this is the wisest of ideas as it gives no flexibility to distribute vaccine based on hotspots or needs. The Dakotas, for instance, are in serious trouble, but with their relatively small population, vaccine just isn't going to get there.

The hot-off-the-presses news from today is that Scott Atlas MD, the Stanford radiologist with no epidemiological or virology experience who was appointed to be a senior adviser to the president's COVID-19 task force has resigned. Good! His blasé laissez-faire attitudes toward prevention have likely cost thousands of people their lives.

As I still have an active California medical license, I seriously thought about calling up the Medical Board of California and filing a complaint against him for endangerment. I am counting the days until January 20th when, with a little luck, decisions on the national level will once again be based on sound science and public health.

We're at 13.5 million cases in the US as we head into December. A month ago we were at 9 million. One third of all COVID-19 cases since the beginning of the pandemic have happened in the last month.

I have this week off. My Christmas preparations are pretty much complete, so I have to find something else to fill the time. The next big thing on my "To Do" list is to go through the bins of ephemera that came out of the house in the move. I'm a pack rat. I keep letters, theater programs, photographs, news clippings—anything that I think I might like to look at again. I used to be very good about scrapbooking it all, but that kind of fell by the wayside with Tommy as he, unlike Steve, had no interest in that kind of sentimentality. Now I have what feels like a few metric tons I have to go through and decide what to save and what to discard.

I've been putting this chore off for a while because it's going to cause me to go through a lot of memories of togetherness at a time when I'm isolated and alone. It would be easier to do with someone, so I could reminisce and tell the stories, but that's not possible at the moment. I'll probably dance around it for another day or two, and then just sit down and start. That's my usual modus operandi. If I find anything terribly interesting, I may scan it in and share it with y'all. Pictures of a time when I had a hair color.

Stay safe, stay well, and be careful out there.

DECEMBER 2020

Another Hundred People

THURSDAY | DECEMBER 3, 2020

DON'T FEEL BAD TODAY.

I've been a bit lazy the last couple of days. I've made starts on my next round of home projects, but I haven't put in the hours and hours they're going to need. Instead, I've spent time reading junk novels, doing a jigsaw puzzle with far too many monochrome pieces, assembling a holiday gift basket for my family in Seattle, and hauling it off to the UPS store for shipping.

However, the thing that still has me screaming inside is the incredible escalation of COVID-19 numbers over the last few weeks. This has been met with a collective shrug by our government. Our current societal story is dominated by the latest shenanigans of various Republican lawyers trying to overturn the presidential election without a shred of objective evidence, and the financial chicanery of the presidential fund raising apparatus, fleecing the flock with *The Grift of the MAGA*.

We are now at 14 million cases of COVID-19. There were nine million at Halloween, less than five weeks ago, which means we are adding 1 million cases a week. We now have over 100,000 people hospitalized nationally which is more or less the inflection point for national systemic strain—and that number is going up. Roughly 2800 people died yesterday alone. That's more than were killed at the World Trade Center on 9/11. In two days, we are losing more citizens than China, with its 1.3 billion people, has lost since the beginning of the pandemic. Their official total death toll since last December is fewer than 5,000.

I expect these numbers, which are horrific, are going to take a sharp increase over December as we have yet to see the impact of the

Thanksgiving holidays. Cases caught over the holiday weekend won't start showing up in hospitals for another two or three weeks—just in time for everyone to start gathering for Christmas, New Year's, and other year-end festivals.

The level of societal denial going on at the moment is breathtaking. I woke up this morning to news that one of our ritzier suburbs is planning on a huge holiday party and dance for the middle schoolers at a local country club. Just what in Heaven makes people think putting 500 tweens in a ballroom bouncing around to the latest hits is a good idea?

I understand parents wanting to provide some normal socialization, but these are not normal times. A recent study from India (which has a different culture, so I can't just generalize), involved hundreds of thousands of cases. Contact tracing showed that the major vector of spread was schools. Children are walking petri dishes for viral illness. They always have been. It's part of the necessary process of developing a healthy body. Put them together in enclosed space, and then have them mingle via their normal behaviors, and they're going to trade germs like crazy—and then carry them back home.

We've reached the point where COVID-19 is becoming a significant stress test on our societal systems. I view it sort of like when structural engineers test models in wind tunnels to determine what sorts of architecture can withstand a category 5 hurricane. We're putting societal infrastructure out there, which has been deliberately hollowed out by various decisions over the last 50 years, and subjecting it to a simultaneous 8-on-the-Richter scale earthquake, F-5 tornado, and wildfire storm. It's no wonder things aren't going so well.

The piece of society I am the most familiar with is the healthcare system. What was once the most advanced health culture, and the envy of the world in the decades following World War II, was changed from a system whose goal was improving American lives into an industry whose goal was improving American business bottom lines, executive compensation, and stock profits. It wasn't deliberate; no one person or thing orchestrated it, but starting in the mid-70s, the sector was taken over by business minds focused on the manufacture of health as measured in data points, and the system was stripped of excess capacity in order to make it lean and mean. Physicians and others skilled in healing lost control of the system to those with skills in accountancy, marketing, and data management.

This coincided with my career in medicine, having entered training in 1984. It has been both fascinating and nerve-wracking to watch this happen. With the stress of COVID-19 out of control, we don't have hospital capacity and we don't have staff capacity. Decisions are made based on financial risks to institutions. We continue to lose smaller and rural hospitals, especially in states which refused the Medicaid expansion for political reasons. (Many of these are the same states in which the infection is spreading like wildfire as the same political trends push the population to ignore sound public health advice).

My generation of physicians is getting pummeled and fed up and will likely begin retiring at a relatively young age. I don't see many of us working into our 80s in the way that an earlier generation did. And we aren't going to have a new generation to replace us as the system pushes graduates into specialties of high remuneration rather than societal need.

The hollowed out educational system is hurting, too. Teachers were having to make do with significant funding cuts as far back as the Reagan era and with salaries so low that many work second jobs to make ends meet. The move from having teachers teach to managing data metrics and preparing students for standardized tests, which came from the No Child Left Behind act, caused another huge issue.

Now teachers are being asked to work two full-time jobs. As in-person classroom teachers and as online teachers to students whose families have opted to keep their children out of the classroom due to COVID-19 risks. It can't be borne. The older generation will retire, and the younger generation will burn out. The lack of leadership from the current administration's Department of Education, run by someone whose sole qualification was donating huge amounts of money to right wing causes, is just icing on the cake.

What can I say about our government? On the federal level, the executive branch decided to politicize a worldwide pandemic into an Us vs. Them exercise, spending months feeding misinformation to the public about risk, public health measures, and basic scientific laws. When the pandemic blossomed out of control, which was inevitable in the face of this attitude, they simply ignored it, kicking responsibility to the states with the results that more conservative states, following federal example, chose to act as if nothing was happening, pouring even more gasoline on the fire.

State governments, with the exception of a few large wealthy states such as California and New York, do not have the resources to deal with global problems. This is the role of the federal government. Things may begin to change on January 20th, but that's still seven weeks away. In the meantime, at current trends, another 7 or 8 million people will get sick, and another 350,000 will die.

So keep up the good fight, wear your mask, wash your hands, social distance, and stay out of crowds.

WEDNESDAY | DECEMBER 9, 2020

I T'S 5 AM AND I'M NOT GOING TO BE ABLE TO GO BACK to sleep after sitting bolt upright at 4, so I might as well do some writing.

I was having one of those narrative dreams. I was watching a film (and was also somehow within its world at the same time). It was a generic rom-com about a 20-something couple who kept meeting cute and awkward, but who were destined for each other. Then, suddenly, there was a hostage situation, and a grenade blast, and one of them ended up dead and kept trying to reach through and correct life to what might have been. That's what woke me up. This overwhelming feeling of loss. I think that's me processing what's going on in the world in metaphorical terms.

At this point, Oliver, one of my two cats, heard me stirring and came over and curled up next to me demanding attention. This is odd.

Oliver has been part of the household since 2008. For the first 12 years, he despised any human contact. He would only appear at feeding time, and Heaven help you if you approached him. Since moving to the condo, he's a different cat. He wants affection and likes to be in the same room with me. He'll even share space with his sister, Anastasia, which he never used to do. He still vanishes if anyone else enters the condo, so he's not a completely changed feline. But clearly, there has been progress here in the area of socialization.

So where are we in terms of *The Accidental Plague Diaries*? The news isn't good. The results of Thanksgiving gatherings are beginning to make themselves known. UAB hospital is now running about 170 COVID-19 inpatients. Back in the spring, it was more in the 40-50 range, and it peaked out in the summer surge around 100 inpatients on the daily census. And these people are sick. You aren't being admitted these days unless you're in danger. Those without significant oxygenation problems or other complications are sent home to recover on their own.

We're at a bit over 15 million cases in the US which means we're adding nearly a million and a half cases a week. The daily death toll in the country is hovering between 2500 and 3000 which is between a Pearl Harbor and a 9/11 occurring on a daily basis. I expect in the next couple of weeks, with more holidays coming, it will surpass 3000 a day, and we're likely to see 100,000 deaths a month in January and February.

Each one of those people was someone who was alive and looking forward to the holiday season a year ago. They were parents, children, siblings, spouses, friends. They had no idea that 2019 was going to be their last chance to celebrate with those they loved. Most of them would still be living if we had a federal government capable of functioning and meeting challenges head on. Perhaps we will have that again, perhaps not. We'll find out shortly.

I've lost a number of patients. The story is usually the same. Younger family members who have not been as careful as they could have come to visit, bringing an unwanted house guest, and an elder pays the ultimate price. As a society, we tend to heave a collective sigh of "So what. They were old." But I can tell you from 30 years of experience in geriatrics that most of our elders have a lot to give and to teach us all about the human condition and who we are as people.

It wasn't so long ago that a well-respected senior physician from a surgical specialty was talking to me at a social event and said to me, "You're so bright. Why did you waste your career by choosing geriatrics?" I've had a lot of successful academic physicians say things like this to me over the years. Usually it's not quite so blunt and couched in more politically palatable terms, but the message is always unmistakably the same: Taking care of the elderly is for losers. I obviously don't think so, or I wouldn't have chosen the field.

Actually, I think it's more that the field chose me. Most who go into geriatrics do it based on some life experience with an elder, a grandparent or great grandparent. It didn't happen that way for me at all. Like most things in my life, there was a great deal of accident and serendipity.

I chose internal medicine as my specialty coming out of medical school because I didn't know what I wanted to be when I grew up. Internal medicine seemed to be the best way to delay that choice. I knew I wanted some sort of rigorous academic training. Having grown up in an academic family, I understood innately how that world works and felt comfortable with it.

Off I went to my residency in Sacramento at UC Davis with only a vague understanding of what I was getting myself into. I did my residency in the late 1980s, a much different world than today. It was before national legislation regarding work hours went into effect, and you were expected to work until your job was done, which was generally an 80-90 hour week. You were on call in the hospital every third or fourth night with no guarantee of sleep. Six months into my first year, the dreaded internship, I was sleep-deprived, lonely, miserable, and wondering if I'd made a huge mistake. (Pretty common feelings among all of us.) Then things started to get better: I met Steve. I came out and began to live a more authentic life. I finished the intern year and schedules got easier. I got the hang of how to do my job in residency and do it well.

Half way through my third year, my program director had her quarterly meeting with me. She looked at me and reminded me that there was no fourth year on the program, and I had better figure out what I wanted to do with myself. That pulled me up a bit short until she told me "Go home and figure out who you are, and then you will know what you should do."

So I went home and talked to Steve about things and realized that I enjoyed ambulatory care, liked talking to patients, believed more in health than in disease, and liked working collaboratively in teams. That made it obvious: I needed to receive my advanced training in academic general internal medicine. So off I went to talk to the head of that division who welcomed me and offered me a fellowship to train to become clinical faculty. On my way out the door, he mentioned the geriatrics fellowship they also offered, and which no one ever wanted.

There I was, seven years into medical training and I had never met a geriatrician, but I was quite capable of reading demographic charts, so I thought it might be a good idea to see what was happening in the area. It didn't take me long to figure out that this was a group of people who thought about medicine in the same way I did. So I signed up for geriatrics training, not out of a specific wish to treat the elderly, but out of a specific philosophy of how I could create and mold systems of care that would be good for all people, just using an elder population in which to do it.

I have always believed that what I do as a doctor is what is good for human beings in general. I just happen to do it for the elderly as the system will begrudgingly allow me to take the time necessary and utilize complementary resources such as nursing, therapies, and social work rather than insist on my getting a patient in and out the door every fifteen minutes.

The health system, in general, understands that geriatric care is important as most of their client base is aging and Medicare is often their largest payor source. However, it has a very tough time understanding the role of geriatrics.

Our system is built on specialization, a breaking down of a human being into organ systems or even further into basic biochemical and physiologic components. You achieve success in the system by becoming a subspecialist. You achieve great success in the academic world (even as a geriatrician) by becoming a leading expert in a very narrow area.

As the system hums along and creates new doctors, there is an implicit bias against general thinking in favor of specialty thinking. Bright candidates are steered toward narrow subspecialties, especially if they involve procedures (highly compensated) versus what are known as evaluation and management (E and M) services which involve thinking and listening and chart research to achieve a diagnosis. If I had a nickel for every time I've heard an attending physician tell a promising medical student a variation on "You're too good for primary care," I'd be a very rich man.

There's an interesting tangent as to why this attitude exists. Procedures are easy to quantify. You can describe them in exact terms. You can distinguish one from another. It's not too difficult to understand what level of expertise, what sorts of ancillary services, and what equipment are needed for each one.

E and M services, on the other hand, are vague. If I am seeing an older person with memory problems trying to distinguish dementia from normal aging change, I do no biopsies; I rely on my experience, intuition, interviewing skills, and simple paper and pencil tests. I will do some lab work and a brain MRI if I am concerned about an interfering undiagnosed medical condition. All of that can take me well over an hour.

We are reimbursed by Medicare (and most other types of insurance) by submitting bills coded through a system known as the CPT. There are thousands and thousands of codes for procedures, but only a handful for E and M services. These codes are proprietary (put out by the AMA), and the committees that create the coding systems consist almost entirely of subspecialists eager to show their worth, but who have grave difficulty with the expansive tendencies of someone like me who thinks backward from their honing down process. Consequently, those of us in cognitive specialties tend to be paid at lower rates.

This has, over the decades, led to a crisis in geriatric care. The number of board certified geriatricians in the country topped out at 9,000 in the 1990s. Most of these took the test without formal training through a grandfathering process. Many of those chose not to recertify or were older and have since retired, so the number of geriatricians currently is closer to 6,000. (It has been estimated that we need about 30,000 to care for aging Baby Boomers, who start turning 75 next month). There used to be about 800 training slots for geriatrics in the country. Due to lack of interest from medical students and residents, many of them have closed. There are now about 400. Only 200 individuals applied for the training programs this past year. UAB, a major university with an excellent training program and track record, has now been unable to attract any trainees in geriatrics for three years running. Those who come up through our medical programs, like most young people, head for brighter lights and bigger cities.

There's been a surge in applications to medical school this last year (up 18%) which some have dubbed the Fauci effect. I think that's wonderful, but those applying this year will not graduate medical school until 2025 and residency until 2028. So even if some of them choose geriatrics, (and I expect we're going to see a huge surge of infectious disease specialists before that), they're not going to be ready until about 2030, the year the very last Boomers pass 65 with the leading edge bumping up against 85—less functional and with chronic disease burden, but not yet into their die-off—in other words, peak age.

Every demographer has been pointing out this phenomenon since the 1970s, but no one has been listening. My planned retirement date is somewhat before this. It's going to be someone else's problem.

The cynical piece of me can't help but wonder if there's someone sitting in the offices of the Center for Medicare and Medicaid Services running spreadsheets of data and calculating what percentage of the Boom needs to die of COVID-19 over the next few years to reduce tax dollars flowing to the healthcare sector over the 2020s and 2030s. I hate to think of it, but I put nothing past the current administration.

Don't be a statistic they can use: Wash your hands, wear your mask, social distance. You know the drill.

SUNDAY | DECEMBER 13, 2020

THE FIRST TRUCKS LOADED WITH COVID-19 vaccine have left the Pfizer plant in Portage, MI and are careening down the nation's interstates bound for an overly stressed healthcare system. With the FDA having granted an Emergency Use Authorization, the first shots will be administered tomorrow, predominantly to healthcare workers on the front lines caring for victims of the pandemic.

It's rather astounding that we have come so far, so fast. The disease was unknown a year ago, was not established in the US until about ten months ago, and only entered most Americans' awareness about nine months ago. Generally, it takes a decade or more of meticulous research to create something like this vaccine, and it was done in less than a year. It shows what human beings can do when they band their collective ingenuity together to solve problems in a crisis. Now if we would just put our minds together and start working on some of the other issues that are tearing our world apart.

There are more than a few myths surrounding the vaccine and what its impact will be on the continued battle against COVID-19.

First, it is not a panacea. The pandemic isn't going to be over, and everything isn't going to return to the way it was next week. Even if a significant portion of the population is inoculated, the virus is entrenched enough to continue spreading, and the basic mitigation measures of masks, hand washing, social distancing, and avoiding of crowds in enclosed spaces are going to be necessary for a while longer. How long is "a while?" I suspect that the earliest that these sorts of things will be able to be relaxed is this coming summer.

Second, despite propaganda coming out of the current administration, the vaccine has nothing to do with them or their actions. It was developed by a small German company BioNTech, founded by Turkish immigrants to that country. Its purpose is to look at the promising new fields of genetic engineering using mRNA. Pfizer came on board for upscaling of manufacture and distribution. Neither company took federal money nor was part of the administration's much touted Operation Warp Speed.

Third, it's not going to be universally available to the general public for quite some time, so don't harass your pharmacist down at the CVS. The vaccine is under federal control and is being allocated to states based on various criteria such as population, the availability of facilities to safely ship and store the vaccine (which must be kept at super-cold temperatures), and disease spread. Alabama is receiving something like 40,000 doses for a population of nearly five million.

There is trepidation in certain quarters about the new mRNA technology used in the vaccine. This is a way of introducing small bits of mRNA into human cells that enables the cells' own protein manufacturing abilities to create antigens to which the immune system then builds antibodies. It's a nifty idea, works fine on paper, and the studies submitted show good efficacy and minimal side effects.

But there are questions: Could this cause the immune systems of certain individuals to react too robustly and make people sicker than the disease would? Did the studies include enough elders with chronic health conditions to know what the vaccine will do when introduced widely to that population? Will issues with transport and storage allow for equitable distribution?

I can't answer any of these questions at this time, but will continue to monitor news and science sources for additional information as it becomes available. Those I know personally with great experience in infectious disease are saying unanimously "take the vaccine," so I'll do so when it becomes available to me. It's likely to be a condition of my continued employment.

My handy dandy coronavirus counter shows that we're up over 16 million cases in the US. It only took four days to add the most recent million. National deaths are at nearly 300,000 and are over 3,000 daily. Here in Alabama, we're at over 4,000 deaths and 300,000 cases. Every hospital in the greater Birmingham area is full. My colleagues are exhausted. I received at least one notice daily last week about a long-term patient of mine being admitted with a serious case. I expect most of them to die. My social media news feed is full of notices of friends asking for thoughts and prayers for their parents, siblings, neighbors, and other connections who have fallen ill.

We're just over two weeks out from Thanksgiving, the peak for cases fueled by travel and gathering. The peak for hospitalization hasn't hit yet. The peak for dying will come sometime thereafter. You can gather for Christmas, and continue to contribute to these numbers, or you can come up with some clever alternatives. The life you save may be your own. At my house, it's going to be Zoom Christmas with the family, and just me and the cats present in person.

It's not all doom and gloom at my house. I've had several productive conversations with a book editor about turning these *Accidental Plague Diaries* into book form and am diving into that project. My Christmas present to myself, a Peloton, has arrived, and I am getting in my daily cardio (my primary care physician is thrilled). I made myself several gallons of mulled cider using Tommy's recipe that I was actually able to recall from memory, and it turned out OK. For my next trick, I'm going to try eggnog using that fifth of Southern Comfort that's been taking up space at the back of my liquor cabinet for the last decade. After a dry spell for the last few months, I'm feeling creative again, and that usually means something interesting should burst forth. I don't know what it is yet, but with luck it'll help with the trying time we all find ourselves in.

Be safe. You know what to do.

THURSDAY | DECEMBER 17, 2020

I T'S THREE WEEKS AFTER THANKSGIVING, and the COVID cases keep surging. I sit here in a state of righteous anger.

I'm sure there's some perfect Yiddish word for it. All the best words for the peaks and valleys of human emotion seem to be Yiddish. (Perhaps one of my Jewish friends can help me out.)

Many times when I've sat down to write these pieces, I've been sad. Sometimes I've been bemused. Tonight, I'm just pissed. It comes from a number of places, but mainly out of the sorts of reporting that I have been seeing over the last 48 hours. The news isn't all bad. The first people are getting the Pfizer mRNA vaccine, primarily my healthcare brothers and sisters on the front lines in emergency rooms, COVID wards, and intensive care units. But even that process is causing a certain amount of anger to boil up.

The initial batch of Pfizer vaccine shipped over this past weekend and was more or less set to go early this week. The storage requirements of super-cold freezers able to maintain -70 degrees Celsius have limited where it can go and how it can be distributed.

For instance, the doses UAB received, as it's the only local hospital with the proper freezers, need to go to people at every hospital system in the region, and the logistics of getting them here to get vaccinated are proving complicated, requiring tremendous planning and triaging regarding which healthcare workers need to be vaccinated first. This is leading to some sniping among colleagues which is unhelpful and uncalled for.

There would be more vaccine to go around but for the ineffectiveness of our current federal government. Pfizer has new shipments ready to go but, in a press release today, they stated they cannot ship as the federal government has yet to contact them to tell them where to send things. This is just the first of many things causing me to blow a gasket or two.

It struck me as insane, during a pandemic with the first potentially helpful tool for fighting it available, that the federal government would somehow drop the ball and not think beyond the first shipment. But then, the cynical part of my brain realized that today was also the day that the Moderna mRNA vaccine was considered by the FDA for emergency approval. It passed committee and, if the process goes like it did last week, will be granted Emergency Authorization for Use tomorrow, will ship over the weekend, and be available next week. That would put two very similar competing products in play.

However, the Pfizer product was not part of the administration's Operation Warp Speed funding and was developed in Germany. Moderna, as an American company, has many well-connected individuals on its board and among its major shareholders who stand to benefit greatly if it gets a greater market share. I can't help but wonder if the ineffectual distribution of the Pfizer vaccine is a deliberate move to help that happen. After it was revealed that Senators Perdue and

Loeffler (both trying to retain their seats in the Georgia runoffs), used their knowledge to divest travel-related stocks and buy stock in companies specializing in body bags, I put nothing past the ruling class and their monetizing of catastrophe.

Of course, the thing that I am most livid about also concerns money. The communications from this past summer between the White House and the CDC that have been passed along to the press show that when science conflicted with a message of "We need to open for business," the messaging always trumped the science.

Much that we needed to know was suppressed. There was a deliberate attempt by the highest levels of the executive branch to institute a policy to infect the entire country for "herd immunity." There were fundamental misunderstandings of just what herd immunity is and how it actually works, but the impression that bursts forth from all of this is a callous disregard for anyone other than the small circles that operate inside the Beltway, and they weren't worried about themselves as, should they happen to fall ill, they would have treatment and support available to them not available to most of the country, so their chances of death or disability would be negligible.

The fact that mainly older people were dying was seen as a good thing financially as there are big savings to social programs if you kill off senior citizens.

The current elder generation becomes eligible for Social Security and Medicare at age 65. Current life expectancy in the US is roughly 79 years, so 14 years total benefit. The average Social Security monthly benefit is $1,400.66 per person, and the average annual Medicare spending per beneficiary is $10,229. That comes out to $27,037 a year in federal spending per person on just those two programs, or $378,517 per person over an average life span.

Roughly 60% of fatal COVID cases in the United States are in the over 65 group. To date, there have been 310,434 deaths. So, the

186,260 deaths of retirees, at $27,037 savings annually, is so far saving $5.036 billion dollars a year in future benefits, and somewhere in the neighborhood of $30-40 billion overall.

We're adding 300,000 cases and 3,500 deaths on a daily basis (an additional savings of $57 million annually in benefits a day). We haven't even begun to crest the peak, so these numbers are going to swell. Don't think for a minute that every Republican Senator and party consultant hasn't jotted similar figures on the back of an envelope somewhere.

Generally, when a government asks a people to sacrifice, particularly themselves (such as during war time), there needs to be a thorough airing of the issues at hand, and the government needs to get the spirit of the governed behind the policy, so that they will be willing to endure the personal pain of what must be endured for the greater good. That's not what we've had here.

What we've had is a deliberate campaign of lies, disinformation, suppression of fact, and general bullcrap which has succeeded in splitting the country into two factions: one trying to do the right thing by fellow citizens, one living in a state of denial. Neither side has been given good information by their government, so they can come together to make informed choices.

SUNDAY | DECEMBER 20, 2020

HERE WE ARE AT THE LEAD-UP TO CHRISTMAS WEEK. The fourth Advent candle, symbolizing Love, has been lit, people should be getting their homes and families ready for sacred traditions, and instead, due to abject failures of national leadership, we're facing more prolonged estrangement, surging cases of COVID overwhelming hospitals and medical staffs, and a brand new social battle about to break out over distribution of vaccine.

We finally have a bright spot in these ongoing tales of the United States in the age of the coronavirus with the arrival of vaccines developed in record time, but, due to the same governmental trends that have botched every other response to the pandemic to date, we're likely to see additional problems before we see solutions.

The Pfizer vaccine has now been out for a week. The Moderna vaccine which received its Emergency Use Authorization this past Friday, is shipping over the weekend, and will be available starting this next week. Meanwhile, hundreds of thousands of doses have shipped so far. But there are hundreds of millions of people in this country, and almost all of them, from a biological perspective, are eligible for vaccination. This leads to a situation of scarce resources and high demand.

There has been no question in anyone's mind that the highest priority for vaccination has to be healthcare workers who work in direct patient care, especially with those who have COVID-19. Too many of them have already become sick. Roughly 2,000 of them have died from occupational exposure to date.

The Pfizer vaccine, with its need for super-cold temperatures, has been distributed through a limited network of hospitals, and the shots are being given as rapidly as they can be administered safely. A second shot is required in three weeks, and part of the distribution plans must include availability of that second dose.

There have been issues with distribution from the get-go. The super-cold temperatures caused logistical nightmares. Doses have remained at Pfizer's plant due to a lack of instruction from federal authorities as to where they should go. There has been speculation that some of the delays are political in nature and have occurred to give Moderna's product a chance to get to the market.

There is an advantage to the Moderna vaccine. It does not require super-cold temperatures and can be kept in a regular freezer. One way or another though, my social media feed of the last week has been full of pictures of happy doctors and nurses receiving their first dose at work before going off to continue the battle. I received mine as well.

I feel a little guilty about having gotten mine in this first wave. I don't do inpatient work on COVID-19 wards. I am exposed occasionally in my outpatient clinic work, but we're pretty good about identifying potentially positive people and handling them by phone and other means, so they won't come into the office and infect other patients and staff.

I got my shot through the VA system as they want me protected, so that I can get back out in the field safely with my rural house calls. I can't help but think, however, that I could continue to do that work telephonically, and that the dose I received should go to someone with more exposure than I.

I hope that the VA is making sure that they are equitably distributing it not just to the doctors and nurses, but to everyone that comes face-to-face with patients—therapists, techs, custodial, dietary. From what I could see of who was waiting for vaccines when I got mine on Friday, they are.

I carry a certain weight of survivor's guilt from not having succumbed to the previous global pandemic of HIV. Having been a young gay man in the SF Bay area of the early 80s, I don't want to carry around an additive burden.

The problem comes once the healthcare community has been taken care of. What then? Various factions, all with perfectly valid claims, have been coming forward demanding their place at the head of the line: the elderly, who are most susceptible to serious disease and death; workers in frontline non-healthcare jobs such as food distribution, transportation, and essential retail; teachers with their exposures to the little disease vectors we call children; representatives of communities of color who want to redress historic inequities.

Over the next couple of months, until supplies grow to meet demand, it's going to get ugly as each group and its advocates jockey for position. I do not foresee a nice orderly women-and-children first loading of the lifeboats. There's one group, of course, that will line jump with impunity and quietly have their needs met: the wealthy and well-connected.

As much as I have amused myself imagining a line of well-heeled Beverly Hills matrons lined up outside of Cedars Sinai, wobbling in their Jimmy Choos and bashing each over their heads with their Jane Birkin bags to be first in the door, we all know that certain lots of vaccine will simply disappear from the supply to reappear in concierge practices and other exclusive care venues not available to the general public. A telling example happened at my alma mater when their health system decided to give their first shipment of vaccine to their senior executives rather than to the staff actually taking care of COVID-19 patients, leading to some very noisy, and well deserved protests, and some PR headaches that will take a while to disappear.

The conservative noise machine now has a problem. On the one hand, they have spent most of the past year minimizing the dangers of COVID-19 and ramping up resistance to basic public health measures that cause little inconvenience. For this reason, we now lead the world in active cases by a long shot, and our curve shows no signs of trending downwards.

On the other hand, those who are behind the propaganda are not stupid and recognize that it's their constituency that is most threatened by rampant spread. They are certainly going to protect themselves but have to figure out how to do it without being called out as flagrant hypocrites by both sides. It makes me angry when I see someone like Marco Rubio, 49 years of age and, to my knowledge, in good health, who has spent the last year supporting the balder-dash coming out of the White House and the even worse behavior of Florida's governor, getting a dose that should go to someone who is in harm's way.

I suppose I should say a few things about the latest out of London where there is a new mutation in COVID-19. Viruses of this type mutate all the time and mutate quickly. The new mutant strain is more infectious than the usual strain and passes more easily from person-to-person, increasing the **R1**, the number of new people each case can infect. It does not cause more virulent disease. It will not cause the vaccine to be ineffective.

Authorities in the UK and EU are trying to lock down the areas where it is spreading to keep this strain contained because, if it becomes more widespread, the number of active cases, and therefore the number of seriously ill, will increase rapidly and overwhelm what the healthcare system can handle. We may be seeing things like this for a while. Don't panic. And carry a towel.

Today is December 20th. It would be my parents' 64th wedding anniversary, and it is the first time in nearly two thirds of a century that my father does not have my mother in this world to help center and complete him, so my thoughts are with him today.

I wonder, sometimes, what my mother might have made of this pandemic? She would have taken it in stride, I'm certain. As a child of the Depression and World War II, and the daughter of two physicians, she would have worn her mask, kept her distance, washed her hands, and come up with plenty of ways to pass the time spending the holidays at home.

Be like Alison.

WEDNESDAY | DECEMBER 23, 2020

I T'S 3:30 AM.

I woke up suddenly at 2:00 AM after crashing around 9:30, so it's going to be one of those first sleep/second sleep nights, or I'm going to have a lot of empty hours before I have to get up and make my way to work in the morning. Fortunately, it's my last work day before the holiday, so I have a long weekend to get my sleep cycle recalibrated.

For the most part, I sleep well, but about every two weeks or so, I have a night or two where all bets are off. I don't worry about it a lot. It's part of being an aging adult. So many of my younger (think 70s) patients are convinced that idiosyncratic sleep patterns are pathologic. They get put on sleeping pills or anxiolytics, not understanding what havoc those are going to cause as they head towards their 80s. I avoid them.

I was having complicated REM-state dreams involving my mother, a journey on foot through the woods which took us and a few friends through houses I have owned and houses of strangers, a couple of quick costume changes, and stairs, lots of stairs. I have no idea what it all means, but as it made me wake up in the middle of the night, I assume I'm processing anxieties. It's not like there's nothing to be anxious about these days between public health issues, politics, and the general state of Western Civilization.

Newly diagnosed cases are running somewhere between 200,000 and 250,000 per day, and we're adding a million new cases every five days or so. The mortality rate at three weeks after diagnosis is holding steady around .16% so 16 of every thousand people diagnosed today will not be here on inauguration day.

The bloodiest day ever for the United States in terms of battle deaths was at the Battle of Antietam on September 17, 1862 with 3,600 deaths. Every day we have more than 225,000 diagnoses, we are ensuring a greater number of lives lost to COVID-19 than casualties from that battle over the following 21 days. 331,000 so far, and the numbers are continuing to accelerate upwards.

On the vaccine front, I am fielding a dozen calls a day from patients and families wanting to know when vaccines will be available to older individuals or those with chronic illness. To all of them, I have the same answer: "I don't know." There has, of yet, been little in the way of guidance from either federal or local levels as to how the vaccine will be allocated or distributed outside of the acute care health system. I will let everyone know when I know.

My social media feed, filled with doctors and nurses, has had two kinds of posts over the last week. Posts of relief and joy from those who have received the vaccine, and posts of angst and frustration from those who are routinely exposed in their work but who have not yet been vaccinated or informed by their health systems when or how they will be. There's not been much in the way of transparency in the system. It's easy to understand the righteous anger at young and healthy political figures who are getting vaccinated before front-line health workers, especially those who have been downplaying the pandemic for political reasons for months and months.

The abject moral and social failure of the highest levels of the federal government is becoming clearer and clearer during this time of transition as more and more energy and media coverage are spent on quixotic attempts to undo an election that was well-conducted under trying circumstances. This, coupled by the cynical playing with peoples' economic livelihoods for partisan advantage, is nauseating.

I understand the game. One side of the aisle is trying to spike the ability of the other side to govern effectively, so they can blame them for failures and take back power later. The ultimate end game appears to be undoing the entire 20th century and, the way things are going both here and in the United Kingdom, most of the 19th as well: consolidating social, economic, and political power back in the hands of a small aristocracy with one set of rules keeping control of the rest through an iron fist of another set of rules.

Of course, there aren't enough of the aristocracy to make this happen without a set of enforcers, mainly the professional classes—those with enough money and assets to think they belong in the club, but who are still dependent on salaries and other earnings for economic survival. They will do the bidding of those on top to protect themselves and their interests. Corporate America's destruction of the pension system with a replacement consisting of IRAs and 401Ks dependent on the success of the stock market ensured that.

This is my peer group, but I saw through this charade years ago and recognized that I still work for money, rather than having my money work for me, and that means that my true economic and political interests are with those lower on the ladder than myself rather than those higher up.

I worry about what may happen to the healthcare system over the next several months. Those of us who provide care will get our vaccines eventually, so our chances of falling seriously ill and missing work will diminish. However, there are only so many of us to go round. Smaller regional hospitals have ICUs running at 150% capacity now. What's it going to be like in a few more weeks? Alabama is a relatively low population state with a well-trained workforce. We've got some capacity, but I see the numbers coming in from Southern California and the Upper Midwest, and I can't even imagine how they're going to begin to deal with things. This may change somewhat after January 20th, but that's still four weeks away, and if 2020 has taught us anything, it's that a lot can happen in a month.

What happens when a new administration can't get federal agencies to be more responsive due to deep damage caused by the current administration? If we go a year or two into a Democratic administration with the same levels of dysfunction and lack of response to the needs of the citizenry that we've had over the last few years, the trust of the people in federalism will likely be irretrievably broken. What then? Devolution of power to states and localities? Civil War? Revolution? We'd love to think that it can't happen here, but I bet the people of Sarajevo, when they put on the '84 Winter Olympics, never dreamed of what would come to them in a decade.

Now it's 4:30 AM and I'm no closer to sleep than I was. Going to get up and have something to eat, disturb the cats, and watch some bad television. It may be the holiday season but that doesn't mean you don't need to wash your hands, wear your mask, social distance, and avoid indoor crowds.

SUNDAY | DECEMBER 27, 2020

THE US COVID-19 CASE COUNTER just passed 19 million. It passed 18 million last Tuesday, was at 17 million on the 17th of this month, 13 million at the end of November, and 9 million at Halloween. That's 10 million cases, and more than 50% of the total, in less than two months, and the numbers show no signs of slowing down. Dr. Fauci, whom I tend to trust on the subject of pandemic disease, was opining early today that things are likely to get worse and worse through the rest of the winter.

So how about the mortality rate? We're at 332,000 deaths. The population of the US in 2019 was estimated at 328,000,000, so we're now over 1/1000th of the citizenry dead in less than a year. I have my personal feelings about a federal government that's presided over the death of a significant portion of its people with what seems, currently, to be a collective yawn, but I'll let you draw your own conclusions.

Maybe I'm using the wrong words here, because the federal government seems to have not presided over much of anything when it comes to either the COVID-19 pandemic or the necessary responses to it, devolving responsibility down to states and regions and, at times, pitting them against each other for political advantage. The end result is a disease that's totally out of control due to a lack of unified vision and messaging to the American people.

Many of my friends are counting down the 24 days left until there's a change of administration, but I'm not holding out a lot of hope for major changes in policy to make themselves felt at ground level much before late spring or summer. We've got a few hurdles to make it over before the inauguration—the special Senate election in Georgia on January 5th and the congressional certification of the electoral college vote on January 6th come to mind. Anything could happen with either one of those given the complete abandonment of public service for private gain and short term political advantage by various clowns in Washington, D.C.

Whether the Christmas and New Year's holidays will have similar spreading effects to Thanksgiving remain to be seen. The travel statistics from airports and the like suggest it's going to be about as bad. The publicity around the fall surge may have caused people to take additional precautions which may mitigate caseload later on, or maybe not.

My Christmas was a quiet day with the cats. I didn't mind it. In looking through my social media feed at pictures of friends gathered by the tree in their immediate family groups, I was struck by the thought that this might be just what American Christmas has needed for a while. The amount of weight that has been put on this one holiday in our country over the last two centuries is more than it can bear. Maybe it's time to start stripping some of it away.

What is American Christmas? It's the Nordic/Germanic Jul (the original Norse spelling of "Yule") Solstice celebration with greenery and lights and feasting. It's the Roman winter solstice celebration of December 25th to which the Christian nativity story was tied. It's the adaptation of the Dutch feast of St. Nicholas that came to New Amsterdam, later New York, and morphed into Santa Claus. It's the Second Great Awakening's reaction against rollicking festivities with its images of still and silent nights of snow. It's the commercialization of the American mercantile world of the 19th and 20th centuries realizing it could be turned into a consumer free-for-all. No wonder we all go into it with expectations so high and a vague feeling of disappointment when it's over.

Tommy and I used to refer to the Christmas season as our annual marathon: decorate house (check), rehearse and sing *The Messiah* with the symphony (check), prepare wigs and makeup for Red Mountain's *Christmas Spectacular* (check), produce and direct the annual children's Holiday pageant for the church (check), prepare dinner and gifts for family (check), host holiday open house for several hundred (check). It's no wonder we rarely went out on New Year's Eve; we were usually asleep by ten.

I miss the results of those days and nights, but not the onslaught and the endless lists and the staying up to all hours. But we did have good times together, whether it was making costumes for the kids, assembly line baking hundreds of Christmas cookies, or making enough chili for a small army. I made Tommy's cider and eggnog this year. I have his chili recipe somewhere but, as it makes somewhere between eight and ten gallons, I won't break it out until I can figure out a way to reduce it somewhat.

The vaccine continues its march across the land with roughly a million Americans, mainly healthcare workers and long-term care residents, having received either the Pfizer or Moderna vaccine to date. I think there's this fallacious idea running around that once we get vaccinated, the pandemic will be over. That's not true.

It's going to take a long time to distribute vaccine to over 300 million. There are huge inequities in the system which will make it difficult for some populations to access it, even if the supplies are plentiful, and there's politicization of the vaccine, although that seems to be waning somewhat as people are getting vaccinated without major ill effects. Be prepared to wear your masks until summer.

I read a great analogy earlier this week as to why we should care about the disease and its death toll. The author compared COVID-19 to a catastrophic weather event. If a hurricane was bearing down on Houston or Miami, would we not board things up and evacuate? It's only going to kill one out of every thousand people, so let's just go about our lives as if everything's normal. It's a great way of seeing how idiotic the laissez-faire arguments that emerge from some quarters actually are.

One one-thousandth is where we are today, and the curve is still trending up. We could easily be at 2/1,000ths or 3/1,000ths by next summer. There are only three mass casualty events in American history greater at this point: World War II at 418,500, The Civil War at 618,200 and the 1918 Flu Epidemic at 675,000. We'll have no problems passing World War II in another month or so, and I won't be surprised if we have a new record by summer.

WEDENESDAY | DECEMBER 30, 2020

W E'RE GOING UP IN PROVERBIAL FLAMES, and I feel like I have a cracked and ancient squirt gun with which to beat them back.

I try to be circumspect in what I say about work, but sometimes the word does have to get out. Six months ago, at the summer peak, UAB hospital had about 100 inpatients with a COVID-19 diagnosis. Then, as the pandemic came under control, this dropped to about 65 inpatients at a time. With the current surge, fueled by Thanksgiving travel and spread from domestic contacts, UAB has much larger numbers, with even higher numbers expected throughout the next few months.

We're a strong and resilient institution with some of the best facilities and personnel on the planet, but there's only so much we can do. Nursing school faculty and students have been pressed into service. I'm on the volunteer list to be called in despite the fact that I haven't practiced inpatient medicine since the last millennium. However, it's my duty and my call as a physician to be part of the team if they need me.

For most of my time during the pandemic, I've been able to help buck up my patients through lockdowns and quarantines, and I was relieved that relatively few of them became ill. I had a few here and there who did. Some were miserable and recovered. Some were barely affected. A few were hospitalized. Two or three died. This past few weeks, it has been different.

I've been fielding calls about diagnoses in my long-term patients three or four times a day. I lost four over the holiday weekend. I know of about ten scattered around various regional hospitals. There's not

317

much of anything I can do for them other than wait. I'm not much for prayer in general, but I think a great deal about them and their families and what they are going through. My patients have mainly been at home. They're pretty compliant with masks and other basic safety measures. Almost all of them have gotten ill at home because of a younger family member coming into the house who hadn't been as vigilant.

In the state of Alabama, there were slightly over 5,000 new cases of COVID-19 diagnosed today per the Department of Public Health. This was out of just over 7,000 tests administered, a positivity rate of 71%. This means that pretty much only symptomatic people were being tested, and we have not been able to even begin testing asymptomatic carriers to tell where the disease is spreading.

Today may be an aberration, but the rolling average for the last week is 41% which is still horrific. In order for a pandemic to be controlled, the positivity rate needs to be routinely and reliably under 5%. When it's over 10%, most public health authorities say it's time to take drastic measures.

I haven't heard a peep out of the governor or the Alabama Department of Public Health recently, and I doubt most of the rest of the public has either. With this kind of spread, the numbers of acutely ill are going to keep increasing to the point where the healthcare system simply can't handle it, but "flattening the curve" is so April. We've moved on.

But wait, we have a weapon, a vaccine!

Alabama has been allocated 128,000 doses in its initial shipments. There are 300,000 Alabamians in the highest priority group (healthcare workers and long-term care facility residents). More vaccine is promised, but we've still got a major distribution problem. As of today, only 20,354 vaccines have been administered since the first Pfizer vaccines became available on December 14th. That's only about

1,200 vaccines a day. At that rate, we'll have the first priority group done around Labor Day.

From what I can tell, vaccines are getting to the state from manufacturing plants but, as the federal government has basically abandoned its role in further distribution to the state level, which has neither the expertise nor the systems to take on so mammoth a project, things are slow to roll out. The holidays, of course, aren't helping.

There are those who say it can't be done any faster. To them, I point to the fact that in 1947, New York City was able to vaccinate all 5 million of its residents for smallpox in two weeks. It can be done, but without effective leadership, it's like recruiting a thousand volunteers to your search and rescue operation, and then not supplying them with maps and telling them to look where they feel like looking.

The new variant that was first discovered in England has seeded in this country with case reports from both California and Colorado. Fortunately, it doesn't appear to cause any worse clinical disease and is as susceptible to the vaccine as prior strains, but it is more transmissible. The most recent figures from England suggest that it is 56% more transmissible than the usual. This doesn't seem like much. For instance, measles is about 1200% more transmissible than COVID, but our brains, which are wired for linear math, don't really get what exponential numbers do until we're overwhelmed by them.

Let us say I have a population of 100 people with COVID and, for sake of argument and easy math, the disease has a transmissibility of 1.0 (its R0 figure) meaning each person can transmit the disease to one other person. Let us say then that they are no longer infectious, so our original cohort of 100 infects 100 more, who then infect 100 more, and so on. At the end of ten cycles of this, there will be ten infected cohorts or a total of 1,000 infected people. If we up the R0 to 1.56, which is the difference between the two strains, our initial cohort infects not 100 people, but 156 people. These 156 then infect

1.56 times as many or 243. After ten cycles of this, you don't end up with 1,000 infected people, you end up with 15,000 infected people. This new strain is not good news and, as we have decided to abandon most mitigation strategies for the holidays, watch out. And wash your hands.

JANUARY 2021

I'm Still Here

SUNDAY | JANUARY 3, 2021

THE US CELEBRATED NEW YEAR'S DAY by surpassing 20 million documented COVID-19 infections.

We hit 10 million cases this past November 9th. It took us only 52 days, less than 8 weeks, to double the case load. And it doesn't look like things are going to slow down anytime soon. We have yet to see the full surge in cases related to Christmas. Those won't peak for another week or so. I wrote a good deal about numbers in the last one of these posts so we're going to skip those in today's entry. They were mind-numbingly bad then and remain that way now.

The most interesting trend to watch over the next few weeks (other than the circus in Washington, D.C.) is going to be how vaccine rollouts proceed with the holidays out of the way and a significant number of first responders and healthcare workers having received their shots. The federal government, with the current administration's laissez-faire attitude toward matters of public health, has devolved responsibilities to states without much guidance, and the states are doing about as well as you might expect—from lines of octogenarians camped out overnight in Florida to officials sneaking their friends and family into vaccination sites in Tennessee.

Alabama is doing a decent job from what I can tell. The only thing I can fault them on is not communicating clearly with the public as to when vaccines will be available for community dwelling people at risk. But I'm pretty sure that's because they don't know themselves about how many vaccines will be available on what schedule, and they want to be sure that whatever system they put in place is going to work as advertised and not fail under the weight of poor planning.

There's been a minor skirmish in the gay community over gay healthcare providers who received their vaccinations and then immediately took off to Puerto Vallarta for a circuit party full of bronzed bodies dancing on the beach. Lots of unmasked/lack-of-social-distancing selfies have been popping up on social media. It reached a height of surreal when, on New Year's Eve, a party boat full of men capsized off the coast leading to the need for a water rescue. No one was physically hurt from what I can tell (although some puffed up egos were likely badly bruised). Nor were there any reports of whether or not the guys on shore sang *There's Got To Be A Morning After* in four-part harmony while this was taking place.

The basic issues seem to be two: first, a flaunting of privilege and second, the possibility of adding to caseloads in a poorer community and country whose healthcare system is straining under the number of cases already present. While I absolutely understand the need for gay professionals working in the relatively homophobic environment of medicine to go let off steam with the tribe, (and I have done so myself), the timing of this event appears to be, how shall I put it, poor.

It would never have occurred to me to try and book such a trip at this moment. I've been leery of even heading for Gulf Shores or Pensacola currently due to the wild spread of COVID-19 in the area. I'm not sure that I would go for the next month or two, even though I will be fully vaccinated.

I miss traveling, I really do. I miss long trips to new places or even weekends in New Orleans or Savannah or at the beach, but I'm doing my best to be part of the solution and to set a good example. Full disclosure: I have put down a deposit for a trip to Europe next fall as I am very hopeful that with a new administration and new approaches to public health policy, we're going to be in a much better position by summer. I am, however, setting it up in such a way that I can walk away from it up to the day before if things are not going well with COVID-19 and making the trip would be irresponsible on my part.

Many people tell me that these essays are helping them understand COVID-19, our healthcare system's response, and what's going on in society. I'm glad to be of service and pleased that these writings, which I took on to help me understand all of this, have found an audience. Of course, this does make me a bit of a role model, and that's always a hard position to be in. I get it at work all the time. New patients and their families come in saying things like "We've heard so many good things about you!" and that leaves me with the sinking feeling that I have to live up to a reputation I may or may not deserve.

I've always been of the philosophy of do the best you can, one patient at a time, and let the chips fall where they may. Because so many of my patients have been either ignored or over-treated by the healthcare system, I can usually make them feel better simply by listening and helping them unlock their own inner powers of wellness. There are days when I walk into work and I'm tired and cranky and would rather be anywhere else, but I put on my physician role and after fifteen minutes or so, I'm Dr. D again and ready to heal what little I can.

This is what makes COVID-19 so difficult for me. There's very little I can do other than watch and wait and treat some symptoms. Viral illness is like that. I have been trying to push a little harder on good health habits as it appears that those with well-balanced health, even of advanced age, are far less likely to develop complicated and serious disease. So I encourage more exercise and a well-balanced diet and talk about supplements where there is some evidence that there might be benefit. I also help get people off excess medication which might harm them in the long run, and I go over the basic mantras of avoiding viral disease like hand hygiene, masking, and social distancing.

I've watched both my husbands die of disease processes I could do nothing about, despite all of my training and intellect. I do my best to keep myself from having to be in a similar position with my patients. I know how to have those "There's nothing more that I or the healthcare system can do," conversations with patients and families, but it never gets any easier. At least with Steve and with Tommy, I was able to sit by their bedsides and hold hands. I can't imagine the pain of having to say goodbye via a borrowed iPad and FaceTime.

So please, all of you, be role models in your own right. You know what to do. The more people who do the right things, the faster this all comes under control. It's been studied. When the privileged are seen flouting rules, the public assumes the rules need not be kept, and we end up in situations like the one we find ourselves in today. Doing the right thing is hard, but it's the right thing to do.

WEDNESDAY | JANUARY 6, 2021

HAPPY EPIPHANY!

Perhaps, in the nation's capital, another epiphany of sorts is taking place in which leaders who have tolerated inexcusable behavior for short term political gain are finally having their eyes opened to the consequences of indulging a segment of the population who have abandoned reason, the rule of law, and other bedrock principles of our constitutional republic.

I will leave it to others much better versed in the ins and outs of politics to opine on the events of today, which are still unfolding. Time will tell if this was a storming of the Bastille or a manning of the barricades of the June Rebellion as portrayed in *Les Misérables*. Hopefully, those on the right side of the aisle are being reminded of the story of Frankenstein's monster, and those on the left that fulfilling a corporatist agenda at the expense of the people may not be the best way to govern going forward.

I am most concerned about today's events in regard to the trickle-down to issues of public health, something I do know a bit about. COVID-19 numbers continue to skyrocket, both locally and nationally. US cases, which crossed the 20 million mark on New Year's Day, are now well above 21 million, and the number of dead in the country is nearly 360,000. There are few hospital beds to be had anywhere in North Central Alabama as ward after ward is transformed from its usual purpose into a COVID-19 unit. My inpatient brothers and sisters are absolutely exhausted, and the onslaught shows no signs of slowing. On a more personal note, I have a panel of roughly 175 house call patients in my charge, mainly elderly and chronically ill. Five of them died over New Year's weekend alone.

What effect is the chaos in the capital going to have on the already inadequate federal response to the coronavirus? Given that the government has pretty much under-responded at every step of the game since a year ago this month, it may not be much.

The biggest issue I see involves federal resources and attention that should be going towards saving the citizenry, but that may get sucked up in the political maelstrom. With uncertainty at the top, bureaucracies will tread water rather than take action, leading to further delays in vaccine delivery or allocation of needed safety equipment and personnel. There's also the issue of the news cycle and the media culture's collective attention span of hours to days. Protracted problems will push COVID-19 news off the front pages, and if it isn't talked about much over the next two weeks, we'll have a certain amount of societal amnesia while the cases increase, the medical system buckles further, and the death toll rises.

The pictures out of DC this afternoon show a lot of people from all over the country bunched closely together and generally unmasked. At the end of the day, they'll board their charter buses and head back from whence they came, having done a lot of intermingling of germs. I wonder if the new more highly infectious UK variant was in the crowd and will use this day of problematic behavior to quickly pop up here, there, and everywhere over the next few weeks.

Most of the left wing protests of this past year, which had equally large crowds, tended to encourage social distancing and mask wearing and, to my knowledge, no major outbreaks of COVID-19 were ever traced to them. That was not true of Trump rallies or Sturgis, and is unlikely to be true of this event.

What does all this mean? I don't know. As I write this, things are still going on at the capitol, but we're just a few minutes away from a 6 PM Eastern Time curfew. Hopefully things will be more orderly tomorrow, and our politicians will start to think themselves out of the pickle they have placed themselves in with their conniving and deal-making and refusals of holding to account of the last few years.

I keep returning to an essay Masha Gessen wrote in the New York Review which was published on November 10, 2016 called *Autocracy: Rules for Survival*. Ms. Gessen, a refugee from Russia who has seen it all, knew what was coming and laid it all out. Listen to your friends who are recent immigrants from more autocratic regimes. They'll tell you how to approach this sort of political turmoil. We Americans have little experience of it, but that doesn't mean it's new to the world.

Before pouring myself a stiff drink and deliberately not turning on the news (I'll be able to learn what I need to know without pundits yelling in my face), I'd like to take a moment to celebrate some of the things that are right with the world.

We've made it into a new year (and those who thought that a mere turning of a calendar page was going to reinvent the world were deluded), but it's nice to know that 2020 is behind us. There's a lot of creative energy bubbling up in arts communities as people get over the shellshock of lockdowns and quarantines and start experimenting with new forms of expression. The *Ratatouille* musical that grew out of amateurs on TikTok adding on to each other's creations helped point the way to what theater can be in isolation and raised $1.5 million for The Actors Fund. I have a couple of projects coming up—a reading of *A Midsummer Night's Dream* in which I am essaying Bottom (fortunately my asses ears arrived from Amazon yesterday) and a full Zoom production of *Tartuffe* in which I am Orgon, being done by the same people who did *The Importance of Being Earnest* this past fall.

Do not despair. We aren't in a civil war yet. Live, laugh, love—just be sure to do it with hand hygiene, masks, social distancing, and not crowding into indoor space.

FRIDAY | JANUARY 8, 2021

IT'S ANOTHER ONE of those sit-bolt-upright-at-3:45-AM nights, my head spinning with half-baked anxieties and bad dreams.

In my REM state just before I woke, I was having my cognitive faculties checked by some unidentifiable power with one of the standard mental status questions. I had just been asked to name as many words as I could that started with the letter "O": option, occidental, orthostasis, omicron... and then I was awake and aware.

I assume I'm processing the bad news of the past few days in my own peculiar way. I deliberately did not watch the live news broadcasts of the Capitol takeover as I have come to the conclusion that televised news is in general bad for my underlying anxiety levels. Instead I read analysis, reportage, and opinion later, all of which was accompanied by plenty of well-composed still photos of what went on.

I'm sure you've seen them too, and for each of us, there is probably one that is the punch in the gut. For me, it was the one of a man flaunting the Confederate battle flag through the rotunda, something that never happened during four years of the Civil War. A close second was a trampled American flag replaced on a stand by a Trump 2020 flag.

The semiotics of flags is interesting. How we put so much meaning into scraps of colored cloth; how they come to hold our most cherished dreams or deepest fears; how even the briefest glimpse of a universally recognized one in visual media, such as the Nazi banner, can immediately change our entire worldview. The last show I did before the shut down, *Cabaret*, immediately shifts in the audience's perceptions with the appearance of a small swastika near the end of the first act. One of these days, I need to read a good book on vexillology if anyone has a recommendation.

We may all be distracted by political theater, but the coronavirus is not going away and continues to pose an imminent threat to the stability of the healthcare system. We're now topping 4,000 deaths daily in this country (that's 30% higher than 9/11 and 40% higher than Pearl Harbor on a daily basis). Our local hospital systems are inundated with beds going into waiting areas. Some people, who require monitoring but are not in imminent danger, are being shuffled into nearby hotel rooms. There hasn't been a day in the last two weeks when I haven't heard of a friend being diagnosed. Fortunately, the majority are young and healthy and seem to be recovering without major incident, but I am also receiving daily calls from friends about grandparents, great aunts, and other cherished elders who are not doing well.

My major thought of the day is that the coronavirus and our politics are fundamentally the same. Something invades the body or the body politic and quietly goes about its business unseen and ignored until all of a sudden it bursts forth in a reign of havoc. On the micro level, the virus enters the body, generally through the respiratory tract. It's a simple organism, a protein capsule containing its basic genetic information that allows it to create the proteins of which it consists. It's so simple that it uses RNA rather than the more involved DNA for its genetic code and doesn't have the cellular machinery to even replicate itself. Instead, its spike proteins attach to host cells, it injects its RNA into those cells, and uses the host's own mechanisms for its replication.

One successful viral attachment can lead to that cell releasing thousands of copies of that virus which then go on to attach to other cells and repeat the process many times over. Eventually, the host's immune system is going to notice the rising tide of invaders and react and the symptoms of disease appear. The devastating consequences of COVID-19 are often the result of an overreaction of the immune system resulting in inflammatory changes which can lead to organ failure and death.

In the same way, one virally infected individual can enter a social group, appear to be healthy, have no signs or symptoms of disease, but shed virus easily to others through close contact and respiratory droplets. If the asymptomatic period is prolonged, the contacts then go on about their business, never realizing they have been exposed and carry it on to others. This coronavirus is infectious, but not as infectious as many other common human viruses, so it's quite depen- dent on human behaviors of congregation to propagate. Transmissibil- ity can be curbed through simple measures such as social distancing and mask wearing. When we refuse to adhere to these simple public health measures, the virus, having no brain or thought, simply takes advantage of our own conscious choices that benefit it. The result of the spread is more and more sick people and, with the traditional gatherings for holidays, the numbers have soared quickly.

Our country's immune system against disease—our healthcare system—is becoming overwhelmed and may start to react in ways due to the pressures put upon it that may ultimately end up being damaging, a sort of institutional auto-immune process. We're just very lucky that COVID-19 has a relatively low mortality rate. If the mortality rate were the same as its very close cousin SARS, we'd be counting the dead in the multi-millions currently.

On the political front, there have been inocula of misinformation, disinformation, and fantasy injected into public discourse. They've bred in the darker corners of the Web such as 4chan and 8chan and Free Republic, and seem to be combinations of regurgitated talking points from the *Protocols of the Elders of Zion, Mein Kampf*, and *The Camp of the Saints*. They have, through widespread social media, entered the minds of those who understand on some basic level that the political system is no longer responsive to the people, but to wealthy donors who fund campaigns.

These ideas have churned quietly in the dark for years, fertilized by a media ecosystem that understood how disaffected people could be mobilized politically, and have been used by political, economic, and religious leaders as a base upon which to amass power and wealth without actually understanding or wanting to do much of anything about the conditions stoking the grievances. The body politic is now fully infected, the showdown at the Capitol was a symptom that cannot be ignored. The responses I see from many in power are like those of most American's to disease. Let's just go down to the urgent care clinic and get a pill, and everything will be normal again.

I don't think that sort of magical thinking is going to help the situation in which we find ourselves. The latest polls show that half of rank and file Republicans are convinced that Wednesday's events are some sort of false flag George Soros/Antifa plot. The usual corners of the conservative media ecosphere are bubbling with "This is just the beginning!" rhetoric. We're going to see more. And what of the immune response? Power protecting itself from those without? Will it be proportional, or will we develop a severe civic auto-immune disease worse than the original infection? I couldn't have imagined the events of this year a year ago, so I have no idea where we're headed.

What can I do? I can get my second COVID shot later today. I'll take whatever after effects it may give. I feel it's my civic and professional duty to do anything in my power to keep the disease from spreading and to set an example. The serious side effects such as anaphylaxis rates among the beta test group of healthcare professionals and long-term care residents who have been vaccinated so far appears to be about 11 in one million. As far as I know, no one has died. The current death toll from COVID in the US is about one in 50. I'll take my chances with the vaccine.

In the meantime, you all know the mantra: Even if you're vaccinated, wash your hands, wear your mask, social distance.

SUNDAY | JANUARY 10, 2021

I T'S COLD IN BIRMINGHAM, but the sun is out, beckoning me to get outside and take a walk or do something else semi-outdoorsy.

I'm still rattled by the surreal events of this past Wednesday and, as more and more information comes to light regarding just what happened on the grounds of the Capitol, I become more and more worried that this particular putsch was not the end of something, but rather the beginning.

For the most part, I've held my tongue on politics over the last ten months, other than the ways in which they intersect with healthcare policy. I don't especially believe in the vituperative name calling and attacking of personality that much of modern political discourse has devolved into. I believe in attacking misguided policies and problematic social trends. It's never possible to truly understand the complexities, judgments, and motivations of an individual without knowing them intimately. It is, however, possible to understand the actions of large groups of people through a study of sociology, economics, and political science. *Le plus ce change, le plus c'est la même chose.*

I've spent years writing political satire for *The Politically Incorrect Cabaret.* When doing that, I have a couple of rules I try to adhere to. Always punch up, never down. Punching down isn't satire, it's cruelty. Make fun of power and positions of power and roles of power, not directly at the humans who inhabit them. It's one of the reasons I have never been able to satirize the current president. It's not possible to separate the person from the power, and that's one of the things that has made him so dangerous to our political norms.

There's a lot swirling out there on the InterWebs about the more violent elements behind Wednesday's insurrection planning additional actions over the next week or so leading up to the inauguration. Whether there is any truth to these rumors, I do not know. I will assume that the Secret Service, as a proud group of professionals, will do their duty to keep things safe for all involved, and that we will have no more paramilitaries stalking the halls of government buildings looking for politicians of opposing beliefs to capture and summarily execute. But do not color me shocked if violence rears up again next week.

The highest levels of government in this country have been lying perpetually for the last four years. Usually it's been about little things that are easily disproved but, without shame, they shrug it off and move on to the next set of alternative facts. This has conditioned all of us, on both sides of the political spectrum, to shrug off lies as par for the political discourse these days. Unfortunately, it has also allowed a lie, The Big Lie that the 2020 election was stolen, to move forward unchecked.

There is not one shred of evidence, other than the usual one- or two-vote errors that turn up when things are looked at with a microscope, that this is true, but it became the underlying motivation for last week's actions. The Big Lie is still out there. It's still motivating a substantial portion of the population. It's still ascribed to by a significant number of national political figures for whatever cynical motives of money or power they may have. It no longer requires Trump for life, and it's going to hover over the Biden administration indefinitely.

The ironic thing, of course, is that there *was* a stolen presidential election in 2000 where everything hung on the state of Florida. All forensic recounts done show that Gore won the state and should have been awarded the electoral votes, but the Supreme Court's intervention tipped things the other way. The loser graciously accepted. There was some protest but no violence. One wonders where we would be today had we had a Gore instead of a Bush presidency in the early part of this century. The Big Lie about a stolen election is unlikely to slink off into the sunset in the same way, and will probably motivate much of what is to come in both congress and the executive branch.

This is all happening in the middle of a worsening pandemic that has dropped right off the front pages. The numbers keep going up. Alabama is diagnosing roughly 5,000 new cases daily, the country is adding a million new cases every five days or so, and the number of dead on a daily basis is now well over 4,000. This isn't going away and, in order to start improving these numbers, an enormous amount of leadership will be required of the incoming administration combined with logistics and resources to make sure vaccines are distributed, hospital pressures are relieved, and appropriate equipment and personnel are in the right places at the right times.

If the Biden team has to spend all of its time shoring up political support and defending itself against The Big Lie, they aren't going to have the energy and the resources to put into fighting the pandemic the way they should. It means that the disease will keep on racing through the country, felling tens of thousands who don't otherwise have to die. And it means that all of my brothers and sisters in health care who have been savaged physically and psychologically by the pandemic will have been written off by society as so much collateral damage, sacrifices on the altar of Big Lie politics.

A personal story came to my attention recently. A good friend, whose family remains in Southern California, is worried about her grandmother. Grandma has had a fall and has some facial fractures and a subdural hematoma. She was taken to the ER and seen there. She needs neurosurgery to drain her subdural, but the hospital is out of the supplies needed to treat her in the OR. Calls to every other hospital in the region reveal no space. She has been sent home to recover on her own the best she can. The family described the ER as a war zone with gurneys everywhere and tents over parking lots to accommodate the dying. Grandma may become a victim of COVID-19 without ever contracting the disease.

The moral of the story? Don't think it can't happen here or that Americans are exceptional. Our healthcare system is buckling due to years of neglect and the moving of its goals away from health to the making of money. It can't cope with the stresses of the pandemic.

I'm hoping the new work week gives me something more positive to write about. In the meantime, you all know the drill: Vaccinated or not, wash your hands, wear your mask, social distance.

FRIDAY | JANUARY 15, 2021

HAVEN'T BEEN ABLE TO WRITE FOR A FEW DAYS.

I don't often get writer's block, but every time I sat down to compose something this week, I would stare at the keyboard for a while and then find an excuse to do something else.

I'm not sure if it's delayed shock and a need to process last week, a creeping sense of hopeless futility when looking at public health statistics around COVID-19, or just a feeling that I've run out of things to say about this peculiar moment in time that we all occupy, when the political and the medical are interlaced in such a unique way.

On the political front, we are just days from a change in administration. I, like most of my fellow countrymen, am waiting with bated breath to see if another shoe is going to drop in Washington, D.C.

The most perfunctory look at the rhetoric spewing forth from the extreme right suggests that the contretemps at the Capitol last week was not the end, and that there are forces out there spoiling for a fight. Will there be more violence in DC this weekend or around next week's inaugural? I can't even begin to predict.

If you'd told me at Christmas I'd be writing about an invasion of the Capitol building with very real physical threats to Congress within a couple of weeks, I would have assumed you were telling a rather cruel joke. Will action spread from the nation's capital to state capitals? There's some suggestion that's possible. Let's just say I don't think anyone will be caught unawares. The possibility of surprise is long gone.

The biggest problem to come out of all this is the continued embrace of The Big Lie—that the election was stolen and illegitimate—by a majority of the Republican Party. There isn't a shred of evidence that this is true (and a great deal of evidence that it is not), but as long as this farcical notion remains in the air, it's going to diminish every accomplishment of the Biden administration.

Politicians, who should know better, but who have cynical reasons for perpetuating The Big Lie for their personal short term political gain, look like they're not willing to concede the truth even for the good of the country. That's going to continue to be a huge problem going forward the next few years, and will likely hamper public health responses and economic recovery. If the federal government is viewed as illegitimate in certain quarters, the motivation for cooperation for the betterment of society will be lacking, and that's going to include the response to the coronavirus.

We're at 23.5 million cases of COVID-19 in the country today according to the Johns Hopkins Coronavirus counter. We will surpass 400,000 US deaths sometime between now and the inaugural. If that number were a city, it would be 48th in population in the US, between Tulsa and Tampa. The winter surge, fueled by holiday travel and gatherings, has shown no significant signs of slowing down either locally or nationally.

The local hospitals are full. The staff are burnt out. I hear stories of horrible conditions from friends in California. Hospitalizations from Christmas should be starting to peak in another week, from New Year's a week after that. Maybe by mid-February we'll start to see better trends.

The vaccines, while off to an encouraging start last month, are bogged down in the same federal morass that has taken down pretty much every part of our public health response to the coronavirus pandemic each step of the way over the past year. Distribution remains problematic. Some of that relates to the logistics of transporting and storing a product that requires specialized temperature regulation and which has a very limited shelf life. (It must be administered within six hours of being drawn out of the stored vial).

This has led to a lot of head-into-wall banging in my VA house call program as so many of those patients live in remote rural areas and are not easily transported to a vaccination center. We're going to have to figure out how to courier doses off to any number of rural homes from Birmingham under a tight clock. And we can't just go house to house. Each recipient is going to have to be monitored for a minimum of fifteen minutes after administration and, given the frailty of the population, thirty minutes is a better idea.

The timeline is tricky: Draw up in pharmacy + get to nurse + nurse driving to far far away + nurse administering and monitoring = a significant number of hours. We won't be able to guarantee more than two or three trips in a day to fit into that six-hour window. Then we have to account for weather, road delays, the occasional flat tire, and chattering families, starved for company, who don't want to let the nurse head off to the next stop.

I am deluged daily with calls, texts, DMs, emails, and taps on my shoulder in the grocery store asking about when so-and-so can get a COVID-19 vaccine. I have only one answer: "I don't know."

All COVID-19 vaccine in Alabama is under the purview of the state department of public health. They have broken the population down into a number of groups. The first, called 1a, included health-care providers and residents in congregate senior facilities. They've made significant progress in getting those vaccines out there.

Group 1b, which includes first responders like police and those with significant chronic health conditions, as well as those over age 75, will be eligible as of this coming week. The state and counties have established hotlines for people to call to make their vaccination appointments. Those hotlines fielded over a million calls in just a week; it hasn't been easy to get through. The last thing I saw was that all appointment slots were full and they were working on a waiting list.

The lack of coherent federal leadership means that pretty much every state is doing their own thing at the moment. Some are prioritizing community dwelling elderly, some are prioritizing those in occupations with more potential exposure such as store clerks and teachers.

The CDC has issued guidelines, but not mandates and, from what I can tell, no one is paying much attention to them. There was agreement that healthcare providers and congregate living seniors needed to be vaccinated first but, after that, it's devolving into a free-for-all. Add to that the so called "Warp Speed" operation of the executive branch that seems incapable of accounting for vaccine—where it is and how best to get it out there—and we get announcements like the one this afternoon where they admitted their highly touted reserve supply which was going to be released to make up for shortages doesn't actually exist.

There is one encouraging bit of news on the vaccine front. A vaccine candidate from Johnson & Johnson is starting to show some encouraging preliminary results. It is not an mRNA vaccine like the currently circulating Pfizer and Moderna products. It uses a modified virus, one which cannot make humans ill, to transport DNA that encodes for the spike proteins of the coronavirus into human cells. The cell then makes and expresses these proteins. The immune system recognizes these as foreign and gears up against them, protecting the person if and when the coronavirus shows up later as the immune system already knows to knock out anything expressing those proteins. The adenovirus that carries the DNA is much hardier than the mRNA transport system of the current vaccines, so it can be stored in a standard refrigerator and, best of all, it's a single shot regimen. Data from trials is expected to be presented to the FDA in late January or early February.

The vaccine is getting out there, albeit slowly. There promises to be a more robust federal response on the public health front starting in less than a week. The weather will begin to warm so people won't be as tempted to gather inside.

Things will get better. I have to keep telling myself that.

In the meantime, vaccinated or not, you all know what to do: Wash your hands, wear your mask, social distance, and stay out of crowded indoor spaces.

This is particularly important these next few weeks as the pesky British strain that's more contagious appears to be starting to spread in this country, and your local healthcare provider really doesn't need the pace of people falling ill to accelerate.

MONDAY | JANUARY 18, 2021

'VE LEARNED TO STEEL MYSELF in recent weeks before opening my news feeds to see what's happened over the last day or so.

I was quite relieved to read through my digests this morning to find that all of the threatened nonsense for the long weekend vowed by those responsible for the violation of the Capitol has not come to pass. There have been some rather desultory state-level demonstrations, but nothing to compare with what came before.

Whether it's because the riot at the Capitol has finally shocked American society out of its complaisance about extremism, or because those forces are simply biding their time until we are all looking the other way to organize and strike again, I do not know. I simply know, due to my study of historical patterns, that The Big Lie of a stolen election, Trumpism, and the bizarreness known as Q-Anon, aren't going away any time soon, and will continue to influence our politics for a while to come.

Martin Luther King Jr. had a dream. I was a toddler when he gave that famous speech. I've heard it and its message my entire life. I've done my best to live up to the ideals of that dream, and to see that my part of the world does as well. I'm human and imperfect, so I haven't always succeeded, but I have kept slowly pushing to be a better accomplice for equality and justice, and I know that's going to be a lifelong challenge.

I'm a white male of the professional class, one whose parents believed in education and in books, so I've had certain systemic advantages through life. Being openly gay has been a disadvantage, but it's also helped me see inherent biases and recognize that correcting those biases isn't any sort of personal attack on me and mine. I think much of the support for the toxic brew of white nationalism, evangelical Christianity, and populist sloganeering that's in vogue these days comes from people who haven't understood this. Whether unwilling or unable, they haven't understood that changing society to allow broader participation isn't about tearing down what is, but about adding to and strengthening it, and allowing others to contribute their inherent gifts. It takes tesserae of all shapes, colors, and sizes to create a mosaic.

When it comes to history and the understanding of social structures and movements, I've always been of the opinion that the underpinnings are economic in nature. Who has the money? Where does it flow? Who gets to adjust those flows in terms of taxation and economic policy?

We're living in a time of extreme wealth. The amount of money our current titans of industry control would make the Roman Emperors blush. And the pandemic has hastened the concentration of wealth into fewer and fewer hands as the economic fallout has hit small businesses far harder than large ones. When I read about fortunes in the billions, I wonder how one even begins to spend that sort of money. For the most part, it isn't spent, it's simply concentrated, and the various net worth lists become a sort of scorecard in the great game of amassing a fortune.

We're living in a time, not unlike that of the Industrial Revolution, when a small number of wealthy white men set national economic policies for their benefit to the detriment of those who actually generated the wealth. In the battle of people versus profits, profits were coming out ahead until about 1848 when various revolutionary reform movements began both in Europe and in the Americas. The pushback, which continued over the next 80-some years, eventually led to fair working hours, the abolition of child labor, the idea of the pension, workplace safety laws, the existence of the weekend, and a thousand and one other things we take for granted.

People were finally valued over profits and the resulting policies led to the post-World War II world with which we're all familiar. However, capital and profit always fight back and, since the 1950s, bit by bit, profit has been renegotiating the social contract in its favor. Pensions became 401Ks, forcing the middle classes to favor economic policies that were pro-capital and market economy. Recipients of social largesse were recast as moochers and thieves. Public investment in infrastructure was curtailed (compare public buildings and spaces in this country with those in any other developed nation to see where that's left us).

When a stress such as the coronavirus hits a society where the balance is tilted towards profit and away from people, you get what we have seen over the last year: an unwillingness to do the sorts of hard shutdowns necessary to control spread; a lack of response of the government to the people regarding the economic pain and anxiety of even partial shut downs; a public infrastructure eroded by neglect that cannot deliver tools such as PPE or vaccine efficiently; a general sense that 400,000 deaths to date is some sort of bearable collateral damage; a general message of "We're all on our own and good luck to you."

Will this begin to change next week with a change of administration? I don't know. The politics may change, but the underlying economics will remain the same without some significant heavy lifting in all three branches of government, and I'm uncertain they're prepared to do that.

In late January, 2020, a resident of San Jose by the name of Patricia Dowd, a woman the same age as I, developed flu-like symptoms. Like most of us, she thought it was no big deal and stayed home treating herself. She died suddenly in her home on February 6, 2020. She was the first known US victim of COVID-19.

Four hundred thousand more have followed Ms. Dowd since then. It only took us five weeks to go from 300,000 to 400,000, and thanks to holiday gatherings, the pace continues to accelerate. We will be at nearly 500,000 deaths on the first anniversary of her passing, more than we lost in four years of World War II and approaching the number lost in four years of the Civil War.

We're well on track for COVID-19 to become the worst mass casualty event in American history. I have hope that we will turn the corner this spring. Vaccines should become more available. They don't necessarily prevent spread, but they definitely prevent the serious forms of the disease that require hospitalization. There is an opportunity, with a new administration, to change the type and tone of public discourse. Better weather will allow more socialization outdoors which is considerably safer.

In the meantime, you all know what to do, vaccinated or not: Wear your mask, wash your hands, social distance, and avoid crowded indoor spaces.

WEDNESDAY | JANUARY 20, 2021

THE CENTER HOLDS, THE REPUBLIC STANDS. We can all go to bed this evening, no matter our political leanings, knowing that there are stable individuals controlling the levers of power.

What does this portend for the future, especially for those coronavirus-related public health issues in which I am most interested? I can't say that I know.

I'm hoping we will begin to see a unified national response, rather than a piecemeal local one dependent on the whims of politics. I'm hoping those in charge bring the resources of the federal government to bear on the vaccination effort and that extant vaccines get into willing arms as quickly as possible. Most of all, I'm hoping that policies will be crafted that will tilt the balance away from the side of profit back toward the side of people.

I have no idea how successful any of these hopes will be in either the short or the long term, particularly this last one. The economic powers that shield capital from the depredations of people with needs are strong and entrenched, and neither political party has taken them on in some decades due to the great costs of maintaining the current apparatus of elective office, particularly the cost of campaigning in the media age. Lofty promises have been made, but results have been few and far between since the mid-1970s when the earnings of corporations began to outstrip the earnings of workers—and those curves have diverged further and further from each other over nearly five decades. That's a lot of societal repair.

I've been talking about The Big Lie regarding the election, the idea of it having been stolen by the Democrats from the Republicans still having currency in some circles, despite no evidence to corroborate this belief and plenty of evidence that the Democrats took both the popular and electoral votes fair and square.

There is, however, an even bigger lie that's been promulgated for decades: that the collapse of earning power by Blue Collar and rural Americans is due to a theft of resources by those below them on the social ladder, whether by undercutting them in the job market or through governmental benefit, rather than due to a redistribution of wealth to those above them through corporate consolidation, multi-nationalism, and control of economic resources outside of the US. This has fed the deep divisions in our country, and they are likely beyond the ability of any one administration to repair.

There is one thing that gives me a great deal of hope and that was on display at the Inauguration in the person of Amanda Gorman with her brilliant reading of her poem *The Hill We Climb*. This young woman, full of poise and meaningful words, captured our current moment perfectly and, to me, is emblematic of the rise of the Millennials and Generation Z to power. She joins the Florida high school students whose work and commitment helped take down the untouchable NRA, the youthful climate change activists, and the committed young people I work with in medicine who are facing the challenges of COVID-19 head on. It's a generation that clearly sees where the old forms and ways of doing things are broken, a generation unafraid of speaking truth to power and moving forward.

The Baby Boomers are not going to relinquish social, economic, and political power easily or gracefully, but time is coming for them. Demographically, somewhere around 15% of that generation will have died by 2030. They will then die off rapidly over the next two decades, roughly 40% in the 2030s and another 40% in the 2040s. A few will linger on, with the last American Boomer passing away around 2080 at the ripe old age of 115. There will be a wholesale changing of the guard in society over the next 20 years, and from what I have seen, the kids are alright and we're in pretty good hands going forward.

We're now, on this 20th day of January 2021, at 400,000 US deaths from COVID-19. Most of these people would have died had this virus arose at another point in modern US history. But, as it coincided with an administration with minimal interest in the commonweal, an accidental plague it did become.

We all have to live with the consequences of this and whatever part we played in allowing it to happen. Our fascination with infotainment over real news and analysis, our wish for quick solutions, our unwillingness to endure discomfort for the sake of others—all of these helped the virus establish itself here in ways that have cost real lives and untold suffering. Now we have the chance to make better choices, but it remains to be seen if we, as a society, will be willing to do this. I hope we are.

In the meantime, I'll still be here—watching, writing, trying to interpret the course of events in ways that help me make sense of this crazy world in which we find ourselves. I'll continue to follow my particular mantra, one which I have been imparting to medical students for decades: The world is saved one patient at a time. I have hope that the plague will recede enough that other things in my life will get back on track, but I am content for the moment with my work, my thoughts, and a little recreation on the side.

Here's to new beginnings, but in the meantime you know what to do: Wash your hands, wear your mask, social distance, and stay out of indoor crowds.

May your vaccine arrive soon should you choose it.

EPILOGUE

Goodbye For Now

MONDAY | MAY 31, 2021

THE ACCIDENTAL PLAGUE DIARIES ARE NOT OVER. (Neither is the accidental plague.) I continue to write my observations on health care, society, and the impact of the coronavirus and will do so as long as the pandemic remains part of my personal and professional life.

For purposes of this volume, however, it was necessary to choose an ending point. Several options occurred to me: New Year's Day 2021? The first anniversary of the declaration of the pandemic? I eventually settled on inauguration day and the transition of federal power which happened on January 20th.

So much of the story of this past year has been bound up in the policy decisions of the previous presidential administration that the day of this change was going to open up a completely new chapter—one way or another. A plague diary under the new administration was likely to be a significantly different document from the one I had been writing.

Will there be another volume in the future covering more recent events? I don't know. This one came about by accident. A second volume strikes me as being a more deliberative choice. I'll trust that the serendipitous events that fill my life will help me make that decision when appropriate.

The months that have elapsed since January as I have massaged and edited this manuscript, have proven more hopeful. There has been steadier federal leadership, a relatively rapid deployment of vaccine, and a spectacular lessening of case numbers, fulfilling my hopes and more optimistic predictions, and so the tenor of any future volume is likely to be quite different than this one.

There's still much that isn't known. Some of the new variants that are significantly more contagious continue to spread. More authoritarian countries like India and Brazil have had major difficulties implementing public health programs to lessen cases. The vaccine is not being distributed widely in much of the Third World due to infrastructure, economic, and political issues.

The pandemic is not American; it is global. Resolving it will require global solutions which are somewhat beyond what our current societies seem capable of.

This Memorial Day, I want to reflect on those who have died to date, roughly 585,000 in the USA alone. A friend of mine suggested (taking a page from the story of the AIDS quilt) that we should create a quilt made of stitched-together cloth masks, one for each victim of the pandemic.

The average mask is about 3 x 8 inches or 24 square inches. Six masks would make a square foot. 585,000 masks would cover 97,500 square feet or two and a quarter acres. For those who have trouble visualising acreage, that's a bit over two football fields.

These were real people who didn't deserve what happened to them, treated as so much collateral damage in a public health versus politics battle not of their own devising, leaving behind shattered family systems and devastated communities. It's going to be some time before we fully come to grips with what that means.

I can imagine being high above, looking down on all those little scraps of cloth, coming together to form a whole like a giant photomosaic. How can we interpret what is revealed? How can we possibly understand and honor all of that sacrifice?

I've had my vaccine. My little corner of the healthcare system is stable. Things theatrical are beginning to open up. The CDC has approved domestic travel for the vaccinated and suggested that resumption of many regular activities is safe for those of us fortunate enough to have received our shots. We aren't out of the woods yet, but the darkness of this past long winter is being replaced by the light and warmth and dreams of summer.

Get your vaccine as soon as practical, whichever one is available. But don't get cocky and discard the good habits that we have all learned over the last year or we could still stumble short of the finish line, and I would rather not be pushed into a new volume of these diaries due to preventable resurgences brought about by bad public behaviors.

You all know the litany: Wash your hands, wear your mask where appropriate, keep your distance—just a little while longer.

AFTERWORD

Next

WEDNESDAY | AUGUST 25, 2021

THE PROBLEM WITH AN ONGOING PANDEMIC is that political and public health developments move much faster than the book publication process.

When I completed this edited manuscript, roughly three months ago, we were at a place of optimism. A truly miraculous vaccine plus a change in administration had led to a rapid decline in cases and promises of a way forward in which COVID-19 would settle into the background of our lives, never fully departing, but no longer a significant challenge for us either as individuals or as a society.

Over the last six weeks, however, a combination of factors including the spread of the highly transmissible Delta variant of the novel coronavirus, a resurgence of organized opposition to masking and vaccines, and political intransigence in more conservative states has led to a backsliding. Cases today, especially in my region of the country, are more or less back where they were when I ended this volume in January.

In the last week or so, I have seen news stories of public meetings in which mobs have verbally assaulted exhausted healthcare workers who are only trying to do their sworn duty of saving lives by advocating sound public health policy, more stories than I care to count of anti-vaccine activists begging forgiveness on their ICU death beds, and stories of hospital after hospital flooded with acutely ill young people who should be at the peak of their lives and productivity, failing because of societal misinformation and failure to care for each other.

I am enough of an optimist and student of history and public health to believe that things will improve and that we will all come through this together. However, given current epidemiologic trends, it's going to get worse before it gets better.

The current 632,000 dead Americans will be joined by thousands more. I will continue to write about these issues, working to make sense of the times in which we find ourselves, and sharing that process with the world. Current publishing models allow for me to update this afterword as quickly as times change. The never-ending saga of COVID-19 will probably prod me into producing another volume of these *Accidental Plague Diaries* at some point. All I can hope is that it does not stretch into a series of three or four books.

Today's young people, coming of age in a pandemic world and malleable enough to adjust to new conditions, are busy studying our current society, its actions and reactions. I have great faith that they will see our mistakes, learn from them and, as they eventually take center stage, enact policies that will keep us out of some of the troubles we have created for ourselves. In the meantime, all I can hope is that we the people start working together, rather than against each other, to bring this accidental plague to an end.

Wash your hands. Wear your mask when indicated. Get your vaccine.

ABOUT THE AUTHOR

Andrew Duxbury is originally from Seattle, Washington. He received his BS in chemistry and biology from Stanford University and his MD from the University of Washington.

He spent his early career at UC Davis in Sacramento where he discovered the fascinating world of geriatric medicine and his first husband, Steve Spivey. He later left the West Coast for the Deep South and the geriatrics faculty of the University of Alabama at Birmingham where he continues to teach and practice geriatric medicine.

After the untimely death of his first husband, shortly after moving to Alabama, he decided to rebalance his life, beginning a second career as a performer and picking up a second husband, Tommy Thompson, along the way.

Tommy also died young, leading to additional introspection and a third career as a writer. Dr. Duxbury continues to muddle through life in Birmingham with his two cats, Oliver and Anastasia, a host of friends, and his trusty laptop.